Epistemology and Phenomenology of Religions

JDV Philosophy Series - 1

Epistemology and Phenomenology of Religions

Creative Insights into Intercultural and Interreligious Dialogue

Salvino Azzopardi SJ
(Professor Emeritus, Jnana-Deepa Vidyapeeth, Pune, India)

Editor
Kuruvilla Pandikattu SJ

Jnana-Deepa Vidyapeeth

&

Christian World Imprints

CWI

First Published in 2018 by

Jnana-Deepa Vidyapeeth
Ramwadi, Nagar Road, **Pune-411014**
jdvoffice@jdv.edu.in
www.jdv.edu.in
Phone: +91 20 41036111

&

Christian World Imprints
Christian Publishing & Books from India
H-12 Bali Nagar, **New Delhi-110015**
info@christianworldimprints.com
www.ChristianWorldImprints.com
Phone: +91 11 25465925

ISBN: 978-93-5148-317-5 (HB) ISBN: 978-93-5148-318-2 (PB)

Cataloging in Publication Data--DK
Courtesy: D.K. Agencies (P) Ltd. <docinfo@dkagencies.com>

Azzopardi, Salvino, 1931-2006, **author.**
Epistemology and phenomenonology of religions : creative insights into intercultural and interreligious dialogue / Salvino Azzopardi SJ ; editor, Kuruvilla Pandikattu SJ.
pages cm. -- (JDV philosophy series ; 1)
ISBN 9789351483175 (HB)
ISBN 9789351483182 (PB)

1. Knowledge, Theory of (Religion) 2. Phenomenology. 3. Intercultural communication--Religious aspects. 4. Religions--Relations. I. Pandikattu, Kuruvila, editor. II. Jnana-Deepa Vidyapeeth, publisher. III. Title. IV. Series: JDV philosophy series ; 1.

LCC BL51.A99 2018 | DDC 200.1 23

Printed in India.

CONTENTS

PART THREE
PHENOMENOLOGY OF RELIGIONS

PART FOUR
RELIGIOUS LANGUAGE

JDV PHILOSOPHY SERIES -1

Since 1893 Jnana-Deepa Vidyapeeth has been pioneering philosophy discussion and debate inspired by prominent personalities like Richard De Smet, Jean de Marneffe, Salvino Azzopardi, Cyril Desbruslais, Noel Sheth, John Vattanky, etc. It has been in the forefront of promoting Indian philosophy and making philosophical thinking relevant for contemporary times. In its effort to reach out to like-minded scholars, JDV Philosophy Series has been visualized as a catalyst for interdisciplinary thinking and contemporary exploration on social issues fostering holistic liberation, integral development and creative engagement.

JDV Philosophy Series (Books published so far)

1. Salvino Azzopardi: Epistemology and Phenomenology of Religions (2018)
2. Kuruvilla Pandikattu & Thomas Karimundackal (ed): Melodies from the Flute (2018)
3. Kurien Kunnumpuram: Freedom and Joy (2018)

PREFACE

It is a great honour for me to write these few introductory paragraphs and I thank the editor wholeheartedly for the invitation. Both Salvino Azzopardi and I obtained our initial formation as Jesuits within the Maltese Province of the Society of Jesus, a province that was established for the duration of seventy years, between 1947 and 2017. We both specialized in philosophy and we both spent many years as professors, serving innumerable students from different parts of the world. Salvino however was my senior by twenty-six years. Consequently, the few times we met during vacation time were always for me moments of inspiration and appreciation. He always left me with a deep impression. I always felt that I had interacted with a person who had travelled a lot in his life, someone who had covered great distances not only in the geographical sense but also in the cultural and philosophical sense.

This book gives us a taste of this richness. It offers a selection of his written work on a particular theme related to knowledge and phenomenology. By knowledge we normally understand the grasping of truth with certainty in some particular domain. By phenomenology we normally understand the study of how things or events present themselves to us, irrespective of our prior scientific knowledge. These two technical terms have been the object of philosophical study for centuries. During these last decades, most philosophers have examined these fundamental notions with great care but restricted their study mainly to everyday objects or circumstances, concentrating their efforts on the strengths and weaknesses of the natural sciences and sidelining to some extent the religious dimension. It is however becoming increasingly obvious that one of the major driving forces of social and cultural change, for the better or for the worse, is indeed religion. It is crucial therefore that philosophers turn their attention to this dimension of human living. We need to examine with great attention questions of the following kind. What is the difference between religious knowledge and religious opinion? What justifies religious knowledge? How can different religious traditions enrich each other and help to arrive a common understanding of religious knowledge and religious experience? What is the correct role of religious language and how is it related to everyday linguistic practice and to technical scientific language?

Within the global effort to answer such questions, Salvino Azzopardi's book is a very welcome contribution. The content of the chapters is especially valuable because it is not the result of serious intellectual effort only but adds to this the fruits of firsthand experience of intercultural and interreligious dialogue. As is explained in the biographical note at the end of this volume, Salvino Azzopardi spent twenty-four years in India. Twenty of these he spent lecturing at JDV in Pune. He studied philosophy at the highest level in both the Western and Indian traditions and travelling widely within the Indian subcontinent exchanging his views with innumerable people of diverse religious convictions. Most of the chapters consist of lecture notes. They do not have the same formal style as monographic studies that are usually addressed to a specialized readership. As lecture notes, they possess a vibrancy and a directness that appeal not only to the mind but also to the heart. They are easily accessible to students and also, at the same time, a pleasure to read for philosophy lecturers. They simplify complex arguments without losing the precious content. They avoid unnecessary jargon and explain every step without assuming prior detailed knowledge on the part of the reader.

The most important feature of this collection is its significance for interreligious dialogue. Such dialogue is essential especially to defuse social and cultural tensions that can escalate and erupt at specific points on the globe with disastrous consequences. Perhaps we can recall a few lines from the speech of Pope Francis that he delivered on September 25, 2015 when he visited the Ground Zero Memorial in New York. This place honors the victims of the September 11, 2001 Al-Qaeda attacks on the World Trade Center. In this speech, he included the following precious thought. "For all our differences and disagreements, we can experience a world of peace. In opposing every attempt to create a rigid uniformity, we can and must build unity on the basis of our diversity of languages, cultures and religions, and lift our voices against everything which would stand in the way of such unity. Together we are called to say "no" to every attempt to impose uniformity and "yes" to a diversity accepted and reconciled." We can reach his noble aim only if we understand the deep philosophical currents that determine how people behave, only if we understand the role of religious language, the impact that religious experience has on private and social life, the role of reason and tradition in the formulation of religious knowledge, and other such fundamental aspects.

In this book, Salvino Azzopardi engages in this noble project fully convinced of the benefits of being both a man of reason and a man of faith. His method and overall attitude constitute a prime example of the opening verses of the encyclical *Faith and Reason*, written by St. John Paul II in 1995: "Faith and reason are like two wings on which the human spirit rises to the contemplation of truth." Salvino

Azzopardi's book is like a ladder by which we are invited to climb up higher and thus attain an enriched level of consciousness. I am convinced that both students and lecturers will find this book very rewarding. They will become more aware of how to make religious claims correctly and how to enjoy religious experiences fully and responsibly. They will thereby grow in wisdom.

Prof. Louis Caruana SJ
Dean, Faculty of Philosophy
Gregorian University, Rome

EDITOR'S INTRODUCTION

Rev. Prof. Salvino Azzopardi SJ is one of the few professors who have impressed me most by his philosophical quest and systematic search which he did both spontaneously and joyfully. In fact, he was one of the inspirations why I myself decided to specialize on the same topic of philosophy.

As I have been teaching philosophy at Jnana-Deepa Vidyapeeth (JDV), Pune, I have been struck by the number of alumni who are fond of Prof. Azzopardi and his philosophical quest. There have been so many requests for his course materials, which he had prepared in the 1970's and 80's.

The various course materials he has prepared about forty years have not become dated, but rather become classic. He was totally at home both in Western philosophy and Indian thoughts. In his philosophy classes he has tried successfully to integrate the wisdom of the Indian traditions with that of the East.

He told me on one of our encounters that every summer he will spend reading and researching on one particular field of philosophy, which becomes his course material for teaching. In this course material, he has integrated vision from East and West or from Christian and Hindu traditions, without giving up his Christian roots!

He was an open-minded person in search of the truth. He enjoyed contemplating. I cannot forget the fact that he had written in large letters some of logical equations. He told me that he will just look at these equations and enjoy the beauty of them! He also enjoyed related to his colleagues and students. His classes were both popular and insightful. He had a knack for making the profound philosophical thoughts both simple and interesting, without watering it down. He showed through his life and vision how philosophy can retain its theoretical nature and can be immensely practical.

Salvino Azzopardi is a multifaceted person, who made everyone at home in his presence. He was truly a thinker, for whom philosophy was his passion. He had been repeatedly affirming that "to be allowed to teach philosophy at Jnana-Deepa Vidyapeeth was a privilege" offered to him.

As a tribute to him, I have collated three of his notes on "Epistemology" (1983), "Phenomenology of Religion" and "Religious Language." Though written in 1980's, they still continue to inspire countless students and can still contribute to the progress of ideas.

It has been my joy to reread and edit this volume, which I dedicate in his honour, so that inspired by Salvino Azzopardi, we can together build a community of open dialogue, mutual respect and collective quest.

It may be noted that the editor has left the paragraph numbering of the author by and large unchanged, since it will help in clarifying concepts through cross-referencing. We have deliberately not changed his language and style, including the use of non-inclusive language, to give a classical sense to his writings.

We are grateful to the President, Jnana-Deepa Vidyapeth, Prof. Selva Rathinam SJ and the Registrar, Prof. Jose Thayil for their encouragement and support. The staff and students of the Faculty of Philosophy, who have been tremendous sources of inspiration, also deserves to be gratefully mentioned. It is a privilege to acknowledge the contributions of both the large campus houses in JDV Campus, De Nobili College, where Azzopardi lived for decades and Papal Seminary, which has been home to me for more than 20 years. Truly we are indebted to Prof Louis Caruana SJ, Dean, Faculty of Philosophy, Gregorian University, Rome for the Preface. Further, I am also grateful to Fr. Ivan Mutharatt and Br Jeril Nirappel for stylistic corrections and suggestions.

Regarding the linguistic style, I have kept the authors language as it is, without introducing the inclusive language. But I may remind the readers that he was very open to people of all colour, religion and gender.

May this book enkindle in the reader a passion for philosophy in general and knowledge or wisdom in particular, just as the author himself was.

PART ONE

EPISTEMOLOGY: ON KNOWLEDGE IN GENERAL

"Those who know the truth are not the equal of those who love it; those who love the truth are not the equal of those who delight in it."

– Confucius

INTRODUCTION TO EPISTEMOLOGY

§1. In this introduction to Epistemology itself, we would like to make the student more and more aware of the importance of Epistemology not only as a philosophical treatise but also, and especially, as a religious endeavor. As a matter of fact, in our understanding of philosophy– which corresponds to the Scholastic and Indian understanding– the philosophical task is eminently a religious undertaking.

§2. Let us put it this way: If I believe in God – both in the sense that I believe that He exists and in the sense thatI believe, trust in Him –my belief if it is to be 'human' must be reasonable. That is to say I must have good grounds why I should believe. I must see, somehow or other, that is I must 'know' what I am believing in and why I am to believe in it. Otherwise, my belief would not be 'human', worthy of a man; an unreasonable belief is simply 'credulity' like belief in ghosts, fairies and mermaids! But if I look around me, I see people who not only do not believe in God but who also claim that such belief is not even possible, that is, that belief in God cannot even be reasonable! I meet other people who claim that even if belief in God were reasonable, one could not be absolutely sure that one's belief is true; at most one could only have opinions about the matter. And of opinions one can never be certain. How else is one to explain the divergence of opinions not only about the existence of God but also about 'who' God is? Some say that by 'God' one is to understand this, others that. Here in India we live in the midst of a great religious pluralism. Followers of one religious tradition claim absolute truth for their religious beliefs, and followers of another religious tradition claim it for their own. If some religious belief of one tradition contradict those of another religious tradition, can one be sure which of them are true and which of them are false? Can I know anything about religious truth? If I can, can I know it for sure?

§3. This perplexity is not limited to religion. Far from it! Take moral matters. All of us are aware how today, perhaps more than ever before, people think differently about so many moral issues. Not only that certain ways of behavior are considered permissible in one culture and are condemned as wrong in another – which is indeed the case – but that even in one given culture, certain ways of behavior once considered permissible were later condemned as wrong – or vice-versa! Within the Catholic Church itself people – and this includes experts in moral matters – differ regarding the moral permissibility of, say, artificial methods of birth-control, divorce, capital punishment, nuclear warfare, etc. We may have often heard Catholics themselves complain that "one does no longer know what to believe nowadays!" Faced with such a perplexity, one is often tempted to despair of ever reaching certainty in moral matters and to leave to each one's conscience to act or behave in the way one thinks to be right. But even then, if I decide to take such an attitude, I can easily remember times, when I once thought something to be right only to have to change my mind later on! So the same question arises: can I know anything about moral truth? And if I can, can I know it for sure?

§4. As if this were not enough, today we hear scientists themselves giving up claims to attain absolute certainty about the very laws of nature and consequently about the indubitableness of scientific knowledge. Contrary to popular opinion, fascinated by the marvelous progress in science and technology, the scientist is only too aware that his knowledge is hypothetical, subject to further verification or falsification. His hypotheses, laws and theories are provisional, not so much descriptive of what things are in themselves as methodical principles of scientific knowledge. But, surely, one could ask, even though scientific knowledge as such (i.e. as methodically and systematically enunciated in general laws and theories) is hypothetical and provisional, and therefore not absolutely certain, the sense-data themselves (i.e. the objects of the senses of sight, hearing, feeling, smelling, tasting) are objects of absolutely certain knowledge. Now the beginner in the study of philosophy will probably be surprised to discover that the reliability of our senses in providing us with sure knowledge has been a subject of great debate in the history of philosophy! As for us though it is true that oftentimes the senses deceive us, we might as well suppose, at least here, that sense-perception is a source of absolutely sure knowledge. But then the important question here would be: is it the only source as some people, including some philosophers maintain? If it is, what becomes of our beliefs in God and in most tents of our faith- which definitely are not objects of sense-perception? Is our moral doctrine based on sense-perception? If not – as in fact it is not –how can I say that I certainly know that murder is morally wrong and that helping the poor is morally right?

§5. Further still. Not only in religious, moral and scientific matters- and for that matter in any learned discipline as such, including the Human sciences like History, Sociology, Psychology where opinions differ and sure knowledge seems to be impossible- but also in everyday thinking we can find ourselves faced with the same perplexity. One day I may think that my friend is good and loveable, later on I discover that he is really selfish. Can I really know others, their qualities and character? Can I, for that matter rely know myself? How often do I hear others- or myself even! - passing wholesale judgments on people, economic or political systems, etc., and later on I discover that such wholesale judgments are simply the result of bias, prejudice, passing emotion, personal interest, social pressure? So was my former judgment true, i.e., did it correspond to the facts? Can I know what the 'facts' are and know them for sure? Very often, and in various fields of knowledge, we tend to consider as 'facts' (realities of a situation, things certainly known to have occurred or be true, data of experience, things assumed as basis of inference) what, on closer examination, are our own 'interpretation', our own emotional response to them. And interpretations and emotional responses differ from person to person in accordance with familial and social background, previous education, temperament and character, present moods and needs, etc. This is an extremely important topic and we shall have to delay on it at some length, later on. But an example or two will make the point clearer. Somebody makes a statement, A Maltese and Indian hear him. The former is offended because the statement is offensive to the Maltese people. The latter sees nothing offensive neither to the Maltese people nor to anybody else. What is the 'fact'? Again. An Indian and an Englishman see the film 'Gandhi'. The former finds it absorbingly moving whereas the latter finds it historically inaccurate and technically poor. Is it a 'fact' that the film is absorbingly moving or is it a 'fact' that it is historically inaccurate and technically poor?

§6. We could go on and on. But what we have said so far is enough to serve our purpose here. Notice that the questions which have been recurring revolve around the theme of knowledge, of true and certain knowledge. The particular questions raised will be partially dealt with in particular branches of Philosophy – in Philosophical Theology (questions regarding the knowledge of God), in Ethics (questions regarding the knowledge of moral truth), in Philosophy of Science (questions, regarding scientific truth), etc.,–but these all presuppose a treatment of the problematic of knowledge, truth and certainty in general. And this is the task of Epistemology.

'Epistemology' (from Greek *episteme,* and *logos,* meaning respectively, 'knowledge' and 'doctrine') can therefore be defined, in a most comprehensive sense, as the philosophical treatise about 'the nature, possibility and origin of true and certain knowledge'. In this sense, it can also be defined simply as 'the theory of knowledge'. The closest Sanskrit word would perhaps be *jnanasastra.* In the West, it is often designated by other words (e.g. Critica, Criteriology, Gnoseology) – with more or less different meanings but often referring to one or other aspects of the whole problematic of knowledge.

§7. But more important than the name or names by which it is called is, obviously, the problematic itself with which it deals. From what we have said so far, this ought to have been made hopefully clear! No wonder that every system of Philosophy (Scholastic, Hindu, Buddhist, etc.) elaborated its own epistemology. No wonder too that Epistemology can easily be considered to be the foundational branch of every system of Philosophy. No wonder that, as we explained in our *Introduction to Philosophy*, (Epistemology) proves to be the most radically self-critical science.

§8. We have divided the treatise into two Sections, or Parts. In the First Section we deal with the more general questions regarding knowledge – its meaning, means of coming to know truly – and hence the meaning of truth and the means to come to know certainly. And since knowledge is not merely an individual affair – we come to know 'together' – we have concluded this Section with an important chapter on the sociology of knowledge.

Most students may not immediately see the importance and relevance of such questions. The questions, as raised in this introduction, cannot fail to let him see wherein the importance- and relevance of these more general and abstract questions regarding knowledge, truth and certainly lie – that is, in the religious sphere most of all. Is it possible to know and speak of God, is it possible to say that our religious belief is true, is it possible to be certain of the truth of our religious belief? All this can be, and in fact is, challenged by atheists or at least questioned by agnostics of all kinds.

Hence, the Second Section which brings all that we would have said in the First Part to bear on these religious questions. In length, it may be shorter – since the foundation would already have been laid in the First Section and all we will have to do is to apply it. A chapter or two of this Second Section will have to be longer than others since certain questions will have to be dealt much longer than they would have been in the First Section (e.g. the question of Language).

§9. We have by-passed many questions usually treated in treatises on Epistemology or treated them only in passing. The criterion of our choice of topics has been precisely the importance and relevance of topics in view of the religious questions.

We have not exposed in detail the views of the various philosophers whom we had to refer to. Such a detailed exposition we have left to the course on the History of Philosophy, Western and Indian. Thus, besides avoiding overlapping and needless repetition, the chief point or points made by the philosopher in question will be brought out in clearer and sharper relief.

Those who do not know Sanskrit need not retain in mind the many Sanskrit terms which are given – except, perhaps, for some key terms which serve them a very good stead in their study of Indian Philosophy generally. We have avoided underlining them (as is usually the custom) to avoid living the pages a cumbersome look.

Again, it is not so important to remember who said what on a given topic but to understand the question at issue and the possible answer.

§10. We have started by saying that the study of Epistemology – and indeed Philosophy in general – is a religious endeavor. To look for Truth – for Wisdom – means 'grappling' with it. In the process, one should expect moments of feeling 'at a loss', of increasing darkness rather than of the expected light, moments even of boredom and of discouragement, but as Gabriel Marcel beautifully puts it, "it is by walking, as pilgrims, on the difficult road strewn with obstacles that we hope to see shining one day that eternal light a reflection of which has not ceased to enlighten us ever since we came into the world; that light without which, we can be sure, we would never have started on our journey."[1]

1 Gabriel Marcel. *The Mystery of Being*, Fr. original, Paris: Aubier, 1951, Vol. II, p. 188.

Chapter 1

KNOWLEDGE AND THE JUDGMENT

§11. The first question with which we shall deal is precisely that regarding the nature of knowledge. But notice how we are asking the question: what are we to mean by 'to know' (and 'knowledge'). In fact, both in the West and in the East, philosophers explain the term(s) differently – in accordance, very often, with their different philosophical assumptions. So the question to ask is not: what is the meaning of 'to know' (or 'knowledge'), but: what I (or you) really mean by this or these terms?

§12. ***a. 'To know'.*** Here we are, of course concerned with a technical (philosophical, epistemological) meaning of the term. In fact, most words, in all languages, have more than one meaning but not all of them are useful in a philosophical discourse. In English, 'to know' can mean, for example, 'to recognize or identify', 'to be acquainted with thing, place or person', 'to be versed in language, skill', etc. What are we to understand by 'to know' in an epistemological sense?

Some authors point out that it is not possible to give an exact definition of 'to know' (or 'knowledge'). Like 'to see' or 'to hear', 'to know' is such a primary fact of experience that one can only describe the activity involved by giving examples. To a man born blind it is impossible to tell him what 'to see' means; similarly, to man born deaf it is impossible to tell him what 'to hear' means. (Of course to a man born an imbecile, unable to 'know' anything at all, it is not possible to tell him anything!).

§13. Be that as it may, we can always suggest at least a loose Definition, or at least description, of what we are to understand by the term in question. The way we prefer to understand the term is this: 'to know' is 'to be aware that such and such is (or is not) the case.' This, obviously needs explaining.

(1) **To be aware:** to be conscious of, to be alert to, and to be cognizant of. For our purposes here, we need not go into all detailed analysis of 'awareness'. Suffice

it to point out that in this commonly accepted understanding of 'awareness', it implies a duality of subject (the knower) and object (the known). An interesting topic which we shall discuss later is whether the subject can ever become aware of himself as subject but not as object. In other words whether there is such a state of object-less awareness. Many Indian Schools of Philosophy maintain that there is, no matter how puzzling this may sound. Hence, the distinction between samvedana or sanjna (object awareness) and cit or caitatiya (objectless consciousness). For the moment, by 'awareness' we shall understand 'object awareness.'

(2) **Such-and-such is (or is not) the case:** this phrase refers to the 'object', what is known. This phrase refers to the 'object' what is known. It denotes a fact, a 'state of affairs', anything which one knows or claims to know. It includes therefore the existence, properties aid relations of things and persons; past, present and likely future events, etc.

(3) **Is (or is not):** this indicates a judgment – an affirmation or negation. In fact, unless and until there is such a judgment, there cannot be knowledge in the way we are meaning the term. To understand this point, we can relate 'knowing' with 'sense-perceiving'; suppose I am given something in my hand. I can see its shape and colour, I can smell and feel its hardness or softness. Still I may not yet know what it is. Only when I say: it's a mango! does knowledge emerge? Of course, in the meantime, I have already come to know many things: for example, that I am holding the thing in my hand, that it is round in shape and reddish in colour, that it is soft or hard, even that it is not a baseball, etc. But notice that in all these fragmentary pieces of knowledge there is always entailed a judgment: it *is* the case that I am holding something in my hand; it *is* the case that it is round in shape and reddish in colour, etc.

§14. *(4)* **Some further remarks**. *A first remark* would be this: the act of judgment Implied in 'to know' need not – and often is not – explicit. When I get to know something, I may not be alert to the fact that I in fact am making this act of judgment. In everyday life, we get to know things spontaneously. Only on reflection can I become alert to the fact that in every act of knowing, an act of judgment is implied. So this act is said to be at least implicitly implied. *A second remark* would be this: 'is (or is not) the case' can, obviously, refer to the past. Suppose I say that I know that Jesus lived twenty centuries ago. This means that I am aware that it is the case that Jesus lived twenty centuries ago. Again when I say that I know that all men will be saved, I am saying that I am aware that it *is* the case that all men will be saved. *A third remark* would be this: to make a judgment is an act, a mental act, whereas we described 'to know' as to be 'aware'. But is 'to be aware' an act or rather a 'state'? 'To know' can refer either to the precise moment when one gets to know something – and in this case 'to know' refers more directly to the mental act. (To 'know' would correspond to the moment when one 'understands' something). But 'to know' can also refer to the time afterwards. Once one got to know something, he keeps on knowing it (till, of course, one is proved wrong or persuaded otherwise). In this case, 'to know' refers more directly to the state of awareness. But this brings us to say something about 'knowledge' (as a noun).

§15. ***b. Knowledge.*** We have been speaking, for obvious reasons, of 'to know' and of 'knowledge' in one breath. In our understanding, 'knowledge' is simply the content of one's knowing, of one's understanding. Some Indian philosophers distinguish 'knowledge' from what is stored up, as it were, in 'memory' – depending, precisely, on what each of them understands by the former term.

§16. The question or questions which we would like to discuss here is whether the way we understand 'to know' leads us to understand 'knowledge' as necessarily true and reasonable. In other words, is 'knowledge'-to be really 'knowledge' (in our understanding of the term) – either true and reasonable or no 'knowledge at all? Does it make sense to speak of 'false knowledge' or 'unreasonable knowledge'? Aren't these contradictions in terms? (Later on, we shall discuss the topics of 'truth' and 'certainty' but what we shall be discussing here is necessary to complete our understanding of 'Knowledge' itself).

§17. **(1) Knowledge and truth**. For the moment, by 'true' (truth we understand the following: 'true' knowledge is that where what is asserted (or denied) corresponds to 'what the case is. If I say that the Rector is in his office and in point of fact he is not, my statement is not true but false. If I deny that I went to Bombay yesterday and in point of fact I did go, my denial is not true but false.

Now suppose that I say that I know that the author of the Fourth Gospel is St John. Later on, in my studies of Scripture, I discover that is not the case. On my discovery will I be able to say that formerly I knew that the author of the Fourth Gospel is St John – or rather that I thought I knew that that is the case, but that, as a matter of fact I was mistaken and did not, know at all? Strictly speaking, then, if knowledge is really knowledge, it has to be true. In common language, however, 'false knowledge' can still make sense but only to the extent that what is meant is that what one thinks one knows is false.

§18. **(2) Knowledge and reasonableness**. A further but connected question is this: is knowledge, no matter how true, but which is based on false or inadequate reasons, knowledge at all? In other words, is knowledge, to be called knowledge (in our understanding of the term), necessarily reasonable (i.e. based on sufficient or adequate reasons)?

Suppose I say that I know that physical evil exists in the world and the reason I give for this assertion is that God could not have created nature in a way other than He has. Supposing that the assertion is true but the reason given is false, can I still be said to really know that physical evil exists in the world? Or to take another example: I hear somebody saying that he knows that abortion is morally wrong and the only reason for that is that it is illegal. Can he be said to really know that abortion is morally wrong? Our answer would be the following: in both cases, given that the claimed knowledge is based on false reasons, the speakers do not seem to know what they are really talking about. Hence their claimed knowledge is no knowledge at all.

That was the case when the adduced reasons are false. But let us take the case when the reasons adduced are not false but simply inadequate. My mother says she knows that sacraments confer grace and the reason for this is that the Parish Priest says so. We shall have to return to such a topic later when one's knowledge is based on the 'witness' of supposedly competent authority. But here our answer to the question raised would be this: given that the reason given is adequate (i.e. reasonable) even if not fully sufficient, the claimed knowledge is real knowledge but insufficient.

§19. 'Truth' and 'reasonableness', are therefore essential, properties, and defining characteristics, of 'knowledge' as we understand the term. But this conclusion raises in its turn another very serious and important question. For if such is the case, can I be said to really know anything unless and until I am certain that what I know is true and reasonable? And is there anything which I can know in such a way? We shall try and tackle this question after we have discussed 'truth' and 'certainty' at some length later. But we shall return to this topic later (§§ 78 ff).

§*20. c.* ***Concepts and propositions.*** We have said that 'to know' implies explicitly or implicitly a judgment – which we defined as an assertion or denial, as an affirmation or denial. We would like here to analyses a little further the nature of a judgment.

1. Unexpressed or expressed judgment. I can make a judgment in my heart of hearts, as it were, or simply 'internally'. When I express it 'externally' (either to myself or to somebody else), I use words which together form a proposition. For example, "God exists!" The proposition is therefore the verbal outward expression of a judgment. Obviously this can be done either orally or in writing.

2. Analysis of a position. Besides, the duality of which we have already spoken implied in 'awareness', there is in every proposition another duality- this time of whom or what something is affirmed or denied (the subject) and what is affirmed or denied (the predicate).

The affirmation or denial itself is expressed by the verb 'is' – either explicitly or implicitly (We recall all this from Logic). A proposition, in modern Western Philosophy, is therefore to be distinguished from a non-propositional sentence (e.g. a command, an interrogation, an exclamation, etc). It is clear that only propositions can be proved or said to be true, or false. (For further details about the kinds of propositions we refer to our Logic, §§ 49-60).

3. Locutions and illocutions. In modern British Philosophy such terms have been common and they throw a certain amount of light on the epistemological questions with which we shall have to deal? 'Locution' stands for the utterance itself, 'illocution' stands for what, besides uttering the words, I am doing. For example, I utter the words: "God loves you". Besides saying these three words (the first speech-act), I may be trying to instill hope in somebody who is depressed. Of course one locution can have more than one illocution – depending on my intention and the situation. (Another term used is 'perlocution' – which, to avoid unnecessary complication we shall here overlook).

Following some authors (1), we can group 'illocutions' under four headings: the *'constatives'*, by which a certain 'state of affairs is affirmed or denied; *'expressives'* by which certain emotions, like wonder, trust, love, gratitude, joy, wish, etc., are expressed; *'commissives'*, by which certain commitments, intentions, decisions are made; and *'prescriptive'*, by which certain commands, recommendations, appointments, etc., are performed. It is clear that only 'constatives' correspond to propositions strictly so-called. We have just said, however, that a sentence can have more than one illocution – which means, therefore, that a given sentence may be considered a proposition in view of its 'constative' locution and a non-proposition in view of its, say, 'prescriptive' locution.

§21. a. **4. Concepts**. If we analyse the proposition a little further, or for that matter, language in general, we discover that often we use such general terms as 'man, animal, soul, tree, book' etc. Now it is clear that 'man', 'animal' etc., do not exist in reality, but only men animals, etc., And yet we often affirm or deny things about them. For example, "Man is created by God", "The soul of an animal is different from that of man". A term denoting a class of beings we call a 'concept'. In scholastic philosophy, it differs from an *idea* in that this simply stands for a mental representation of an object. Notice, however, that in western philosophy, these terms are used differently- oftentimes in accordance with different philosophical assumption.

Since 'concept', as said, denotes a class of beings, it is a universal idea (i.e. of that whole class). The question just referred to, namely how is it that we can affirm or deny things about realities which, as universals do not exist, has given rise, both in Western and in Indian Philosophy (significantly enough!) to what has come down to be known as "*the problem of the universal*". All kinds of positions have been taken ranging from that which maintains that concepts are mere words, images of singular objects, constructions of thought (*apohas*) without any objective foundation in reality (*Nominalism*) to the other 'extreme position which maintains that concepts correspond to realities existing in themselves (*jati*) (*Radical Realism*). The problem is treated not only in Epistemology ("what is the epistemic value of 'concepts'?) but also in Psychology ("how do we I really form 'concepts' in our mind?") and in Metaphysics ("does the concept refer to a universal reality itself existing in itself, i.e., externally to man's mind? If yes, where and how?").

§22. We shall refrain from discussing this problem. Already in the middle Ages, an author cynically remarked that philosophers had spent more time discussing the problem of the universals than Alexander spent in conquering the whole world. (What would he have said had he lived up to today?). It is that kind of problem which has given to Philosophy a bad name and made it seem to many much ado about nothing. Still, one cannot deny that the assumptions and conclusions of a philosophical stance taken on the problem oftentimes have important consequences on one's philosophical system as a whole. This will become clearer later. Suppose, for example, I say that all man can know are his sense-impressions or the images left-on His senses by the objects. I would have to conclude, then, not only that the 'concepts' are mere images but that I cannot know anything at all which is not sense-perceptible. Can I know, then, anything about God? What becomes of my religious belief?

Any book or treatise on Epistemology usually treats this problem. As for us, we take the following stance. Whose assumptions and conclusions will become clear during the rest of this treatise. (It agrees with the stance taken by Scholasticism and other Indian Philosophical Systems including-Kumarila's Mimamsa, Dvaita, Saiva Siddhanta and Jaina).

1. Man is capable both of having 'percepts' (e.g. when I see a particular, singular man) and of forming 'concepts' (e.g. of 'man' in general).[2]
2. This is possible because of essential properties common to particular, singular objects. Man is capable perceiving these properties, 'abstracting' them from the objects, as it were, and think of them as identities applicable to many.
3. Concepts have epistemic value – i.e., they serve in our knowledge of reality. Without them no language would be possible nor any progress in the natural sciences themselves. To deny this value to concepts would be to deny any cognitive value to the language by which this denial itself is expressed.
4. As such (i.e. as universal ideas), concepts are the result of man's understanding of reality – of objects in their singularity and in their commonality of properties.
5. Now as the proposition is a verbal expression of a judgment (cf. supra) so a noun is a verbal expression of a concept, a conventional sign which we use to refer to it. It can also be a tool, or instrument, which we use to express, the concept. But as in the judgment, so in the forming of a concept, much activity on the part of the knower is involved. By means of concepts and judgments man 'constructs' reality' making it intelligible.

---

2 See Salvino Azzopardi *Logic*, I9a-19d for a further understanding and distinction between concept', 'idea', 'image', 'notion', etc.

Chapter 2

KNOWLEDGE AND THE 'PRAMANAS'

§23. The question of how we come to know has been treated much more fully and insightfully in Indian Philosophy, we think, than in Western Philosophy. Indian Philosophy speaks of the 'sources of knowledge' (pramanas) or means by which we can come to know and to know what. We shall, however, overlook the controversy in Indian Philosophy regarding their number, whether one could count them as one (as in the system of the Carvakas), two (as in Buddhism and Vaisesika), three (as in Samkhya), four (as in Nyaya), five (as in Mimamsa) six (as in Vedanta and Kumarila's Mimamsa), etc., up to no less than ten! Whether a way of arriving at knowledge is to be considered genuine or not is certainly not an idle question, but whether such a way is implied in another way is, according to us, not so important. Many schools differ from others recording the number of such ways sometimes because they do not consider certain ways to be genuine, but, oftentimes, because they consider certain ways to be implied in others and therefore not independent sources of knowledge.

We shall consider only those ways which both in the West and in the East are considered to be the more important.

§24. So in this chapter we shall follow the order usually given by authors writing on Indian Epistemology, integrating theories and insights of Western Schools of Philosophy and adding our own comments and reflections. Note, in this respect, that whereas we, in the first chapter, already made it clear that what we mean by 'to know' (or 'knowledge') is essentially to know truly and reasonably, Indian philosophers distinguish between 'jnana' (or 'buddhi') – unfortunately often translated into English as knowledge- which can be either true or false, and 'prama' which is necessarily true (and which, therefore, corresponds more to what we are calling 'knowledge'). Pramanas, are therefore, strictly speaking, ways or means to obtain prama, true knowledge. But, in point of fact, what is after meant by the term is ways and means, or sources, of knowledge which can be either true or false. So to avoid confusion, we shall reserve knowledge only to essentially true knowledge (prama) and use 'cognition' – which is not such a felicitous word, either! – to stand for knowledge which can be either true or false ('jnana or buddhi') (2).

1. PERCEPTION (PRATYAKSA)

§25. Sense -experience is certainly one of the ways of how we come to know. It is not only just one way, but certainly, the chronologically first and most basic way of man's coming to know anything at all. Certain philosophers maintain that this is not the case since of certain things we have 'innate ideas' independently any sense-experience. We shall discuss this topic later, but, generally speaking all schools of Philosophy, except, for certain extreme positions of Western RATIONALISM, sense-experience (perception) to be a genuine means of knowledge – even though, dependently on their respective psychology, they explain its 'mechanism' differently. The reason then why we would like to delay on such a seemingly obvious fact is that, on the one hand, some maintain that only sense-experience is a genuine source of knowledge, thus denying any knowledge of what is not sense-perceptible, or at least, of what is not verifiable or falsifiable by sense-observation (EMPIRICISM) and, on the other hand, others maintain– including St Thomas and the Scholastics generally – that our knowledge of God, and religious language, though possible, take their origin from sense-experience. It is clear how both of these positions affect – though in a different way – our understanding of "religious faith and belief! We shall limit ourselves to certain important points.

§26. a. It is not much of a difficulty to say that since our senses often, deceive us – a question already raised in the Introduction – the senses, or sense-experience, are not a reliable source of knowledge. The fact of this possible deception simply proves that it is not the senses which 'know' but man by means of his senses. We have already pointed out that knowledge, all knowledge, implies a judgment. And in passing this judgment, man can certainly err- not because, however of any radical unreliability of the senses but because of some extrinsic factors like hastiness in the judgment, ignorance of some physical fact, etc. And what is more, even if we accept the fact that contrary to what common sense-experience, qualities of objects (like color and sound) are quantities (e.g. measurable wave-lengths), the sense-organs have still to be presumed to be reliable to produce regular wave–lengths (through the nerve-system) so as to be correctly 'interpreted' and known by the brain and to be 'measured' on the appropriate instrument.

b. But one big lesson we can learn from RATIONALISM, especially of the Idealistic type, is that sensations are not simply passive registering of the sense-data. A lot of active 'interpretation' on the part of the knower – by his reasoning faculties takes place in every act of perception. If, as we have just said, it is man who knows (and not the senses), all that goes in the making of a man, goes into his perception and understanding of reality. Many things which we think are mere objects of sense (e.g. space!) are man's 'construction' – originating, yes, from his sense-experience, but rationally 'built up'. And not only his reasoning faculties, but his emotions, etc., color the picture man draws of the world around him. This is a very important point and we shall return to it later.

§27. c. **The sense-organs**. Both Indian and Thomistic Psychology speak of external and internal senses. The external ones – to which correspond five kinds of external perceptions – are the visual, auditory, tactile, olfactory and gustatory. The internal one, in Indian Psychology, is the manas or antahkarana. It is the perception of myself seeing, of myself hearing, etc. It is operative also in the perception of external objects – when I perceive something, Iperceive myself to be perceiving the object – but the immediate object of perception by the manas is the 'myself'. Of course, those who deny a 'self' or those who reduce it simply to a chain of perceptions (empiricists of all kinds, both in the West and in the East) do not posit such an internal sense (This is an insistence where one's epistemology is fashioned by one's psychology!). Those who do, either posit it or account for the perception of the self either through inference or some other kind of higher perception (see below). This internal sense corresponding to the 'central sense' in Thomistic Psychology by which man is aware of himself and of his activities, is able to distinguish between his different sensations and activities and to integrate the data of the external senses thus referring them to a common, definite object.

§28. d. **Indeterminate (nirvikalpaka) and determinate (savikalpaka) perception.** We mention this distinction both because the terms often recur in Indian philosophical literature and because it serves to bring out a point which we insisted upon earlier, namely that every perception, indeed every act of knowledge (prama) entails a judgment. Unlike some commentators, but like some others, we do not understand this to be a distinction between two kinds of perception but rather as an insightful analysis of two stages in the process of any act of perception. "At first I perceive something vaguely without being able to say what exactly it is that I am perceiving. This is the indeterminate perception. It is only when I perceive what the thing, when I am able to say what it is, that I can say that I am really, determinately perceiving it. And this, of course, entails a judgment.

§29. **e. Normal (laukika) and supernormal (alaukika) perception.** This is a very intriguing distinction and it is worth giving it some thought. Besides the normal perception (of the six kinds mentioned above), Indian Philosophy speaks of a supernormal one. It is supra- normal because whereas the former is due to the 'contact' (sannikarsa) of the sense-organ with the object, the latter is not, and yet it is still considered to be a 'direct' apprehension of the object and therefore a perception.

This supernormal perception is of three kinds: The *first* is the (direct) apprehension of the 'universal' in the object, for example of the "cowness" in the cow (Those who hold this view can be counted among the 'radical realists' whom we referred to when we mentioned problem of the universals, §21!). The *second* is the perception of an object which is not proportionate to the sense-organ by which it is normally perceived. For example, on a hot day I see a picture of the sea and I feel cool. Now the usual explanation given to this is that the sight-experience is associated with a past experience of coolness so as to produce, as it were, a two-fold sensation (the visual and the tactile). Illusion, according to some, can be explained in this way. I see a rope in the dark and I perceive a snake. The presented object (the rope) is mistaken for the represented object (the snake of a past experience) due to this association. This is intriguing because also in Christian mystical literature, we come across authors who speak of, for example, 'touching', 'smelling', and 'tasting' spiritual realities. Some commentators understand this as symbolic language, but others do not fail to speak, in this context, of 'spiritual faculties' – distinct both from mere intellectual knowledge on the one hand and from ordinary sense-perception on the other.

§30. The *third* is more intriguing still. It is yogic (yogaja) perception of recondite or subtle things, in remote places or times including the past and future, due to an intense illumination of the mind obtained in deep concentration. It is intriguing not only because all schools of Indian Philosophy, including the 'heterodox' ones, claim that such a supra-normal perception is possible (it is the paramarthika perception of Jainism, the bodhi of the Buddhists, the kaivalya of Sankhya-yoga and the aparoksanubhuti of Vedanta), but we find the same claim in Christian mystical literature. It is interesting, in fact, to compare and contrast, in this respect, for example what Patanjali and St John of the Cross have to say on the matter. Both speak of the power of knowing and foretelling future events, of knowing the exact time of one's death, of knowing and reading other people's minds, and of a certain kind of "knowing all things", etc. St John, speaking of the power of knowing events happening in one's absence, remarks that such "knowledge derives from the illumined and purified spirit of those who have reached perfection or are close to it" (Ascent, II, 26).

We could interpret all this in a variety of ways- apart from dismissing it as "just talk"! We could, for example, interpret this kind of perception – together with the other phenomena which, it is claimed usually accompany it like supra-human strength, ability to go without food or drink for an extraordinary length of time, etc. -as a symbolic description of the powers of apperception of the deeper (or higher) levels of human consciousness.

Today we often hear of a "sixth sense" or even, more generally still of "extra-sensory-perception" (ESP). Claims are being made that experiments, scientifically conducted, are proving that the range of human perception is much wider and deeper than hitherto commonly supposed.

2. INFERENCE (ANUAMANA)

§31. According to Indian philosophers only perception is a means of direct (aparoksa) cognition. All the other means are means of indirect (paroksa) cognition that is of cognition obtained through the means of some other cognition directly perceived. That is why those philosophers who recognize only two pramanas do so, mostly, because they reduce all means of indirect cognition to inference. Anumana, as is clear, can be understood both as a way of reasoning and as a means of obtaining cognition. Now, as a way of reasoning we have studied it in Logic; here we shall be concerned with it as a means of obtaining cognition that is we shall examine its epistemic value (does inference lead to true cognition?) and not its formal structure. Logic, as we recall, deal with the validity, not with the truth, of argument. In other words, given that A is B and that B is C, it surely follows that A is C. I prove that A is C because there is an invariable connection (vyapti) between A and B. Logic does not question the truth of his invariable connection (i.e. that if A, then B). So here the question is: supposing that I cannot establish this connection, how can I say, how can I infer that A is C? If I can, this can only be done by perception and my alleged inference is already implied in it – it is not a means of obtaining new cognition, it is not really a means of obtaining cognition different from, and independent on, perception! One can clearly see the seriousness of this difficulty. Most of our knowledge is inferred from other known truths (or claimed truths) and not directly perceived (including most of our religious knowledge). What becomes of it if it is shown that all our knowledge is only of objects directly perceived (and sense perceived at that) or no knowledge at all?

§32. It is interesting to note that most of the objection raised by ancient Indian empiricists (the Carvakas) against inference as a means of—true knowledge have found an echo in some modern philosophers in the West (e.g. Hume and J.S. Mill). Let us examine carefully such objections.

1. *Objections against inference*

a. For inference to yield true-cognition, it is obviously necessary that the major premise [premiss is in the copy], as well as the minor premise, be true now even if the minor premise can easily, be recognized as true – since it is an object of direct perception, how can the major be recognized to be true since it is not such an object of direct perception? For example: Whatever begins to exist, must someday cease-to exist; you have begun to exist (i.e. you have been born); therefore, you must someday cease to exist. Now how can I come to say that "whatever begins to exist, must someday cease to 'exist? Is that unconditionally, i.e., necessarily true? How do I know? Have I sense experienced all things – not only of the present but also of the past *and* future? Such a statement is a generalization which cannot be proved to correspond to facts.

b. Even then, even supposing that I can sense-perceive some things which begin to exist and then cease to exist, how can I say that they cease to exist because they begin to exist (as the statement implies). In other words even if 'decay' was an essential characteristics of those things which I sense-perceived to have ceased to exist, how can I say that all other things are, in this respect, similar to them? How can I form a 'class' of things (characterized by the same characteristics)? What I sense-perceive is this particular thing and that particular thing, but not any 'universal'!

§33. c. If sense-perception is unable to establish the unconditional truth of the major premiss and the meaningfulness of the universal concept, neither can other alleged means (e.g. the internal sense, testimony, etc.) for all these alleged means pre-suppose the truth and validity of inference – which here is being rejected as a valid means of true cognition.

d. Besides, even if we were to grant that the major can be accepted as true, inference can yield no new knowledge for the conclusion (which is supposed to be the new knowledge) is already implied in it (which one is taking as the already known). And this makes the whole process of inference a vicious circle. To continue with our example: for me to say that "whatever begins to exist, must someday cease to exist", I must already know that "you must someday cease to exist" – how else could I use the term "whatever"?

e. In sum, and in more Indian technical terms, inferential knowledge (*anumiti*) is not genuine knowledge, knowledge in the true sense of the term (*prama*) since the invariable concomitance (vyapti) between the middle term which is supposed to serve a sign (*linga*) – in our example, "whatever is born" – pointing to the major term to be asserted in the conclusion (lingi) cannot be known.

f. Of course, those empiricists who are also 'pragmatists' ('true' is what is 'useful') recognize the pragmatic value of inferential knowledge for day-to-day life. But they rule out certainty in the strict sense in such matters contenting themselves with probability. Logically, the categorical assertion is reduced to a hypothetical one: If whatever begins to exist must someday cease to exist. ...

§34. 2. *Genuineness of inferential knowledge*

It is clear that such objections against the genuineness of the process of inference and of inferential knowledge thus supposed to be obtained rest on the assumption that apart from sense-perception, no knowledge (true and certain knowledge) is possible. But it would not be too difficult to show to prove his point, the empiricist has to use concepts – without which no discourse is possible! – and inference itself without which no argument is possible. Here, therefore, the empiricist position is either 'meaningless' or self-defeating. It is an instance of 'exercised contradiction' (see our Logic, § 54 note).

The concept is not always, as the objections suppose, a 'sensation' obtained by a mere sense-object (as we have said), nor is it even 'an idea derived from a complete enumeration' of the objects it denotes. Here again the 'problem of the universals' pops up again! Though the concept has both a 'collective' use (said of all the class as a whole) and a 'distributive' use (said of all the members of the class in particular), the 'universal' concept refers to the common characteristics of the objects which it denotes. How it is formed (Nyaya: by a supra-sensible apprehension of their common aspects, *samanyalaksana pratyasatti*) is indeed a very disputed question, but its epistemic value, at least as a tool for true discourse and genuine knowledge cannot be disputed without falling into self-contradiction.

§35. It is clear too that every inference comprises both a deduction and an induction (See our Logic for their nature and complementarity, §§ 65-66 and §§ 122-130). The vyapti can only be known by the induction. And it is the epistemic value of induction which is at the root of the objections against the genuineness of inferential knowledge. Unless and until one is prepared to posit some kind of 'insight' into the "whole process of obtaining any knowledge – including perceptual knowledge - one cannot start even talking meaningfully about anything at all. This leads us to the very *important* topic regarding the 'intuitive' or 'insightful' power (as distinguished from the 'discursive' or 'argumentative') of human understanding – something which we shall discuss later.

As to whether inference can yield *new* knowledge – even granting that the conclusion is implied, in the major premiss – the answer seems to be that to come to an explicit awareness of what is only logically implied in an already known truth is surely a process of every act of understanding. Whether or not one is prepared to call this newly, explicated awareness 'knowledge' depends on one's understanding of the term. Similarly, as to whether inference can only yield certainty (and not merely 'probability'), we shall have to discuss the nature of certainty – another important topic indeed! – later.

§36. Finally note that such important Schools of Indian Philosophy as Sunyavada Buddhism and Advaita Vedanta restrict inference as a means to obtain genuine knowledge of sense-objects, that is, to empirical reality. They deny that it can be used to come to know 'meta- empirical reality' (for example, 'religious truth'). For this something else – which cannot be said to be a 'means' at all! – is required. We shall discuss this topic later too. The topic is certainly one of the *most* important ones which we discuss in the Course!

§37.3. *Kinds of inference*

Since we speak of the kinds of inference in our Logic, we need not delay on this topic here. We content ourselves with briefly recalling them. Western logicians speak of and treat separately 'education' or immediate inference (an inference of one proposition from another) and, more importantly, 'deduction' and 'induction' (two forms of mediate inference, the former from a general truth to a particular instance, the latter from particular instances to a general truth). In 'induction' they distinguish further between 'perfect induction' (or 'complete' since it is arrived at after a complete consideration of all the instances in question) and 'imperfect induction' (by incomplete enumeration, by analogy, by elimination).

§38. Indian logicians speak of induction and deduction in one breath, as it were. We recall that the syllogistic structure as expounded by them clearly brings out how the actual process of reasoning, is both inductive and deductive, formal and material at the same time. This has both advantages (for it mirrors in a better way what happens in actual fact when we reason things out, and, on the academic plane, it impedes Logic from falling into cold formality) and disadvantages (because one can easily overlook distinctions, e.g. between the logical or linguistic aspect of human discourse from the epistemological aspect – as in fact, happened with certain schools of Philosophy as we are going to see).

§39. Be that as it may, Indian, logicians distinguish between '*svartha*' and '*parartha*' inference. This brings out well the distinction between that spontaneous inference in daily life, a psychological process done by and for oneself, and that statement in a formal syllogistic structure used mainly to convince others about the validity and truth of one's conclusions, – But more importantly still, Indian logicians distinguish between three types of inference: the '*purvavat*' (when the inference is from cause to effect, the middle term, or *linga*, being this cause), the '*sesavat*' (When the inference is from effect to cause, the *linga* being this effect), and the '*samanyatodrsta*' (when the inference is from the invariable co-presence of two 'things', the *linga*; being one of the two).

§40. We recall also the Indian classification of inference based not so much on the '*linga*' as on the different ways one can arrive at establishing *vyapti*. Hence, we have '*kevalanvayi*' (noticing how the '*linga*' is always related to the '*lingi*', the middle term to the minor), '*kevalavyatireki*' (noticing how they are never related) and '*anvayavyatireki*' (noticing how they are related in such a way that when, there is the one, there is the other, and when one is not there, the other too is not there).

§41. 4. *Fallacy as unsound inference*

In our Logic we also devote much space to 'fallacy' (*hetvabhasa*). So, again, we refer to what we say there. We simply recall that in Western Logic, only the topic of the fallacies treat of the 'truth' (and not simply of the 'validity' of inference. Appeal, is made, in the case, of 'material' fallacies to common-sense. Indian Logic treats only of these material fallacies. It bases them on the fact that what *seems* to be the reason (*hetu* or *linga*) is no reason at all. Hence, it lists the five characteristics of a true *hetu*: must be present in minor term, must be present in all instances of the major term, must be absent whenever the major term is absent, must not be incompatible with the minor term, must not be such it could be contradicted by stronger reasons.

3. TESTIMONY (SABDA)

§42. If we stop to consider, we shall be surprised to discover how much of our knowledge is based on, derived from, the 'word' (*sabda*) – witness, testimony of other people. Not only our knowledge of past events (historical knowledge), of remote places and people and of so much data established in the different sciences, but also our knowledge of so many things regarding our own selves is so dependent on the word of others. For example, how do I know when I was born, who my parents are, whether I have been baptized or not – unless on the word of others? (Knowledge which is thus based on the word of others we shall henceforth call 'belief'). This is eminently true of much of our religious belief. In fact, religious believers are 'believers' because they trust the witness of their respective Scriptures (e.g. the Bible, the Qu'ran, Sruti). And many among them-whether they are Christians, Muslims or Hindus – go as far as to say that religious truth can *only* be known on such a witness. This, of course, raises great difficulties to both of those with an 'empirical turn of mind and – but for opposite reasons – of those with a 'rationalist' turn of mind.

Still, at least as a means of true cognition on the intra-sensible world' (as distinct from the supra-sensible), most schools of Philosophy whether in the West and in the East recognize 'testimony'- under certain conditions – as a genuine means of true cognition, even though they differ as to whether it is completely independent on other sources (e.g. perception and inference), its range and 'certainty'.

§43. 1. Kinds of testimony

Testimony can, of course, be either oral or written. But Indian philosophers speak, more importantly, of 'drasta' (testimony, whether general or scriptural, regarding perceptible objects) and 'adrsta' (that regarding non-perceptible objects). Or again between 'laukika' (non- scriptural) and 'alaukika' (or 'vaidika', scriptural).

Significative is the reason for this latter distinction in Indian Philosophy. Some like Nyaya hold that the Vedas are the word of God who as an omniscient and most truthful is eminently to be relied upon. For others (e.g. Mimamsa) the Vedas are eminently reliable precisely because, unlike human testimony, they are not the word of any 'person' (*apaurseya*) whether human or divine, but are the embodiment of eternal truths. (Apart from the mimamsika theory of the eternality' of the word, which is hard to prove, we could however remark that if by 'Vedas' one were to understand the books themselves, they are certainly the work of man, the seers, but if by the term one were to understand the truths themselves, truths of course, cannot be said to be 'the work' of anybody not even of 'God' Himself!).

§44. 2. Testimony and reliability

For testimony to be a genuine source of true cognition, it must to have been frost proved to be reliable, i.e., trustworthy (*aptavacana*). And many factors, here, have to be taken in consideration. And with regard to Scriptural testimony, still more. All of which makes testimony, as a genuine source of true cognition, a little problematic!

a. In general. What makes a witness 'credible' (trustworthy, reliable)? Apart from his truthfulness (not intending to deceive), he has to prove his 'competence' (knowledge ability, his being in a position to assert what he is asserting, his authoritativeness – the nature and degree of which, of course, depending on the subject-matter. Recall, in 'Logic' the 'fallacy of assumed authority'!). The credibility of one witness can be enhanced if it is confirmed, or corroborated, by that of other witnesses.

§45 b. Scriptural testimony. Besides, trying to understand what the witness asserts (and here all the work of 'hermeneutics', the science of how to interpret written texts, especially ancient ones) and trying to understand *religious* texts – religious language, as we are going to see, has specific characteristics – one has to try to establish, as much as possible, their authorship, their integrity and their authenticity. Which is not saying a little!

Once these conditions are observed, to 'believe' would be reasonable, and hence source of 'knowledge' (cf. §18). As to 'certainty' –later!

4. COMPARISON (UPAMANA) and ANALOGY

§46. Cognition by 'similarity' is differently understood in Indian Philosophy. Some (Nyaya) understand by it that existing between a word and its connotation. To take the classical example: a villager is told by a forester that 'gavaya' is a wild animal which resembles a domestic cow. Later the villager sees an animal as the forester described it, and comes to know that 'gavaya' means this kind of animal. Others (Mimamsa and Vedanta) understand by it that existing between a remembered object and an actually perceived one: the villager sees the similarity between the cow which he remembers and the wild animal which he is now actually perceiving. The knowledge of this 'similarity' – which, according to these thinkers in their different understanding of the term, is a different kind of knowledge and therefore requiring a different kind of means to obtain it – is 'upamiti'. This, however, is a debatable point in Indian Philosophy. All the other schools do not see in 'upamana' an independent means, or source, of knowledge but reduce it to a combination of perception, memory and inference.

§47. 1. Heuristic value of 'comparison'

What we are more interested in is the heuristic value of 'comparison' (i.e. its usefulness in the whole process of understanding). Both students and teachers know very well the usefulness of the 'example' in learning and teaching. Check a word in the dictionary; you read its meaning and definition, and still you do not understand what the word means. Somebody explains it by giving an example. You immediately understand.

What is more is this. But here we have to widen the *scope* of 'upamana', to include the coming to understand non-perceptible realities, or at least the words used to denote them (like God, soul, heaven, etc.), from a certain kind of 'similarity' between perceptible realities and them. Of course, the Vedanta would not recognize the usefulness of upamana in this way, for according to it – as we have already hinted and shall see later – Ultimate Reality cannot be known by any pramana.

Its usefulness is limited, according to it, to the knowledge of similarity between a remembered perceptible thing and another actually perceived thing, and vice-versa. Still the way Sabara (a mimamsika) explains upamana- as the "knowledge of an unperceived object as being similar to some known object" – seems to justify this wider scope. As a matter of fact, the upanisads – or for that matter all the religious literature of the world- do make use of this 'similarity' to speak of Ultimate Reality and to bring the reader to 'understand' what they are talking about. Upamana, in this respect, can at least serve to evoke 'insight' (a word which we have used before – in §35 – and which we shall examine in some detail later).

§48. 2. Analogy

In this wider understanding, 'upamana' comes close to the Scholastic 'analogy' about which we shall have to say a lot of things later on. But be it noted already that, as understood in Scholasticism, analogy is not made use of to 'prove' the existence of supra-sensible realities, it is rather, or at least principally, a way of predication – that is, a way of speaking meaningfully (intelligibly) of what exceeds the grasp of sensible perception and thus to arrive at a better understanding of what is meant by the words used to refer to it. The simile, the metaphor, the myth, the allegory, the parable, the model – terms which we shall explain later – are all heuristic functions of the 'example'.

§49. Be it noted, in passing that the frequent discussion whether a *pramana* is or is not reducible to another – whether, that is, it is a specific way of arriving at true cognition independently on all others – is, if we are not mistaken, to the insufficient distinction between the 'logical' and the 'epistemological' aspect of human understanding. This is one of the disadvantages hinted at above of treating them together in one breath (see §38). In fact, people who try to show that, for example, 'comparison' is reducible to 'inference' how logically it is so: If A is similar to B, B is similar to A; A is similar to B, Therefore B is similar to A; But to say that is one thing, to say that in the actual process of understanding (epistemologically), that is the exact way of coming to understand one thing because of its similarity to another, is a different question!

5. POSTULATION (ARTHAPATTI) and HYPOTHESIS

§50. Here again, 'postulation' is a little differently; understood in Indian Philosophy and the question whether it could be reduced to another pramana (inference) is raised again. Some (Mimamsa) understand it as the cognition of a fact which has to be assumed or supposed in order to explain two seemingly contradictory facts. Others (Vedanta) understand it as the cognition of a fact which is similarly to be assumed or supposed to explain a seemingly unexplainable fact – whether this fact is known – by perception or by Sruti.

As usual we shall not discuss whether 'postulation' understood in either or both senses is reducible to inference, but as have done with 'upamana' we shall try to bring out its heuristic value – which, we think, is very great.

§51. 1. Heuristic value of 'postulation'

Notice, first of all, that 'postulation' rests on the 'insight' (once again!) that two seemingly contradictory facts *must* have an explanation to account for this seeming contradiction, and that, similarly, a seemingly unexplainable fact *must* have an explanation. To have noticed this is important for what we shall have later to say about 'insight'.

Secondly, let it be noted that the kind of 'postulation' in question or assumption, or supposition, corresponds to the 'hypothesis' used in Sciences to explain the laws of nature. Here the 'insight' is there *are* laws of nature, there is a kind of constancy in the behavior of physical phenomena and that given the proper conditions and with the proper instruments they can be progressively known.

52. But even in daily life and in Philosophy, the 'postulation', or 'hypothesis' has its usefulness to understand reality. In Western Philosophy, the term 'postulate' is mostly associated with Kant. Kant claims that though such supra-sensible realities as the existence of God, the immortality of the soul and human freedom cannot be proved by (speculative) reason, they have to be 'postulated' by (practical) reason. This topic will be studied in detail both in the History of Western Philosophy and in Moral Philosophy. But here we content ourselves with showing the function of 'postulation' in human understanding. To make this clear we link the idea of Kant with the more recent question in Western Philosophy whether one can 'deduce' the fact that man is physically 'free' from the fact that he is morally obliged to do good. (Whether one can 'deduce' a 'can' from an 'ought'). Now supposing that that man ought to do good is a proved fact, or truth, one cannot logically prove or deduce from that fact that he is physically free – that is, one cannot do so from

the mere meaning of the words 'can' and 'ought'. But epistemologically unless and until one assumes or supposes that man is physically free, it would be absurd to say that man is morally obliged (ought) to do anything. This is the kind of postulation which Kant according to us, must have had in mind. Postulation is certainly a genuine means to attain knowledge.

We ourselves, in our various courses, do make much use of 'postulation' to explain either seemingly contradictory facts (e.g. the existence of a loving and omnipotent God and the existence of evil) or seemingly unexplainable facts (e.g. the existence of religious pluralism).

§53. 2. The nature of a 'good' hypothesis

As distinct from 'proof' which one can logically show whether it is true or false, a 'hypothesis', by its very nature, can only be shown to be appropriate or inappropriate, arbitrary or well-grounded, reasonable or not. And this depends on whether the 'hypothesis' fulfils certain conditions – and this applicable to any hypothesis whether it is used in Science, in Philosophy or in any other field of knowledge.

a. A hypothesis must be based on good or sound reasons. For example, if my hypothesis for the cause of cancer (a seemingly unexplainable fact) is that it is caused by the devil and my reason for saying so is that all Diseases are evil and evil can only be caused by an evil being, my hypothesis can be shown - on medical, philosophical and theological grounds, to be unsound.

b. The hypothesis must give a reasonable explanation for all the relevant facts. For example, it must explain, in our case, how is it that occurs mostly in advanced age, that it can attack many different organs of the body and the blood itself, that it can but rarely occur in young age, that it responds to certain treatment but not to others, etc.

§54. c. The hypothesis must be internally consistent. If some elements in the hypothesis contradict some others, the hypothesis is not consistent. If, for example, the hypothesis says that cancer is caused by viruses and says too that it is responsive to cobalt treatment in its early stages because cobalt destroys microbes which are not known to produce any virus then there is something wrong with my hypothesis!

d. The hypothesis must be coherent with other well-established medical facts or any other known truths. If, for example, the hypothesis says that cancer is such a disease that it simply cannot be caused by anything, it is not coherent with medical or philosophical well-established truths.

§55. There are other (minor) conditions which a 'good' hypothesis must fulfill. In Science, for example, the simpler the hypothesis, the more appropriate is it considered to be. But for our present purposes what we have said is sufficient, we think, to give an indication of what a 'good' hypothesis is and of its heuristic function. Needless to add that a hypothesis remains always 'open-ended', that is, it remains always provisional, subject to correction, serving as it does as a supposition or conjecture for further study. It may eventually have to yield place to a 'better' hypothesis, that is, on one which is grounded on more, or more solid reasons, or which explains better, or more, facts, or, finally, which is more internally consistent or more coherent with other truths established in other fields of knowledge.

§56. 3. Difference between 'arthapatti' and 'hypothesis'

Our last, remark on 'hypothesis' brings out the difference between 'arthapatti' as understood in Indian Philosophy and 'hypothsis' as understood in Western Philosophy. Whereas hypothesis, as said, is, by its very nature, provisional, that is tentative explanation, arthapatti, or postulation can be said to be certain. If man ought to do good, I can certainly postulate that he is physically free. Without being a logical implication (cf. Logic), it is an epistemologically sure way of gaining true cognition. Of course, the conclusion arrived at can subsequently be proved either false or not the only possible true one. But this means that like in perception or inference the conclusion can subsequently be proved false even though perception and inference can be said to be, in themselves sure means of obtaining true cognition. This brings out a second difference between 'arthapatti' and 'hypothesis'. The former stands for the means of obtaining true cognition itself, that is, as a 'pramana', while the latter stands for the supposition.

§57. Whether or not the 'knowledge' obtained through postulation, and much more the hypothesis itself, can be called 'knowledge' in the true sense depends, as we have had the occasion to remark before, on what one understands by the term. In the first chapter we have made it clear that it belongs to 'knowledge' (in our sense of the term) that it be true and reasonable. As we have just pointed out, it belongs to the very nature of 'hypothesis' (in our sense of the term) that it be founded on solid grounds and hence that it be reasonable!

6. 'ANUPALABDHI' AND OTHER 'PRAMANAS' IN INDIAN PHILOSOPHY

§58. We mention these other 'pramanas' as found in Indian philosophy not merely for completeness sake but also, we think, one or two have to be given, the consideration they deserve. Each has been recognized as a genuine 'pramana' by one or other of the Indian Schools. The big and ever-recurring question is, again, whether it is to be considered as a specific 'pramana', whether, that is, it is independent of and reducible to any other one.

§59. 1. 'Anupalabdhi'

The question is this: if the existence of a perceived object is known by direct perception (*pratyaksa*), how is its absence, or non-existence, perceived? Only some (the Advaitins and some Mimamsikas) require a specific 'pramana' for this - which they call 'anupalabdhi' (variously translated as 'non-perception', 'non-cognition', 'non-apprehension'). The others claim that perception or inference is sufficient to explain the cognition of the 'non-existence' of an object. Reasons and counter-reasons are given. This, to our mind, is another instance where professional philosophers can give philosophy a bad name (like in the case of the 'problem of the universals')! Be that as it may, it is to be noticed that 'non-existence' is spoken of here as a predicate. In fact, Vaisesika counts it (*abhava*) among the '*padarthas*' (supreme classifications of all knowable objects). Hence, considered as such, 'non-existence' of a thing can be spoken in terms of 'an object', as 'something' to be known and one can even speak of the different "kinds" of 'non-existence' (as Vaisesika in fact does). Western logicians would today say that that is a misuse of language for, according to at least many of them 'non-existence' is a negation of something and not 'something'. Even 'existence' itself cannot be said to be a 'predicate' – at least not in the same sense as the other predicates are. (Cf. our Logic, where we speak of predicates, predicables and categories. – Notice, finally, that the Advaitins do not say that 'non perception' of anything leads to the knowledge of its 'non-existence'. Only 'appropriate non-perception' (yoga) does so, i.e., when it is only a question of an object which is perceptible (and not, therefore, of supra-sensible, supra-perceptible realities).

§60. 2. 'Sambhva'

It is the way of coming to know the existence of a thing, not directly and immediately as in perception, but from the existence of another thing in which it inheres or is included (sam + bhava). Of course, this inclusion cannot be merely a possible or accidental one, but necessary and certain. Thus, I cannot come to know the holiness of a priest from his 'priesthood', but I can come to know, it is claimed, that a thousand includes a hundred. This is clearly a case of 'implication' but Nyaya considers it as an instance of deductive inference. But is it really any kind of inference at all? Isn't it rather that kind of implication which is immediately seen as self-evident and expressed in analytically true propositions – e.g., the whole includes and is greater than the parts? This is not an inference in as much as it is not deduced from another proposition. But if it is not, if it is self-evident, needing no proof, is not this another instance of 'insight'? We shall return to this topic later.

§61. 3. 'Aitihya'

Aitihya, or tradition, is recognized by the Pauranikas (believers in the Puranas, ancient sacred treatises) as a genuine 'pramana'. This is easily dismissed by some because, they argue, tradition can either be traced to reliable sources, in which case it is an instance of 'testimony' (sabda) and not a specific 'pramana', or be not traceable to any reliable source – in which case it is not a 'pramana' at all (The Puranas, in fact, have no known author. They are said to have been compiled by Vyasa, himself a legendary figure). But it seems to us that this dismissal is hasty. It is true *if* tradition is reduced to a way of knowing because of the reliability of the one giving witness, it will be an instance of testimony. But if tradition is seen as a way of knowing on the ground that, for example, the fact that it lasted for a great period of time, believed in by so many people, is indicative, by itself, of its reliability (irrespective who the author(s) may be, then the knowledge gained there from is certainly 'reasonable'. Here is an 'insight' which has remained perhaps unexpressed!

§62. 4. Cesta

We speak today of 'non-verbal communication'. The Tantras (body of religious Saivite literature) speak of 'cesta', gesture, like bodily movements, facial expressions, etc., which can be a source of knowledge. That such gesture can be a means of communication, there is certainly no doubt. But it is not clear how it can be considered as a 'pramana'- unless in the same sense as any verbal or written communication can be said to be such, that is, as a source of meaning.

§63. 5. 'Parisesa'

This is a way of coming to know something by the 'elimination' (parisesa) of those objects which are not it – that is which are distinct from and not identifiable with it. It is interesting to compare this process with what in Scholasticism has come to be known as 'the way of remotion'. We shall have to speak a lot about it since according to St Thomas it is the 'principal way' to come to know and speak about God. It is a way which in fact is constantly used in mystical literature including the Upanisads.

But even as applied to the knowledge of perceptible things alone, some do not acknowledge it to be a specific 'pramana' by itself but reduce it to perception or some other 'pramana'. Here again what we remarked before applies here too: not sufficient attention is given to the distinction between the logical and epistemological order. Be that as it may, let it be noted that in Scholasticism, this 'way of remotion', like 'analogy' is not used to 'prove' the existence of God, but as a way, not indeed of predication since this is precisely a way of negating attributes (hence its other name as 'way of negation'), but of coming to know what is meant by the word 'God' – precisely by saying what 'God' is not!

Chapter 3

REASON AND INTELLECT

§64. We are entering here a very delicate area. Our answer to many epistemological questions depends, to a large extent, on what we shall be trying to establish here. Hence a word of warning: In Philosophy, different Schools, or even different authors of the same school, use often the same words with different meaning. This naturally is often the cause, or at least one of the causes, for philosophical disagreement. This disagreement is increased when the original terms used by an author in his native tongue (Sanskrit, English, French, German, etc.) is translated into another language!

To apply all this to the topic we are going to deal with in this chapter. The words 'reason', 'intellectual', 'intelligence', 'mind', 'insight', 'intuition' and a host of others are fluid: they can and often are, used with different meanings. The same author himself may not be always consistent in his usage of words. So one has to be extremely careful to understand what the author means by the word and the context in which he is using it. (The intention of the author, or speaker, as expressed in the word is referred to, in Indian Philosophy, as 'tatparya').

1. INSIGHT

§65. In our exposition of the different 'pramanas', we often, had the occasion to point, in passing, to the necessity of postulating some sort of 'insight' to account for the psychological process of the 'pramana' in question. Thus, for example, we have seen it at work, so to say, in the formation of the 'universal concept' (§ 34), in induction (§ 35), in the heuristic function of analogy (§ 47) and of postulation (§ 51), in 'sambhava' and 'aitihya' (§§ 6C-61). The nature and function of 'insight' in every process of understanding has, in recent times, been exhaustively and convincingly brought out in his by now famous *Insight: A Study of Human Understanding.*[3]

Here we simply define the term *as apenetration with the understanding into (insight) some self-evident truth.* This insight is therefore required if we want to account for any way to come to know anything at all - unless, of course, we prefer either to reduce such process to mere sense-perception- a position which we have already argued is self-contradictory (§ 34)- 'or to opt for a kind of universal skepticism (which says that we cannot know anything at all) - a position which besides being self-contradictory for the same reason, is not even human!

§66. But what is a self-evident truth? And can we really claim that there are any? Unlike an inferred truth – i.e., a truth deduced or derived from another truth by the processcalled 'inference' comprising both deduction and induction (and which we have already examined; §§ 31-41) – a self evident truth is one which is not thus inferred but is 'seen' to be true directly and immediately. It is seen to be so by 'insight'. They are said to be 'a-priori'. Here we have to be careful. We have to distinguish between what in the whole process of understanding comes first (prior) in time and what comes first logically. Now in time, perception (and experience in general) comes first. And this is acknowledged, at least generally, in Scholasticism as well as in Indian Schools of Philosophy. As the Scholastic adage has it, "There is nothing in the mind which has not first been in the senses." But logically – in the same way as a 'conclusion' is drawn from the premises – what comes first is the explicit or implicit awareness of the self-evidence of the truth in question. To put all this in another way: a self-evident truth is one whose verifiability does not depend on sense perception or any other means. (It is in this sense, and only in this, that a self-evident truth is said to be 'independent' of perception or experience). All this will become clearer when we give examples of a self-evident truth.

2. REASON

§67. As we have already hinted 'reason' is one whose meaning is fluid and is the cause of much misunderstanding. In the West, since the time of Descartes, 'reason' has come to refer to that power of the mind to draw, by inference one truth from another. It is also in this sense that the Sanskrit term 'manas' is often translated (but seen also § 27). But both in scholasticism and other Schools of Philosophy in the West as well as in most schools of Indian Philosophy (except the empiricist schools in either West or East) claim for the mind the power to 'see-in' evident truths and even – but this is naturally more disputable as we are going to see later- to 'see-in' supra-sensible, supra-perceptual, truths. And if have to conclude from what we have said earlier that this 'insight' is required in all the process of human

3 Lonergan, Bernard J. F., and Frederick E. Crowe. *Insight: A Study of Human Understanding.* Toronto: University of Toronto Press, 2005.

understanding, we have to conclude that there exists in the human mind this power of insight. (Whether or not they are to be considered as separate faculties or separate powers of the same mind is another, less important, issue). And to be able to distinguish this power (or act) of insight from the power (or act) of inferring, we shall distinguish between 'intuition' and 'reason.'Intuition we define as: *the immediate apprehension by the mind, without reasoning of self-evident truths* (At times 'insight' and 'intuition' are used 'interchangeably'). Reasoning, we define as: *the process by which we come to know* through perception, thinking and reflecting, inferring.

3. INTELLECT

§68. It is useful to recall here that it is *man*, who comes to know, understands, etc., and not the mind, or the intellect, or reason, etc. Such a 'schematization' is useful only as a model (a "schema") to help us understand the whole process, and possible range, of human understanding itself!

Now by 'intellect' we can understand either the all-comprehensive human faculty, or power, of understanding, of coming to know – of whose, therefore intuition, reasoning would be different aspects or acts. Or else for this all comprehensive faculty we use the term 'mind' and reserve the term 'intellect' to the power, or act, of intuition alone. We prefer to do the latter.

The question of vocabulary is very important, as we have said, to avoid confusion. Still it remains secondary. The interesting question is to see what 'self-evident truths' we can speak of. We can speak of these truths as 'necessary truths', i.e., that they cannot fee denied without contradiction – exercitively or logically. By definition, they cannot be 'proved' (for otherwise, they would be 'inferred' and not immediately seen, or intuited). But this does not mean that they are explicitly (clearly, thematically) adverted to. It is only in a philosophical study such as this, can one become fully aware of them – aware that in any previous process of understanding of his, one had, even without his knowing, to presuppose them, and that, therefore, they were the immediate data of his consciousness.

§69. Let us illustrate this by a simple and commonly used example. Somebody tells me that the three angles of any triangle are equal to 180 degrees. I do not see this immediately. But then he draws a line to prolong the base, draws a parallel line to the opposite side of the triangle and starts explaining. While I follow his explanation, I am perceiving the figure, I am thinking and following his argument, etc. So far I have been 'reasoning'. I discover that his conclusion has finally to be based on the truth that things which are equal to the same thing are equal to one another! This, of course, is 'common-sense', he does not need to go on and, prove it. And even if he tried, he could not. So, I come to know that the three angles of any triangle are equal to 180 degrees by 'reason'. I know that things which are equal to the same thing are equal to one another by 'intellect'!

§70. In fact, in Logic and Mathematics, we can discover that many truths are known 'intuitively': in fact, all the basic principles of both are so known. Of course, modern Symbolic Logic considers these as 'tautological implications' or 'tautological equivalences' (see our Logic §§199ff) and uses them as tools for meaningful discourse and correct argumentation without stopping to consider whether, as the scholastic adage has it, "the rules of thought are rules of being itself", that is whether we think in such and such a way because our mind is fashioned that way but because reality itself demands it. (We shall return to this point when we discuss Kant who has got something very definite to say about the matter!)

§71. One could ask whether these self-evident truths, being as they are so 'formal' could really be counted as information about the real world, whether, that is they can be really said to form part of 'knowledge' and not rather as directives for right thinking. Well, apart from the fact that here it all depends on what one means by 'knowledge' (something which we discussed in our first chapter), the remark which we have just passed answers the question. Scholasticism singled out some self- evident truths which are informative about reality. And it is because they are so informative that they can be expressed as rules, or directives, for right thinking. These self-evident are known as 'first principles 'and studied in Metaphysics. For example the *Principle of Identity* (if A is A, then A is A and non-A is non-A; expressed as a logical rule: if a proposition is true, it is true), the *Principle of Non-Contradiction* (if A is true, non A is false: if a proposition is true, its contradictory is false: we shall discuss later whether this principle is so self-evident that it cannot be that some Indian school of philosophy deny it as it is often alleged), the *Principle of Excluded Middle* (either A or not A; proposition can be either true or false, not both). Again, the *Principle of Sufficient Reason* (Being is not absurd; it must be intelligible), the *principle of causality* (contingent Being must have a cause to explain its existence), the *principle of finality* (who ever acts, acts for a purpose).

§72. At first sight, these principles seem trite, obvious ("self-evident"!) without much consequence. But recall when you started learning geometry and started by learning the 'axioms'. They too may have seemed so, and yet you later learnt that without them you could not have progressed, step by step, to the understanding of the theorems which gradually became more and more complex. This brings us to another remark which is important. These self-evident truths do not serve 'premises' of a conclusion. From them, in fact, nothing can logically be inferred or derived. They serve rather as a *basis* on which a truth (from which another truth is to be inferred) is ultimately shown to be true or because of which it is true.

§73. But it is not only in what, concerns our knowledge of reality (the speculative order) that we have to presuppose certain self-evident truths, but also in what concerns our knowledge of right 'behavior' (the practical, or moral order). In our *Ethics*, we begin our reflections by precisely trying to single out certain self-evident moral truths, the immediate data of moral consciousness. (E.g. the good is to be done, evil not to be done and this applies to all men, and in an objective and not merely objective way, etc.). Indeed, in our *Philosophy of Religion*, we similarly try to single out some self-evident religious truths. (E.g. the existence of an object of ultimate concern, supreme significance, absolute worth, in man's deepest consciousness – no matter what this object is called).

§74. Two final remarks 1. A 'self-evident truth' can be compared to but also contrasted with Kant's 'synthetic-a-priori judgment' and the 'necessary true proposition' (or 'tautology') of contemporary western Logic. All refer to something which is known to be absolutely true and certain, but this 'something' is, in the first case, a law of mind as well as being, in the second case, the formal structure of the proposition which can be said to be unexceptionally valid, and in the third case, the universal and necessary form (category) of the subjective judgment.

2. Many other functions are ascribed, in the philosophical literature of the world, to the "intellect"- depending, precisely, on what is meant by the term. But we have thought it extremely important to make the student aware of the place, or role, of 'insight' - indeed of 'insight' into self-evident truths- in the whole process of 'coming to know' and this not only to understand better the 'pramanas' but also to equip ourselves better when we come to the central topic of our course, namely, *can we come to know God and meaningfully speak about Him?*

Chapter 4

KNOWLEDGE AND TRUTH

§75. In the first chapter, we have said that in our understanding of the term 'knowledge' is essentially true. We saw that this corresponds to the Indian term 'prama'. We said too (§17) that by 'true' we were provincially meaning 'corresponding to what the case is'. Now, in the history of philosophy, both in the west and in the East, we come across various understanding of the term 'true' (or 'truth'). From each we can learn a lot. So, before we definitely settle for what we are going to understand by 'true', it is good to examine carefully these various understandings. The question which is usually raised in this context is this: what is the criterion, or test, of truth? That is how I am going to know that what I am affirming or denying is true or false? In any case, an understanding of what one means by 'true' can help us answer the question which we already raised in the first chapter (§ 19) whether I can be said to really know until and unless I am certain that what I know is true (and reasonable).

§76. 1. Preliminary Remarks

1. It is clear that no matter the different understandings of the term 'true' which we shall be here exposing, we are here concerned with the term as qualifying a judgment (expressed or unexpressed in a proposition and of a proposition of the 'constantive illocution' type, §§20-21). In other words, we are here concerned with *epistemological truth*. In fact the term 'true' can be used to qualify a person or a thing. (E.g. "he is a true patriot", or "this is true whisky" – by which is meant, in the first case, 'ideal', in the second 'genuine'). In Metaphysics, one usually distinguishes between this 'epistemological (or logical) truth' (as opposed to error), from 'moral truth' (as opposed to a lie) and 'ontological (or transcendental) truth' (as supposed to non-being). In our *Logic*, we took pains to distinguish between 'truth' and 'validity'. But do know that often, even in philosophical literature, these two words are used inter-changeably.

§77. 2. Now, speaking of the 'criterion' or 'test of truth, we have to clarify the notion of 'evidence', for clearly that principle or standard (criterion) by which, we judge whether a judgment is true or false is precisely 'evidence'. But what is evidence? We have already (§ 66) spoken of a 'self-evident' truth as one which is seen 'directly and immediately' but at that stage, we took 'evident' in the generally accepted meaning of the term. Here we have to clarify the notion a little better. By 'evidence' we, therefore, mean that *clarity (obviousness, conspicuity) serving to indicate (attest to) the truth of the judgment.* Roughly speaking, it can be called 'proof'. I say that Mr X is in his room. What is the evidence, – or proof – that what I am saying is true? It may be that I just saw him going into his room. For me it is 'clear' (evident) that what I am saying is true. Or it may be that I have just been told by a reliable parson. In this case, for me it is 'clear' that what 1 am saying is true. Now since – as in the latter case the reliable person may have been mistaken and therefore what is 'clear' to me (subjectively speaking) may not have corresponded to the facts (i.e., to the truth, objectively speaking), the question arises what kind, or degree, of 'objective evidence' is required- if this is at all possible! – for me to say that 1 am absolutely sure that what I am saying is true. This brings us, once again, to the problem of 'certitude' which we shall be treating later. Still, the notion of 'evidence' as expressed here is sufficient, we think, to follow intelligently the admittedly difficult problem regarding 'truth'!

§78. 3. Apart from the question about 'certitude', two other questions have to be distinguished. It seems to us that a greater agreement on this question regarding 'truth' could have been achieved in the history of Philosophy, whether in the West or in the East, if these two questions had been better distinguished. The first question (the semantic) is this: what am I going to understand by the term 'true'; the second question (the epistemological) is this: if the criterion of 'truth' is 'objective evidence, is this 'objective evidence' possible at all and if it is possible, what amount of clarity is sufficient and necessary for me to say that I am certain of what I am affirming (or denying)? These two questions (or sets of questions) are so distinct that I could, for example, find myself able to say what I mean by 'true' and still unable to say that no 'objective evidence', in any field of knowledge, is at all possible.

§79 4. Whereas in the west (especially in more modern times) this distinction could have helped in the context of the discussion about 'truth', in India, it could have done so in the context of the discussion about 'cognition' (*jnana*, *buddhi*). The question raised and enthusiastically debated was: what is the nature of '*true and valid* cognition' (i.e. prama). Most schools of Indian philosophy agree on many points. But when the viewed question arises as to whether the truth or validity of cognition is 'intrinsic' or 'extrinsic' to it, opinions differ. Some say that cognition as such (jnana) can be either true or false, valid or invalid and hence truth is extrinsic to it (Nyaya). Others say that cognition as such is always true and valid and it is only accidently (e.g. by the defects of the instrumental cause) that it can be invalid and false, and therefore truth and validity are always intrinsic to it and only falsity and invalidity are extrinsic to it (Mimamsa). Again, others say that cognition as such is always false and invalid and it is only through extraneous factors (e.g. Like achieving an intended aim) that it can be true and valid, and hence truth and validity are always extrinsic whereas falsity and invalidity are intrinsic (Buddhism), etc. A very careful perusal of the points at issue can reveal that here the two questions (the semantic and epistemological) are dealt with in one breath whereas it would have been better to distinguish better between the two. In fact to ask whether truth and validity belong to cognition intrinsically or extrinsically can be resolved into the question – not what is the nature of cognition? – but what are we going to understand by cognition? (This is the semantic question!). Now if we agreed to call 'cognition' *only* true and valid cognition, then the question whether truth and validity belong to it intrinsically or extrinsically would not arise for it would have been solved by the very understanding (definition) of the term. Once we would have agreed what to call 'cognition', than and only then would we pass to the other question regarding the possibility and type of objective evidence sufficient and necessary to meet our already established meaning of cognition (the epistemological question). As we proceed to examine the theories of truth (in the West and in the East) we shall keep the distinctness of the two questions always in mind.

§80. 2. Theories of Truth

1. The Correspondence Theory

This theory says that truth is "the adequation of the mind to the object". In other words, truth is the correspondence itself between what I affirm or deny to what is really the case. This has been our provisional understanding of 'truth'. The majority of Indian Schools of Philosophy agree that *prama*, knowledge, must correspond to what really the object of knowledge is in itself.

Some, however, raise the question: how can I know that what I can affirm or deny really corresponds to what the case is? In other words, how can I know that the object *as* known corresponds to the object *as* it is in itself? For if I had to turn my attention to this very 'correspondence' I would still know it *as* known, but would it, in its turn, correspond to what it is in itself? And so on and so fourth ad infinitum! 1 cannot jump out of my mind, as it were, so as to be able to 'compare' what I know and the object of my knowledge as it is in itself and thus to see whether they correspond to each other or not.

Kant says: don't worry, you can never know the object as it is in itself (noumenon), for this remains always unknown and unknowable; you can only know the object *as* known (phenomenon), as it appears to you and moulded by certain forms of your mind (categories). The Scholastics say: don't worry, you do know the object as it is in itself; in fact the object as known is really a kind of 'sign in which' (signum quo) not the image of the object as it is in itself is known, but directly the object itself.

§81. On this particular topic, the Indian Schools of Philosophy are also divided. Two main trends appear; one says that truth is 'self-validating' (svatah-pramanyavada), the other says that truth has to be validated by something other than itself (paratah-pramanyavada). We do not intend to enter into the details of these two trends (the former, best represented by Samkhya, Mimamsa and Vedanta, the latter by Nyaya-Vaisesika), but we make some reflections of our own.

We have tried to show that in *every* way of coming to know we have to presuppose some 'insight' (i.e. into some 'self-evident' truth – *if*, of course, we do not want to opt for a kind of universal skepticism which, we have seen too, is self-contradictory and therefore philosophically untenable). This is why too the 'infinitive regress' which we have just mentioned is not only not-necessary and impossible but also required only by a universal skepticism. In the whole problematic of knowledge, the real issue, as the Vedanta has clearly seen, is not so much the possibility of knowledge but the possibility of error! (It is instructive to observe that many philosophers in the West, when they come to tackle the problem regarding the possibility of knowledge – the *Problema Criticum* – find themselves obliged to justify the very legitimacy of raising the question). Still this does not mean that in every way of coming to know, this 'insight' is had immediately. It is only when one starts questioning the validity of the truth in question that one can come to 'see-in' that self-evident truth on the basis of which this truth is finally affirmed. It is in this sense that, according to us, truth is its own guarantor, its own validation. Though this can be more clearly seen in the 'formal sciences' (like Logic and Mathematics) and in perception it can also be seen in every way of coming to know since these, no less but surely even more mediately are finally based on a 'self-evident' truth.

§82. All this will become clearer when we compare and contrast with the other theories of truth about which we shall be speaking presently. But the way we understand 'correspondence' is to see in it the 'definition' of what we mean by 'truth' and not as some modern commentators of Nyaya, for example, as a 'test' of 'truth'. We make use of the 'test' or 'proof' to see whether the judgment (or the proposition) is true or false. If I manage to obtain sufficient and necessary 'evidence', then I know that the judgment is true, otherwise I may either still be doubtful, or if the evidence is sufficient and necessary that my judgment is false, I know that it is false. But then, supposing that I know fully know that my judgment is true, I do not need to have 'test' the already established 'truth' of my judgment by some other non-cognitive means (e.g. by its usefulness). If I do still feel the need to have further tests, it means that I am still doubtful about whether my judgment is true or false. And if I simply want to show *why* (not whether!) my judgment is true, then I have to initiate a process of reasoning which I can come to see finally rests not on any non-cognitive consideration (e.g. usefulness) but on some 'self-evident' truth.

§83. Still because some fail to disentangle themselves from the difficulty regarding the possibility of ascertaining whether the 'correspondence' is itself true or false, or simply whether it is true at all (for it may happen that I may not be able to see that it is false, and yet I may not be able to see that it is true either), they seek to find some other meaning of 'truth'. The epistemological difficulty leads them to solve the semantic question differently. Notice already the two questions getting involved with each other once again.

§84. 2. The Pragmatic Theory

PRAGMATICM (from Greek 'pragma', deed) is that doctrine, or trend of thought, according to which the value of an assertion lies solely in its practical bearing upon human interests. In this sense, it can also be called ULITARIANISM (from Latin 'utilis', useful). So, concretely, suppose I asked whether it is true that fire heats, the pragmatist would answer: well, if you put water or food on it, will it heat or not? The answer is definitely yes. So, according to the pragmatist, all you need to know to see whether what you are saying is true or false is whether it serves you a good purpose. If it does, it is true; if it does not, it is false, or at least not-true. It is clear that here 'true' is reduced to 'useful'. Or more precisely still, the question whether "fire heats" corresponds to objective facts or not is either considered as impossible to ascertain or as use-less. At first sight, this may seem very attractive (and practical!) idea, but if universally applied it can and does have disastrous consequences not only in the realm of Philosophy but and especially in that of Religion, as we are going to, see. Still, a lot can be learnt from such a trend of thought.

§85. In the West, best known for pursuing such a trend of thought are C.S. Peirce (the "father of modern pragmatism" and coiner of the term), J. Dewey (calling his philosophy "instrumentalism") and William James. *The first,* a scientist and logician, applied his theory mostly to scientific assertions (but also to Ethics). If a proposition yields results in the field of scientific enquiry and as such is accepted by the scientific community, that proposition is true. *The second* applies his doctrine not only scientific assertions, and thus to the formation of a scientific theory, but also to all assertions we use in the solution of everyday problems. If our solutions are useful and if our theories by which we try to reconstruct the ever changing flow of life are verified by life itself, our solutions and theories can be called true. *The third* speaks more in terms of 'meaning' or 'view' of life. If an assertion, and the view of life which is thus made up of such assertions, function satisfactorily in my life, if in other words, it gives meaning and purpose to my life, then that assertion and view of life are true. Of course they may be meaningful, or relevant, to me and not to you. In that case they may be 'true' to me and not to you. James applies this also to religious propositions expressive of religious beliefs. And in this he is followed by others more recent thinkers of whom we shall speak later in a related but different context.

§86. In India a similar approach to 'truth' can be discerned, as could be expected, in Carvaka, the Indian Empiricism par excellence. As we have seen, this School of Indian Philosophy – like its counterpart in any part of the world – accepts perception alone as a source of knowledge. But we are not to suppose that the Carvaka philosopher was so stupid as to refrain from cooking his food because of his skeptic philosophical stance regarding the possibility of knowing for certain that whenever one puts his food on the fire, the fire cooks it (something known by inference and not by perception)! Any knowledge obtained in any other way except perception does have value – only practical (pragmatic!) value. Thus Jayarasi, who even denied the truth of perceptual knowledge (and the existence of the four physical elements generally accepted by the Indian Materialists), is not unaware that in spite of all denial of theoretical knowledge, practical life can and should go on (9).

§87. When, however, modern commentators on Indian Philosophy speak of 'pragmatism' in India, they single out Samkhya as its best representative, or at least which attaches more importance to the practical value, or 'workability' (arthakriyakaritva) of true cognition. But isn't there a big misunderstanding here? Samkhya, like for that matter all the Schools of Indian Philosophy (except Carvaka, of course) considers valid (yathartha) cognition as one which corresponds to the facts - and therefore these can all be grouped, in one way or another, under the "Correspondence Theory of truth". But when they – all of them – speak of the test of truth as 'successful activity' (pravrttisamarthya), do they mean this in an epistemological sense or in a religious (and in a way ontological) sense? It has to be constantly borne in mind that these schools of Indian philosophy are chiefly interested in the attainment of 'moksa'. So the test of true (in the sense of 'genuine', §76) cognition is whether such cognition is or is not conducive to the desired end. Its 'pragmatic' character has little to do with the western meaning of the term!

§88. A lot can be learned from an epistemological pragmatic approach to 'truth'. We already have had the opportunity to speak of the value of a 'working hypothesis' in scientific enquiry. Not only that but, as we pointed out too, of the set of hypotheses which make up a theory – and this too in religious knowledge (§§ 52-55) – one cannot really ask whether they are true or false but whether they are appropriate or inappropriate, arbitrary or well-grounded, reasonable or not. Till, of course, reasons, ultimately founded on some self-evident truth, do not provide sufficient evidence to prove them true or false, they are to be considered 'true' in this pragmatic sense. 'Truth' is here understood, rightly, as 'usefulness'.

Reality, after all, – from the smallest atom to 'God' – is so mysterious, at times so puzzling, that we have to be humble enough to admit that in most things we know things only "in so far" as we can and in accordance with our limited capacity for knowing. This approach, far from being a skeptic one, or a purely subjectivistic one, equips one with a certain openness to the ever-present but ever-eluding Truth. As St Augustine says, "We look to find, we find to look again" (10). Much of our knowledge of Reality is a 'construction' of it in such a way as to make it intelligible to us, but in such a way too that remains always provisional, hypothetical.

§89. And this is particularly true when from the level of 'facts' we pass on to the level of their 'significance'. That there is somebody in front of me is a fact, and it is a fact too that she is of such and such description. But is it a fact that "she is the most beautiful girl in the world"? Is this a 'propositional judgment' subject to be proved true or false. If not, is it not 'true' to anybody, including to her passionate lover? If it is 'true' to him, what is meant by 'true' here? Does it not mean 'significant'? Take such other judgments: "my work is my life", "my family is my world", "love is my breath", "humanity is a community", "history has a purpose", "good and evil are in perfect harmony", "God is a loving Father". What is 'true here and what is 'false'?

Further still, what does it profit a man to know all there is to know if finally all his knowledge serves him for nothing, least of all to be, or become, what he is supposed to be or become? Can I really call that true (i.e. genuine, worth-while, knowledge)? If not what is then 'knowledge'? Is it not that purposeful knowledge, that knowledge which alone can serve him truly to achieve his final destiny? And what is the meaning here of 'true' and 'truly'? Is it not that that knowledge which serves no useful purpose, which does not, or cannot, result into a fruitful activity, a sterile knowledge? And if it is, can it still be called true knowledge?

§90. All this is, of course, is true – and profoundly so. We shall return to these questions later when we shall deal with language and its functions, especially religious language. But from the epistemological standpoint, the Pragmatic Theory of Truth needs, according to us, to be severely qualified. *Firstly*, scientific 'knowledge' and scientific 'truth' cannot, without much further ado, be taken to be the paradigm of 'knowledge' and 'truth' in general. To do so would presuppose certain presuppositions which would be themselves subject to non-scientific 'proof' – and hence to a non-pragmatic concept of 'knowledge' and 'truth'. *Secondly* from a semantic point of view, it would be arbitrary to define 'truth' stipulatively since there *is* a conventional (everyday) meaning of the term. All one could say is that in such and such a field of knowledge, or in any kind of 'hypothesis' it would be inappropriate to speak of 'truth' but of something else – something which we did ourselves -or, that in such a case, one cannot come to know the truth at all! *Thirdly*, from a religious point of view, belief, no matter how 'significant' it is, or should be, would lose all its religious value (and therefore its 'significance') if it could be shown to rest on no real foundation – i.e., with a basis in reality. A false conviction may still be 'significant' to somebody but this does not make it 'true'. *Fourthly*, to say that 'truth' is relative (i.e. known only progressively, and in accordance with the capacity, and 'interpretation' of the knower, and as 'significant' to him or not) shows only that one has to distinguish between different fields of knowledge, different functions of language, different levels of understanding, and different kinds of 'illocutions' (§20). RELATIVISM (which says that no objective truth can be known at all, and, therefore, in no sense at all, can one say to be absolutely certain about anything) can be shown to be like Skepticism, exercitively self-contradictory.

§91. 3. The Coherence Theory

Because of the difficulty we discussed with regard to the 'correspondence' theory, some interpret 'truth' as coherence between a proposition and other well-established true propositions. If it can be shown that this proposition does not contradict these well-established propositions, then it can be called 'true'. As is clear, this theory presuppose that before we start asking ourselves whether a proposition is true, we would have already agreed explicitly or implicitly, on certain other propositions as being true. For example, we ask ourselves whether the proposition "abortion is murder" is true or false, we shall have first to agree on whether following prepositions are also true or false, namely, "to kill a person unnecessarily is murder", "the unborn child is a person", "abortion is to kill a person unnecessarily". Now supposing that we agree that these propositions are true, it follows that our original proposition can be seen to be 'true'. In other words, it is logically implied by, 'not in conflict with, coheres with, the previously agreed-upon truths.

§92. In its simplest form, this theory equates 'truth' with logical implication. As could be expected, LOGICAL POSITIVISM (about which we shall be speaking later) renounces all idea of truth as correspondence with facts and interprets it as correspondence or coherence with propositions themselves. Or to put it differently, for it the 'facts' are the propositions themselves.

But in its more radical form, this theory is the epistemological aspect of that more general theory according to which the laws of thought not only are the laws of being itself (§70) in the sense that they correspond to them, but are the laws of being in the sense that they are their origin. So the primacy is given not to being over thought but to Thought (with a capital T), over all beings. And if Thought is essentially consistent, then if one could work out a logically consistent view of Reality, this must necessarily reflect Reality as it is in fact. And a given proposition, or judgment, if it coheres with this whole logically consistent view of Reality, is true, otherwise false (IDEALISM) (e.g. that of Spinoza, Hegel in the West, to a certain extent that of Sankara in India).

§93. In India all the Schools of Philosophy accept, of course, that true cognition is characterized by 'self-consistency' (samvada) and 'uncontradictability' (abadhitatva) – by which latter term is meant 'not being contradicted by another true cognition', in other words, coherence with other known truths. But, as far as we know, the Logical Positivist theory which reduces 'truth' only to coherence of a proposition with a set of other propositions previously accepted as true is not found in India.

§94. Here again we have a lot to learn from this theory. When a judgment is expressed in a proposition – in a proposition which is made up of concepts, notions, etc., – it is expressed in fact in a particular 'linguistic field' where not only the truth of the propositions but also the meaning of the concepts themselves are mutually related. And there are more than one 'linguistic field' (or as it is sometimes called 'universe of discourse') such as the scientific, the esthetic, the legal, the economical, the moral, the religious, etc.[4] For example, the proposition "Man is composed of body and soul" may be true in a Scholastic philosophical 'linguistic field' (where 'man' 'composed', 'is, 'body' and 'soul' have a specific meaning, and the truth of the judgment depends on the truth of many other related judgments, like "being is composed of matter and form", "spiritual acts cannot intrinsically depend on matter", etc.) but that same proposition may be either false or at least unintelligible in another 'linguistic field' (as in Samakya's or in MATERIALISM, etc.). A proposition in a Euclidean geometrical 'linguistic field' may be false or unintelligible in a non-Euclidean one; a logical proposition in a two-valued logical 'linguistic field' may be false in a three- valued logical one, etc.

§95. In our *Philosophy of Religion*, we take pains to show how a religious tenet(e.g. "Christ is the son of God" in Christianity, or "Atman is Brahman" in Vedanta) can neither be made intelligible and much less said to be true or false except within the whole context of its respective religious tradition, which is, as it were, its "matrix". Hence, the meaninglessness of trying to understand a 'text' out of its 'context' (11). Hence, too the misunderstandings which can arise if one tried to compare and contrast different philosophical, religious, etc., opinions, beliefs, doctrines before one has made sure that one has first understood each in its respective, "linguistic field'.

§96. All this is therefore very true. Still does logical coherence enough to say that something is 'true' (in the generally accepted meaning of the term')? We have already remarked that to give a simulative definition to an already conventionally agreed-upon meaning of a term is arbitrary. But apart from this semantic question,

4 Each of these, in its turn, can be considered to contain within itself many 'linguistic fields'. Hence the different philosophical systems are different 'linguistic fields'. Similarly, the different religious traditions are different 'linguistic fields', etc. And one could go on seeing different 'linguistic fields' contained even within one philosophical system or in one religious tradition, etc.

it is clear that proponents of the logical coherence theory of truth are led to such a definition of theirs because of the epistemological difficulty we discussed with regard to the 'Correspondence Theory'. More directly still, one could point out that this theory does not solve this same difficulty. For its presupposition (that before we start asking whether a proposition is true or not we have to have already agreed to consider other propositions as true) requires that we would have already settled the logical coherence of each of these latter propositions with still other propositions. The 'infinite regress' would be require here too. (And it would be no answer to say that as a matter of fact, we 'inherit' the truth of these propositions from society. The question here is not how in fact we come to know from the time of our childhood up, but how we can philosophically understand 'truth'!). Recall that we too required self-consistency and coherence in any 'good' (i.e. appropriate) hypothesis. But we added too that precisely because as such a hypothesis remains a hypothesis, it would be out of place to ask whether it is true or false. Or in other words, we did not consider hypothesis as such, in spite of its logical self-consistency and coherence, necessarily true (§§ 53-55).

§97. So while 'true' can in the formal sciences (Logic, Mathematics) be considered to be the equivalent of 'logical consistent' precisely because formal sciences, by their very nature, do not refer to any specific object (fact, state of affairs), it cannot be so considered elsewhere. So, can we at least agree that if a whole system of philosophical understanding of Reality (i.e. not simply propositions) is in fact self-consistent and coherent, it does mirror it as IDEALISM believes? The difficulty here is that it is not impossible to imagine two perfectly self-consistent and coherent systems of the sort which are not compatible among themselves, or even contradictory to one another. In this case, when we have two or even more such systems, the question arises which of them is one to call 'true' – supposing that in virtue of the principle of contradiction, they cannot be all called true. There could be many answers to this question. One could, for example, say that on further analysis one can always discern, in what one had at first sight mistaken to be a perfectly self-consistent and coherent theory, inconsistencies, in such a way that one would finally realize that there can be only one logically self-consistent and coherent view of Reality. Or, one could answer, Reality can in fact be mirrored in two or more such systems, provided that they are perfectly self-consistent and coherent, even though they are not compatible (but not contradictory). Again, one could answer that what seems to be contradictory on a logical, epistemological, level, need not be contradictory on the meta-logical, trans-empirical, level (i.e. the level of Reality as a whole in its ultimate causes), etc. All this would be interesting to discuss (as we do in our *Philosophy of Religion* but it is clear that ultimately, on the epistemological level, if a self-consistent and coherent view of Reality is to be said to be true, whether or not it is the only possible one or not) it is not just because it is so but because it would have been shown to correspond to what the case is, i.e., to the nature and structure, etc., of Reality itself.

§98. 4. The Performative Theory

To understand this theory, we must go back to what we said about 'illocutions' (§ 21). We recall that these are kinds of 'speech-acts' which we do – perform- when we say something. Now when I say, for example, "It is true that the world is round", According to some (e.g. F.P. Ramsey), I am certainly not giving any more information about the world in the first case than in the second. All I am doing more when I add, "it is true that..." is adding emphasis, style, or indication as to the position the statement has in the whole of my argument.

§99. Others, however, are not slow in remarking that this is a confusion between a first-order assertion' (in our case, 'the world is round' where something is said or stated about the 'world') and a 'second order assertion '(in our case 'it is true that the world is round' where something is said or stated about the whole proposition as a whole, namely 'the world is round'). Now some (e.g. P.F. Strawson) while pointing out that 'true' (or 'false') occur only in 'second-order assertions' see in the use of the term 'true' a sign of the speaker's affirmation (and in the use of the term 'false' of his denial). Thus, to keep to our example, when I say, "it is true that the world is round" ("That the world is round is true") what I am doing is indicating that I agree (believe, am convinced, concede, affirm) that the world is round. Hence, the performative function of the term 'true' (and correspondingly of the term 'false') (12).

§100. The distinction between 'first-order assertions' and 'second order assertions' is well made. In our *Logic* (§ 19f) we speak of the distinction between 'first intentions' and 'second intentions' – but that was with regard to 'concepts'. As a 'second intention' concept is a concept of a concept, so too a 'second-order assertion' is an assertion of an assertion. In "The world is round", the logical term of the proposition serving as its 'subject' (the 'what' something is said about) is 'the world'; in the proposition "That the world is round is true", the logical term is not 'the world' but the whole proposition "the world is round". Something is said about this whole proposition – and what is said is that it corresponds to what the case is.

Now it is undoubtedly true that when I say "It is true that the world is round" I am doing something more than giving information about the world. I am doing something more, namely I am indicating that I too believe, affirm, agree, etc., that the world is round. It would make no sense to say, "It is true that the world is round, but I do not believe it (or am not convinced of it)." If I was not convinced of it, I would not say that it is true in the first place. Not only are the two propositions not identical, but their 'illocutionary load' is different. Whereas "The world is round" has one 'illocution' (a constative), "It is true that..." has two: the constative and the expressive, the former affirming something about the world, the latter expressing some attitude (in this case of belief, agreement, conviction, etc.) of the one who affirms. It is only of constatives that the question of 'truth' arises, as we have seen. So by reducing a constative to an expressive is neither logically nor epistemologically sound, and the question of "truth" remains unsolved.

§101. Other authors (e.g. A.J. Ayer) similarly reduce moral propositions (e.g. "abortion is murder"), esthetic propositions (e.g. "the girl is beautiful"), and indeed religious propositions (e.g. God exists") to mere expressives. We shall return to him later. But the same criticism could be addressed to him as the one we are addressing to the Performative Theory of Truth in general. Still, one big lesson we could learn from it is that even in religious language, propositions do often have a big expressive illocutionary load (and not simply constative). When I say, for example, "God is a loving Father" I am not simply making a statement of fact (or of on alleged fact) but I am expressing some attitude, or attitudes, of mine! (13).

§102. 3. ERROR

When one discusses 'truth' one cannot help mentioning 'falsehood' for 'falsehood' is the opposite of 'truth' (in all senses, ontological, moral and logical, § 76). If, in the logical, or epistemological sense, 'truth' is the correspondence between what is affirmed or denied to what the case, 'falsehood', in the same sense, is the non-correspondence between the two. If a true judgment (or proposition) is that which corresponds to what the case is, a false judgment (or proposition) is that which does not, etc. And if 'truth' lies, strictly speaking, in the judgment, as we have said, so does 'falsehood'. Now, when I pass a true judgment, I am right, when I pass a false judgment, I am wrong. In the latter case, I commit an *error*, I am mistaken. (Of course, I can be more or less mistaken, as I can be more or less right in my judgment. If I said that the distance between Pune and Bombay, by train is 100 kms, and you said that it is 150 kms, whereas, in fact, it is 192 kms, I would be more mistaken than you. Of course, you would also be mistaken, but jour judgment would be 'closer' to the truth than mine).

§103. Indian philosophers seem to have been greatly intrigued by the very possibility of error. We have seen how they distinguish between 'cognition' (jnana) and 'knowledge' (prama). It is only true and valid cognition (yathartha jnana) which is 'knowledge'. Depending on their further understanding of 'knowledge', however – whether it should be characterized by novelty, uncontradictedness, indubitability, etc., – they characterize false and untrue cognition (ayathartha jnana) somewhat differently. Some therefore would include in it the simple fact that one does not know or ignorance (avidya), or doubt (samsaya), or opinion (uha), or even dreams (svapna), indeed hypothetical argument ('tarka') or - but only according to some few, what is simply reproduced in memory (smrti) or recognised by the memory and actual perception (pratyabhijna). But what seems to hare intrigued them most is *perceptual error* (viparyaya, or 'illusion'), that is, error made in sense-experience.

§104. Now one could ask how it is that Indian philosophers were so intrigued by this kind of error, by 'illusion'. How is it that all the Schools of Indian Philosophy go to such lengths to examine the source of error and to describe not only the psychological process involved in 'illusion' but also the ontological status (i.e. the kind of 'existence' or 'non-existence') of the object of 'illusion'? It is a fact that 'perception' is the one 'pramana' on whose reliability all the Schools of Philosophy (in the East as well in the West barring some radical Rationalists) agree. Is it also because the Indian Schools of Philosophy, like most of those in the West (particularly Scholasticism) place perception at the origin of all our knowledge? (We have already discussed the distinction between 'origin' in a temporal sense and 'origin' in a logical sense, 'dependence' in time and 'dependence' for verification, § 66). That could be *one* reason, for it is clear that unless perceptual error is explained, the whole epistemological fabric would be threatened if it is true that perception is at the basis of all knowledge. *A second reason* perhaps could be this: we recall that 'true' (in the sense of fruitful, important) knowledge is that which leads to salvation (moksa, mukti). The very possibility of error in perception would have, directly or indirectly, disastrous consequences for one's salvation itself if, again, knowledge is required for 'salvation' and the basis of all knowledge is sense-perception!

§105. Be that as it may, the different Schools of Indian Philosophy explain 'illusion' differently. For example, as the 'apprehension' ('khyati' of an object existing at least in part, of a non-existent object, of an object which is both existent and non-existent, of a synthesis between what is existent and non-existent, etc. We shall not go into all that. But it would be good to see how Advaita explains it – not so much for what it says about the possibility of 'illusion' as for its description of something which cannot be said to be real (sat) or unreal (asat) or even real and unreal - at the sametime (sadasat)!– Advaita explains 'illusion' as 'maya'. I see a shell and mistake it for silver. The shell falsely appears to me as silver. Now this 'false appearance' is obviously not real for it is not the appearance of the shell, but neither is it unreal for it is something, i.e., an appearance, and not 'nothing'. It cannot even be said that it is real and non-real at the same time in the sense that the apprehension of 'this' is real and that of 'silver' is unreal. Of 'maya', Sankara' says "that it is 'unspeakable and undefinable'. But what is more important to remember is that Sankara makes great use of this idea to account for our mistaking what is really real (Sat, namely, Brahman) for what is only apparently real' (Asat, the world of visible and tangible phenomena). Is this an instance where one's 'metaphysics' determines one's epistemology? (Even if that were so, there is profound truth in Sankara's doctrine – as we shall see later!).

§106. In the West, the very possibility of perceptual error could at least partially account for the many trends in Western philosophy which sought to base knowledge, or at least to finally explain it, on purely rational grounds and not on sense-perception. We already have had the occasion to touch on this point in a different context when we referred to RATIONALISM (§ 26) and the fundamental role of 'reason' in the 're-construction' of the objects of perception. But in this particular context, we wish to refer to all kinds of trend of thought in Western Philosophy which in a kind of Idealist way (§ 97) sought to base knowledge on an 'apperception' of universal and abiding 'Ideas' like Plato, or on some absolutely sure and indubitable "clear and distinct ideas" like Descartes – or, in a different sense, on the 'a-priori' forms of the mind itself, like Kant, etc. All of these distrusting the – reliability of sense-perception because of the possibility of perceptual error and the ever-shifting nature of our knowledge based on sense objects and perception, looked for a surer footing for knowledge. Seeing that the 'formal sciences' do not depend on sense-perception for their truth and justification, Spinoza tried to build up his whole philosophy "in the manner of geometry" (starting with axioms and definitions and proceeding with theorems) and modern Logical Positivists do not hesitate to take Mathematics as the paradigm of knowledge.

§107. We need not repeat here what we have already said about the fundamental reliability of sense-perception (§ 25-26). No matter how perceptual error is to be explained, it is to be noted that if we can speak of perceptual error at all, i.e., if we somehow or other can come to detect it and show that it *is* an error, it is because, paradoxically enough, sense perception is fundamentally reliable.

In English, however, by 'error' we do not mean perceptual error alone. He can commit errors – be mistaken – in drawing false conclusions from given data (in 'inference'), in believing unreliable witnesses, etc. But here again, if we can speak at all of 'error' at all, it is because of our capacity for truth! The 'primary datum', then, whether in perception or in any other way of coming to know, is our capacity for the truth! But the ever-groping mind for the truth, the-wonder and mysteriousness of Reality and the admittedly limited means to attain it, the spatio-temporal conditioning and historicity of man, the physical and psychological barriers (disease of the senses, weariness and laziness, bias and prejudice, inadvertence and non-chalancy, etc.), remains always subject to error – but also and at the same time capable of recognizing the error and overcome it. But this means too that man's knowledge of Reality remains always partial, imperfect, relative (not 'relativistic'!), certain up to a certain extent and uncertain up to another... And this brings us to the question of certitude.

Chapter 5

KNOWLEDGE AND CERTITUDE

§108. During the course of our reflexions so far we have often had to raise the question about 'certitude' (or 'certainty'). Thus, when we explained what we meant by 'knowledge' and how, in our understanding of term 'truth' and 'reasonableness' were essential characteristics of it. We had already to raise the question whether, if such were the case, it would be possible to say that 'we knew' anything for sure, i.e., with certainty (§19). Again, when we discussed the validity of 'inference' we referred to the empiricists' understanding of it as yielding only pragmatic probability but not 'certainty' (§ 33e). Again, when we discussed 'testimony', we concluded that 'belief' could certainly be considered as 'reasonable' but left the question of 'certainty' till later (§ 45). – The problem of certitude became more acute, of course, when we discussed 'truth' (§ 77). It is clear that it is one thing to say what 'truth' is and what it is not, it is quite another to say whether, and to what extent, I can be sure (certain) of the 'truth' (no matter how it is understood). Some Indian Schools of Philosophy (e.g. Samkhya) too characterize true cognition as 'certain' (asamdigdha) – i.e., as subjectively certain and not only objectively 'uncontractictable' (abadhita).

§109. 1. The notion of 'certitude'

Scholastics generally define 'certitude' as 'the firm assent of the mind to the truth, based on evidence'. This definition is certainly a good one, but we prefer to explain 'certitude' in our own way. And the way we understand it is simply this: 'the conviction that such and such is the case." The following explanation will hopefully make things clear.

1. Conviction. In our understanding of the term, 'knowledge' is 'the awareness that such and such is (or is not) the case' (§ 13). The motion 'of 'certitude' as

'conviction' adds to the notion of 'awareness' the Scholastic 'firm assent' but not so much as an act performed here and now but rather an a psychological state of mind resulting from it. (This is partly determined by the usage in modern English of the terms used here, like 'assent'). Another word for 'conviction' is 'persuasion'. I can be aware of something, that such and such is (or is not) the case but depending on what the case is (as we are going to see) I can be more or less convinced or persuaded that that is so.

This can even be made clearer is we compare and contrast other possible psychological states with regard to whether such and such is (or is not) the case, as follows:

§110. 2. *Conviction and Evidence*

What makes all the difference between that state of mind when one 'doubts', or that state of mind when one simply 'thinks' that such and such is the case, and that state of mind when one is 'convinced' ('persuaded', 'certain') that that is so? In 'doubt' one has reasons for and reasons against that such and such is or is not the case. One is indecisive, wavers, between two reasons, or sets of reasons. When one 'thinks' that such and such is, or is not, the case, one is inclined towards one side more than to the other. One has formed a'probable opinion' about the matter but still hesitates to say definitely, unwaveringly, that it is so. Notice that this admits a whole gamut of degrees – depending precisely on the force of the reasons towards which he is inclined to accept. It is only when one definitely decides for or against one side, when he is no longer afraid that there can be any – reasonable room for doubting and therefore that he can be mistaken, that one is convinced and says that he is sure, certain, that such and such is or not the case. And the reasons because of which he is moved to take such a step or to find himself in such a state of mind – are precisely that we have previously called the 'evidence' (§ 77). Needless to mention that this is merely an analysis of the psychological process involved. In actual life, it is often gone through spontaneously, unreflectingly.

§111. 3. *Conviction and Truth*

'Conviction', therefore, refer to this state of mind 'truth' refers to the correspondence itself between what is asserted or denied about whether such and such is, or is not, the case. 'Conviction' is 'subjective', 'truth' is 'objective'. One can, in other words, be convinced that such and such is, or is not, the case and if this does correspond to what in fact the case is, one is right; otherwise one is wrong. In the latter case his conviction is erroneous (§ 102).

§112. 2. *Kinds of Certitudes Possible and to be Expected*

We are going to touch here on a very important question. In fact, many everyday doubts regarding the possibility of being 'sure' ('certain') about different things –

including, for example, moral and religious matters – can and in fact does lead to a certain kind of skepticism, if not about the possibility of being sure of anything at all, at least about the possibility of being sure of certain matters. We have already raised so many questions in this regard in our very Introduction! Often we become aware of so many opinions given on certain matters, one saying this and another saying something completely different and contrary to the first that one is tempted to despair of 'knowing what to believe any longer'! An analysis of the different kinds of certitude – which are possible and reasonably – but only reasonably! - to be expected in different matters can help us sort things out.

§113. In a sense, it is true, one is either certain (convinced) or one is not. Strictly speaking, it would make no sense to say that I am 'more or less' convinced. What I am really saying is that I have a strong opinion on the matter but I am not yet convinced. And we have distinguished between the state of mind implied by saying that one has an 'opinion' and that implied by saying that one is 'convinced' ('certain'). Generally, Scholastics point out that the difference between the possible kinds of 'certitude' is not due to the degree of 'firmness' of assent, nor is it due to the difference in the fields of knowledge, but on the kind of evidence available according to the case. Strictly speaking, this is, according to us, correct. But following our own line of exposition, and keeping to our own understanding of the terms ('knowledge', 'truth', 'certitude', 'evidence'), we, here again, proceed in our own way.

§114. If certitude is based on evidence, we prefer to distinguish between the different kinds of possible and expected certitudes on the basis *both* of the different fields of knowledge and consequently of the different kinds of evidence.

a. Logical certitude. Here we are in the field of 'formal' field of knowledge, the realm of pure ideas and the relationships between them – as in Logic and Mathematics. The evidence of the truth of the propositions is obtained by analysis of the terms and definitions used. No other means of verification is needed – or indeed possible. Here, the truth is expressed in analytical propositions which are therefore 'necessary true' propositions (or 'tautologies') and can be seen to be such even before ('a-priori') their application to other fields of knowledge. And the certitude thus based on such kind of evidence, admitting of no possible or conceivable exception, can be called 'absolute'. I am absolutely certain (by a kind of 'logical certitude') that if A = B, and B = C, then A = C. I am similarly certain that 2 + 2 = 4. Again I am similarly certain that it is either raining or not raining. Similarly with definitions: I am certain, in the same way, that if I define a 'rational animal' as man, then that man is a rational animal is for me absolutely certain!

§115. *b. Ontological Certitude.* Here we are in the field of the knowledge of being as being, the realm of visible and tangible realities but considered from the point of view of those characteristics which they have in common to the extent that they are beings, existents. This realm could be considered as the counterpart, as it were, of the logical realm – if we are prepared to admit, as we pointed out before, that the 'laws of the mind' (the logical realm) are based on the 'laws of being itself' (the ontological realm). The evidence of the truth of the Judgments is obtained, certainly first from general experience (including sense-experience, but more directly from a reflection on the nature of the judgment itself as judgment. Of course, there can be other methods, but ultimately certain laws of being itself can be 'insightfully' discovered – what we have called 'first principles' (§ 71) – which not only are self-evident (cannot be denied without contradiction) but also serve as the ultimate for any further knowledge of reality. The 'self- evidence' in question here, however, is not merely logical but ontological, and the contradiction would not be one of the terms (contradiction in terms) but a judgmental one (an exercitive contradiction). Here, the truth is expressed in 'synthetic-a-priori judgments (in our sense, not necessarily Kant's). And the evidence thus based on such kind of evidence, again admitting of no possible or conceivable exception, can also be called 'absolute'. Thus I am absolutely certain that I exist, that I can know at least southing for sure, that what is and cannot not be at the same time, etc. (These principles are explained in detail in *Metaphysics*).

§116. We would like to make an 'excursus' here – as we announced earlier – since some think that ancient Indian Philosophers did not accept the Principles of Non-contradiction and of the Excluded Middle. The relevance of this will become clear later when we shall discuss religious knowledge, truth and certitude! But since this is a bit over-technical, the student can *by-pass* it at least till much later.

As we have seen, Sankara (and Advaita in general) says that 'maya' can be said neither to be 'real' nor 'unreal' nor 'both real and unreal'. In terms of 'logical values', Advaita, unlike Western Logic does not operate with a 'two-valued logic' (i.e. 'true' and 'false') – but with a 'three-valued' one, i.e., true (real), false (unreal) and 'indescribable'. Hence, the relation between 'true' and 'false' is not a contradictory one but only a contrary one. That is to say, if 'p' (standing for a thing, concept or proposition) – is false, one cannot infer that therefore 'non-p' is true (for it can be neither false nor true) or in other words, to say that 'maya' is not real (false), one cannot infer that therefore it is real (true). But does all this really disprove the" Law of Non-contradiction and the Law of Excluded Middle. We think not. (Later on, however, we shall try and explain that these laws – and a 'two-valued' – operate only when what is asserted or denied are understood in a univocal sense. When we apply it to religious language, they have to be applied in a qualified way). Even a 'three-valued logic' can be ultimately reduced to a 'two-valued logic': either what you are saying is true (that a 'three-valued logic' is possible and valid) or it is false!

§117. A similar position is held by the Buddhist Nagarjuna (and Madhyamika in general). Of no object whatever can we say that it is 'real' (for 'real' means existent in its own right, non-related and non-originated), or 'unreal' (for somehow it exists, it appears), or 'both real and non-real' or 'neither real nor unreal' (for in these two latter cases, that would be mere gibberish). This is the famous way of arguing 'according to the four 'categories' of thought and speech (catuskotis). Notice, first of all, that Madhyamika makes use of this destructive dialectic not to deny the empirical value of logic, truth and knowledge, but simply to show that from an 'ultimate point of view' (we shall return of this important topic later), the phenomenal world is not the 'really real' – which is indescribable and beyond these categories of thought and speech. Secondly, it is clear from the third and fourth category, the statements would be gibberish precisely because they would express contradictory propositions! Only if 'real' and 'non-real' were understood in an analogical sense, would the statement be intelligible. So, once again the catuskoti logic does not disprove the Principle of Contradiction and that of the Excluded Middle, as we understand them. But from this Madhyamika logic a lot can be learnt with respect to the use of logical language to speak about reality 'from an ultimate point of view'!

§118. Again, something similar (but not quite) is found in the Jain doctrine regarding the 'indeterminate' and 'multi- faceted' reality (anekantavada). No one thing can be understood thoroughly for that would require that one knew it from all points of views and in all its relations. Only from an 'ultimate point of view' can one know everything (kevalajnana). So, from the everyday and empirical point of view, we have always to qualify our judgments as 'somehow' (syat) true or 'somehow' false (This is the Jain 'syadvada', theory of knowledge).

Seven forms of judgment (saptabhanginaya) are recognized: (1) somehow S is P (e.g. somehow he is a son); (2) somehow S is not P (e.g. somehow he is not a son - in relation either to his own son or to somebody other than his parents); (3) Somehow, S is P and is not P (e.g. in relation to his parents, he is a son but in relation to anybody else, he is not a son); (4) Somehow S is indescribable (avaktavyam) (e.g. somehow I cannot say what he really is, for to do that I have to know him in all his relationships, and in himself); *the fifth, sixth and seventh forms* are the conjunctions of the fourth and these ones respectively. Much can be learnt from this theory - particularly with the 'relativity' of truth and speech (§§ 90,107) and the advocates of this theory do not make use of it to deny sure and valid knowledge (in fact they accept perception, inference and testimony as pramanas) but to show how empirical knowledge and truth always remain one sided, one faceted. And on this plane, the principle of Non-Contradiction and that of the Excluded Middle remains valid.

§119. *c. Physical Certitude.* Here we are in the field of the knowledge of things, of their properties and ways of acting, the realm therefore of science. The evidence of the truth of the laws of Nature is obtained by, first of all, sense-perception, verification or falsification by laboratory - conducted experiments of hypotheses formed, etc. Here, the opposite of a given law is not, at least theoretically inconceivable. Its truth is subject to our further understanding of how nature works, so to say. In this field, the only possible certitude we can have – and the only one to be expected is 'physical certitude'. It is not 'absolute' but 'hypothetical' – in the sense that I can say, "yes, I am sure on the possible evidence given so far." Hence I can say I am sure, certain, that the sun will rise from the East, that action and reaction are equal and opposite, that the volume of a gas at constant temperature varies inversely with the pressure, etc. (We need not to have recourse to the possibility of 'miracles' to explain the hypothetical kind of 'physical certitude'. The language of modern scientists about the 'provisional' character of all scientific laws is enough).

§120. *d. Moral Certitude.* Here we have to be careful for unlike the previous usage "of the term'certain' (or 'sure') which is a philosophical technical one, the usage of the term'to be morally sure' is also an everyday common one. We often use such expressions as, "I am morally sure that the exam is postponed till next month" – by which is meant that "I am pretty sure that...", "I have good pre strong reasons to believe that…" etc. So we have to distinguish between at least three meanings of 'moral certitude'.

1. 'Certitude' in the field of knowledge of Ethics which studies how man should behave, the general norms and principles which should help him judge what is 'right' or 'wrong' both in general and in the practical day-to-day situations, especially in 'conflict-situations', etc. We are all aware how, especially today, how certain questions regarding the moral justifiability of certain actions (e.g. nuclear warfare, capital punishment, abortion, birth-control, etc.) are debated. We are all aware too that certain ways of behavior or of action which in the past were morally justified, today they are morally condemned (e.g. slavery), or vice-versa (e.g. exacting interest on loans). This uncertainty can lead one to say that no certitude at all can be had in 'moral matters' and each one is to let himself be guided either by one's conscience or, at most, by the current customs of one's people. The disastrous consequences of such a position can easily be ascertained. The thing is that people expect a kind of certitude in 'moral matters' which is neither possible nor even to be expected.

§121. So, how is the 'evidence' of the truths in moral matters obtained? Here, of course, different methods can be and are used. If one based one's Ethics on the immediate data of (moral) consciousness – which, as we said, can be seen to be 'self-evident' (e.g. the good is to be done, evil to be avoided; if man ought to do what is right, he can do what is right; man ought to fulfil himself as a man; etc.), then some truths in moral matters can be known with absolute certainty. This part could be considered as a part of Ontology itself and thus of the ontological certitude is possible. But as for the rest, evidence is obtained by good arguments which bring us to the third meaning of 'moral certitude'. We shall examine a second meaning first.

§122. 2. A second meaning of 'moral certitude' is that which can be had in the field of knowledge of human nature, its psychological make-up, man's social relationships, his history. This is the realm of the Human (or Social) Sciences. What kind of evidence can be obtained for the truths of these Sciences? Naturally much depends on each Science. Sociology or Psychology use different methods than that of History, for example. Depending on the way evidence is obtained, and therefore the nature of the kind of evidence obtained, the kind of certitude possible would be different. But both Sociology and Psychology study certain human behavior constants. These, of course, are different from those constants studied and formulated as 'physical laws' – for here man is, because of his freedom, less predictable than things. But if I am told that "an exploited class will sooner or later revolt", that "a given culture is largely determined by its economy", that "the population growth is inversely proportionate to technology and urbanization", what evidence can I have for that and how do I obtain it? It is clear that the evidence here is obtained through observation (which today is conducted on very scientific basis). The certitude based on such evidence cannot amount to 'physical certitude' – the field of knowledge, to start with, is different, and consequently the kind of evidence obtained in both is different. Precisely because this evidence, in most of the Social Sciences, is based on the observation of the usual ways of human behavior ("mores"), the certitude which is only possible here is 'moral certitude' (in this second sense).

§123. 3. A third meaning (and the fourth one which follows) of 'moral certitude' is taken more from the everyday usage of the term and has nothing to do with any particular field of knowledge. Whenever the *only* evidence I have for a given truth is 'testimony' (witness, the spoken or written word of a reliable person) the only certitude which is possible and to be expected here is 'moral certitude' in this third sense. And no matter what the field of knowledge is. About a given law of nature, the scientist can have 'physical certitude' but a non-scientist, who relies on his competence and reliability, can only have about the same matter 'moral certitude'. We spoke at some length about this kind of knowledge based on 'testimony' and its 'reasonableness (§§ 42-45) and how, in point of fact, most of our knowledge is thus based on it. We need not repeat all that here.

§124. 4. A fourth meaning, as important to bear in mind, of 'moral certitude' is when the evidence, no matter what the field of knowledge is, is based on good reasons. 'Testimony' may be one – but if it is the only one, then we have 'moral certitude' in the third sense. Here one has to have more than that. Notice that even in Science, the scientist may start by having good reasons to form a hypothesis. At that stage he has moral certitude about the truth of his hypothesis. 'By further research, his moral certitude can become physical certitude. But in the Human Sciences, the greater amount of reasons makes the truth more probable, never a physical one (unless one proves that the question at issue is a physical phenomenon!) When we spoke of 'moral matters' we said that apart from a small amount of truths, the greater part are based on good reasons. Of these we can only have 'moral certitude' in this fourth sense. This needs not dismay us. On the contrary this should liberate us from that anxiety to look for absolute certitude where such a thing is neither possible nor to be expected!

§125. As can be seen 'moral certitude in the fourth sense is 'stronger' than the one in the third sense. Actually, 'moral certitude' in the third sense is the weakest of the lot but still it could, given the nature of the case ("How can I be sure who my parents are?) Or the actual conditions of the knower ("How can I be sure that there are a North and South Pole?), it is the only 'moral certitude' to be expected. But notice that often moral responsibility demands that, given the nature of the case and the actual conditions of the knower, the latter should not content himself with it, e.g. the doctor in the exercise of his duties with the patients, the counsellor with the counselee. Hence, the distinction between 'ignorance' (absence of that knowledge and moral certitude expected) and 'nescience'(absence of that knowledge and moral certitude not expected from one).

§126. *e. Religious certitude.* Here we are in the field of religious knowledge. But a lot have first to be said before we can adequately tackle nature of religious certitude, the kind of evidence on which it is based, how we go about obtaining such evidence, the nature of religious truth and kind of language it is expressed in – indeed our whole Second Section is devoted to study such questions. All we have said so far in this First section meant to clear the ground for the religious epistemological question!

§127. But by way of anticipation, lest we should leave the question of 'religious certitude' hanging in the air, so to speak, we could from now pass the following remarks:

a. In our way of proceeding where we are distinguishing meanings of certitude (or kinds of certitude) on the basis both of the field of knowledge and, consequently, on the kind of evidence possible in that field, it is already to be foreseen that the kind of religious certitude possible and to be expected, given the specificity of the field of knowledge concerned - supposing that religious knowledge is possible and genuine knowledge – will be specifically different, at least at some stage or level of the process by which one obtains it, from every other kind.

§128. b. It is an observable fact that most people 'inherit' so to say, religious belief from their parents, their educators, etc., – who in their turn 'inherit' them from their own parents, educators, etc. Hence, the conditioning factor here wrought by 'society' on one's religious beliefs (and for that matter on other beliefs of his, whether political, social, etc., – we shall come to this topic presently). This, of course, raises the question whether and to what extent such conditioned religious knowledge is genuine knowledge. But that is not what concerns here directly. What concerns us here is to observe that at the beginning – and in most cases, throughout one's life – man's religious belief is based on the witness, testimony of others. We discussed the conditions under which it could be considered 'reasonable' (under 'sabda', §§ 44 ff), but, at any rate, the 'certitude' based on it can only be 'moral certitude' in the third meaning of the term explained above).

§129. c. Even at a higher (or deeper) level, when one starts thinking things out for oneself, if his religious beliefs remain based on the evidence of his respective Scriptures ("written testimony"), his certitude can only be 'moral certitude' – and his religious beliefs remain 'beliefs' (§ 42). Still, if at this stage, one sees more and more reasons to confirm, corroborate, justify, his religious belief – indicating the reasonableness of his act of believing in those particular Scriptures and in their contents, answering difficulties which may arise in a reasonable way, showing the untenability of opposite beliefs in a fairly convincing way, etc. – then he can be said to be 'morally certain' in the fourth sense of the term. A 'convergence of probabilities' (Newman), in this respect, can even amount to something like, but perhaps not quite,' ontological certitude' – if, that is, this convergence can be seen to point to, or to be finally based upon, a 'self-evident truth' insightfully intuited (§§ 65-66).

§130. d. Many great philosophers, who were at the same time great religious men, claim something further – and herein lies, according to us, the specificity of 'religious certitude'. And this is the more noteworthy since these men belong to different religious traditions. They claim a direct perception of supra-sensible Reality, of reality in its ultimate Significance (§§ 89-90), in its Ultimacy (or ultimate causes). Hence, they distinguish two levels of reality (the empirical and the transcendental) two levels of experience (the vyavaharika-drsti, and the paramarthika-drsti, -according to Vedanta, Jaina and Buddha, and the rational and sapiential according to Christianity), and hence too two levels of knowledge and of certitude. But all this leads us straight into the Second Part of this course. But before that we would like to pass some remarks on another interesting topic.

Chapter 6

KNOWLEDGE AND SOCIETY

§131. When we spoke of the 'means' (or 'sources') of knowledge, we together with many Schools of Indian and Western Philosophy, listed 'testimony' (sabda) as one of them – indeed as one of the more important. We returned to this important topic again when we discussed religious belief is the context of 'certitude' (§§ 128-129). But already in the questions raised in the Introduction and in this latter context, we pointed out the possible difficulties which can be put to any epistemological theory. In fact, knowledge is not merely an individual affair, it is also a social phenomenon. Man being the social and historical being that he is, his thought and knowledge are greatly affected, and to a large extent molded, by his environing society. As history makes man as much as man makes history, so too society makes man as much as man makes society. This is being realized more and more today. So whereas what we examined under 'testimony' applies mostly to that means of knowledge whereby the individual as individual comes to know something by consciously accepting the 'word' of a reliable person or authority, what we are going to examine here applies mostly to those factors whereby the individual as a social being, or group of men and women considered collectively, come to obtain certain 'belief systems' by unconsciously letting themselves by affected or influenced by the surrounding social structures. By a 'social phenomenon' we mean something which can be studied, as to its nature, roots, foreseeable consequences, by empirical techniques, and procedures (e.g. urbanization, kinship, social deviance, etc).

A 'sociology of knowledge' is today a respectable part of Sociology. It studies knowledge as a social phenomenon. Still as a discipline in itself, it is somewhat differently understood (cf. Scheler, Mannheim and the wider scope given it by Berger-Luckmann). More importantly for us, more recent sociologists of knowledge do recognize the distinction that is to be drawn between the sociological issues (e.g. what the 'social determinants' of knowledge are) and the philosophical epistemological ones (e.g. the validity, relativity, historicity of knowledge). It is clear that in a treatise such as this, it is precisely these philosophical epistemological issues as related to the sociological issues which will be our concern here. So what we intend to do is to list down some of the main issues raised by sociologists of knowledge (as given by R. Merton, one of the more important contemporary American sociologists to have paid attention to the sociology of knowledge), and then we proceed to make our own reflections.

1. SOCIOLOGICAL ISSUES

§132. 1. Where is the existential basis of mental productions located? Social bases: social position, class, generation, occupational role, mode of production, group structures (university, bureaucracy, academies, sects, political parties), "historical situation", interests, society, ethic affiliations, social mobility, power structure, social processes (competition, conflict, etc.).

Cultural bases: values, ethos, climate of opinion, Volkgeist, Zeitgeist, type of culture, culture mentality, Weltanschanungen, etc.

2. *What mental productions are being sociologically analyzed?* Spheres of moral beliefs, ideologies, ideas, the categories of thought, philosophy, religious beliefs, social norms, positive science, technology etc.

Which aspects are being analyzed: their selection (foci of attention), level of abstraction, presuppositions (what is taken as data and what as problematical), conceptual content, models of verification, objectives of Intellectual activity, etc.

§133. 3. *How are mental productions related to the existential basis?* Causal or functional relations: determination, cause, correspondence, necessary condition, conditioning, functional interdependence, interaction dependence, etc.

Symbolic or organismic or meaningful relations: consistency, harmony, coherence, unity, congruence, compatibility (and antonyms); expression, realization, symbolic expression, 'Strukturzusammenhang', structural identities, inner connection, stylistic analogies, logico-meaninful integration, identity of meaning, etc. [Merton points out the ambiguity of some of these terms].

4. *Why [are] manifest and latent functions imputed to these existentially conditioned mental productions?*

E.g. to maintain power, promote stability, orientation, exploitation, obscure actual social relationships, provide motivation, canalize behavior, divert criticism, deflect hostility, provide reassurance, control nature, coordinate social relationships, etc.

5. *When do the imputed relations of the existential base and knowledge obtain?*

Merton distinguishes between 'historicist theories' (confined to particular societies or cultures), and 'general analytical theories'.

2. PHILOSOPHICAL REFLECTIONS

§134. 1. *Man comes to know with his whole being* – including his social being. As we have said, man is essentially a social being (i.e. a being who, to fulfil his potentialities as a man, necessarily needs to grow and live with other human beings). So he comes to know 'with' others, in a relationship 'with' others, in a community 'with' others. It is not enough to say – but this was a big insight on the part of St Thomas Aquinas – that "it is not the intellect which understands, but man with his intellect"; it is necessary to specify that man understands (comes to know) with his whole being, and since his being is a social being, he does so with his whole social being. Man does not think, reflect, judge, etc., in a vacuum, so to say. He certainly can do so all by himself, closed up in a room, but his 'being' (interests, certain pre-suppositions and assumptions, his tastes, his emotive responses, his already formed convictions, etc.) is already moulded by the society he lives in and when he comes to think, etc., he thinks with all his 'being' understood in this social sense. (We are not impugning here the validity of the 'means of knowledge' (pramanas) what we have just remarked on 'testimony' (§ 371), applies to them all).

§135. 2. *Given the 'socialness' of man's being by which he comes to know, man's 'objective' knowledge is existentially conditioned.* As understood here, 'objective' is not opposed to 'subjective' but refers to man's knowledge of exteriorly existent objects, persons, and events. It excludes the awareness of 'self-evident truths'. If there is one thing on which all sociologists of knowledge seem to agree is that 'thought' in so far as it is not 'immanently determined' (i.e. self-evident) has an extra cognitive basis (not derived from reasoning but from some factor in his social existence). Of course, sociologists of knowledge differ widely as to what to include under 'thought' and in 'extra cognitive basis'; they widely differ too what one is to understand by 'conditioned' (see § 133), (3).

a. *'Self-evident truths':* this is required by the sociology of knowledge itself – it its findings are to be accepted as true, or even as more 'appropriate' than contending theories. But this is not to say that their understanding and formulation are not also existentially conditioned, for, according to us, they are.

b. 'Conditioned': not 'determined' in the sense that it cannot change. This, in fact would be to go against experience itself, as we are going to show presently. 'Conditioned', therefore, in the sense of more or less influenced. And the more this influence is unconscious, the greater it is. Most people may never become aware of this extra-cognitive influence on their whole knowledge or process of thought.

c. 'Existentially': i.e. by the extra-cognitive factors of his 'social beingness, so to say, therefore by his 'existence'. As a social being man is essentially a 'historical being'- the product of the place and *time* he lives in. And by 'time' we do not mean simply mean chronological time (years and century) but chairological time (opportunities, needs, situations, problem, achievements, etc., which all go to characterize a specific moment of history from another)!

§136. 3. Given the existential conditioning of man's objective knowledge, this remains necessarily 'relative'. This is already implied in the Scholastic dictum: "whatever is received in the mind (i.e. whatever is known) is received (i.e. known) in accordance with the nature of the receiver". And if man, as stated here, is essentially a social and historical being, whatever he knows, he knows in accordance with his social and historical nature. – We have often had the opportunity to distinguish between 'relative' and 'relativistic' (§§ 90, 107, 118). In this respect we could recall too the Jain 'syadvada' and the Buddhist 'catuskoti' logic. In this context too, we cannot help passing some remarks about the opposition Kant's theory encountered all throughout its history. Fearing the relativism and the subjectivism to which it could lead, philosophers fought it might and main. No matter its merits and demerits as a philosophical theory of knowledge, we do feel inclined to accept his basic contention that 'objective' knowledge remains necessarily relative. (Understood in the light of the Jain and Buddhist theories, to us it makes a great deal of sense. And the findings of the sociology of knowledge – in spite of differences of opinion among the theorists themselves – point in the same-direction!) That is 'relative' to the knower – which on the one hand explains the possibility of science, and on the other hand explains that the thing-in-itself (is matter energy? and what is energy?), the soul (do I really know myself?) and 'God' (as we shall see in the Second Section) remain unknowable by mere discursive reason! (Haven't the opponents of a 'relative' theory of knowledge been existentially conditioned by their very fear of relativism and subjectivism, and their insistence on 'absolutism' in human knowledge, often religiously inspired?).

§137. 4. *A relative 'objective' knowledge presupposes an unconditionally true theory.* This forestalls any objection to what we are saying here – and answers, at the same time, the usual objections against such theories as those mentioned in the previous paragraphs. In fact, it could be objected that if what we are saying here is true, it can only be relatively true. Aren't we too, in saying that we are saying-: existentially conditioned? And if it is relatively true, isn't it relatively false too? Aren't we getting trapped in a kind of skepticism which we have earlier shown to be exercitively contradictory? – Something similar to what we said regarding 'first- order assertions' and 'second-order assertions', and 'first intentions' and 'second intentions' (§§ 98, 100) must be said here too. The referent of 'objective knowledge, as we said, is exteriorly existent objects, persons, events; the referent of a theory is different, it is, in 'our case, 'objective' knowledge itself, made up as it is of second-order assertions, second intentions. There is no contradiction in saying therefore that 'objective' knowledge is relative, but what I am saying know, and my theory about 'object-ive' knowledge is absolutely true. And this is certainly to be pre-supposed if any theory is to be considered true. 'Syadvada' cannot, and in fact does not, include itself among the 'relatively' known objects of its discourse; neither does the 'catuskoti' Logic. Contrary to what many of their opponents think, they are not self-contradictory. And, as can be seen, therefore, they are not to be confused with or mistaken for a kind of skepticism. A radical skepticism *is*, as we have shown, self-contradictory. But only a 'radical' one – i.e., which includes itself as 'object' of its skepticism!

§138. 5. *Awareness of man's existential conditioning implies possibility of growth in human freedom.* To be able to speak at all of man's existential conditioning means that one has to become first aware of it. Surely many people, if not most, never become so aware. But to become aware of it means that one is not so conditioned that one cannot 'distance' oneself, as it were, from it and cannot 'de-condition' oneself, at least up to a certain extent and progressively. This is at the basis of our distinction between 'conditioning' and 'determining'. And experience bears us out. Did it not over happen to us that we became aware that what we believed once to be true was simply the result of our having been told in early childhood (or later), something which we had always taken for granted and never questioned but later, due to several factors (e.g. having been challenged to 'prove' its truth or having confronted with different beliefs) have come to 'change' our belief – and what is more to have done so consciously even knowing that we are doing so because we are being 'influenced' by others'! This explains too, how it was possible that individuals can go against the 'current' (generally-held beliefs or opinions, etc.) and change the thinking of their time! Society makes man as much as man makes society! It is true that this process of 'de-conditioning' may take time and remains always partial. It may take place first on the 'head-level' and only with conscious effort will it take place, if at all, on the 'gut level'. But still, this proves that man is fundamentally free (i.e. existential conditioned yes, but not absolutely determined in his thought and knowledge). But it proves at the same time that man is only 'fundamentally' free. Full freedom, if at all possible, is not something given at the very beginning of man's existence: it is a goal to be achieved, a task to be performed! – Finally note that to 'de-condition' oneself does not mean to 'throw overboard' all one has learnt before. It means that once one has become aware of the possibility of his having been so conditioned to think and act in such and such a way, one now tries to think and judge for himself and act accordingly. Many things we have learnt before (parents, educators, etc.) will be now accepted, in full awareness, for their own merit. A sociology of knowledge, as somebody put it, is not a sociology of error – but, precisely, of knowledge! This brings us to the following point.

§139. 6. *Relative 'objective' knowledge explains possibility of different perspectives on Reality and Knowledge itself which may be but need not be mutually exclusive.* Another way of saying that man is 'existentially conditioned' is to say that man is 'existentially situated', i.e., placed, essentially, in a particular place and time in history. Hence, man's 'objective' knowledge is also 'existentially situated' (cf. the German 'Sitz im-Leben'). This means, however, two things: (a) the extent that he is 'free', or at least, that he has the possibility to grow in human freedom, to the extent that he can become more and more aware of 'self- evident truths' (which are not space and time-bound), to the extent, finally that that he is capable of 'unconditionally true theory' (§ 137), he is not so 'existentially situated! (b) But, as far as his 'objective' knowledge is concerned, man can become aware not only of the 'relativeness' of it but also, and consequently, of the possibility of different partial, necessarily one-faceted perspectives on Reality (Truth in an ontological sense and on the phenomenon of Knowledge itself. Hence, the possibility of different metaphysical and epistemological systems. What is more, he can become aware that while all need not be true (the possibility of 'error' § 102 ff), always remain a possibility) or equally 'adequate', yet they could be complementary and not mutually exclusive. A 'partial knowledge' can be, and necessarily has to be, completed, enriched, by others. (Again, it would be no objection to say that what we are saying here is only partially true and therefore partially false. Here, the referent of our discourse is neither 'objects', nor even 'objective knowledge as in § 137, but theory, itself. As we speak about a concept of a concept and of an assertion of an assertion, here we are speaking of a theory of a theory, a 'meta-theory'. Any objection to what we are saying here has to place itself on this 'meta-theoretical' level of discourse).

§140. This is why, the better to understand the thought of an author or of a philosophical or religious movement, one needs to try and understand, as much as one can, his or its 'situation': where and when, the economical, social, political, religious circumstances of the time and place; the author's biography, his character and temperament, his surroundings, his needs and intentions, etc.

A sociological analysis would perhaps yield interesting results in this area. How is it that in the West Empiricism flourished mostly in Anglo-Saxon countries whereas Idealism in Germanic counties (Which is true even today)? What is the 'existential basis' for the one and the other? Surely Marxism would be better understood not only as a philosophical movement but as the thought of Marx if it is seen to be 'situated' in the age of the Industrial Revolution and in the biography of Marx itself. Similarly with Existentialism seen as 'situated' in the period between two world wars and in the life-history of such men as Sartre and Gabriel Marcel. Darwin's theory of 'natural selection' could perhaps be better understood if seen as 'situated' in his current competitive economic order and Freud's theory of the 'super-ego' as 'situated' in a social order which demanded as too rigid obedience and subjection to familial, political and religious authority. Again, Buddhism can be better understood if seen as 'situated' in the Bramanic period of India in the 6th century B.C., Islam in the polytheistic period of Arabia in the 6th Century A.D., Christianity in the Roman period of Palestine in the 1st Century, etc., etc. This brings us, in its turn, to still another point.

§141. 7. Existentially-situated knowledge, while explaining possibility of cultural pluralism, does not necessarily mean cultural relativism. We have said that a relative 'objective' knowledge explains possibility of different perspectives of Reality (and knowledge itself) which may but need not be mutually exclusive. Another way of saying this is that cultural pluralism is possible, cultural relativism is not. – It is perhaps not so easy to define 'culture'- but by this term we mean, in short, 'the belief and value system of a given society' (belief system = mythos; value system = ethos). A 'culture' is expressed in the literature, music, architecture, politics, morality, philosophy, social order, economic order, religion of that society. 'Society' again is a difficult word to define; it can have different meanings according to the purpose which links it together. (Thus we can speak of the familial society, the political society, the international society and a philatelic or swimming society, etc.)! In our context, by 'society' we mean, 'a people with a common, collective, idea of itself'. (cf. the similar conception of E. Durkheim who speaks, in this respect of a 'collective consciousness'). It is this 'idea' which a society gives to itself (of its 'ideals') which is mirrored, so to say, in its culture.

§142. That a cultural pluralism is a fact is, of course, an observable phenomenon. But the possibility in question here is the epistemological one, i.e., that different cultures, though different, can be complementary and not necessarily mutually exclusive. 'Cultural relativism' is a different thing altogether. It says that even though cultures (in their philosophies, theologies, etc.) are mutually exclusive (contradictory to each other), given that culture is existentially based or existentially conditioned (i.e. necessitated by the actual state of affairs of the society), given too that 'truth' has a mere social function (i.e. to serve the coherence of a society- a pragmatic function, cf. Durkheim), there is no way of judging the 'truth' or 'falsity' of their respective tenants of belief. We have taken pains all along throughout this course to show that such a philosophical position is untenable. For this would mean that the Nazi culture which demanded the slaughter of 6,000,000 Jews during World War II cannot be subjected to a 'value' judgment. In the same way, the American culture which accepted slavery as part of its economic system up to the last century was immune to a 'value' judgment!

§143. Some final remarks. Today, because of intra-national and inter-national communications, 'societies' are no longer so closed as before. And the more they let themselves, consciously or unconsciously, be influenced by other societies and their cultures, both on a national and inter-national level, the more likely they be enriched and complemented. Today, it is easier to speak of a 'world society'- and consequently of a 'world culture'. The common factors which would constitute 'the idea' this world society has of itself would be perhaps minimal and so would therefore be those factors which would constitute the 'world culture'. But this idea would be perhaps enough to justify a cultural pluralism, within itself. And in such a cultural pluralism, as it already exists to a great extent today in many countries and as, we may hope, it will be in the future, man will be more able to grow in that human freedom which we have spoken of (§138). And Truth, indeed , makes man free!

PART TWO

EPISTEMOLOGY: ON TALKING ABOUT GOD

Chapter 1

RELIGIOUS KNOWLEDGE

§144. We discussed what we meant by 'knowledge' in Part One. We said that by 'knowledge' we meant 'awareness that such and such is (or is not) the case'. In our further explanation we said 'knowledge' is essentially true and reasonable, otherwise it is no 'knowledge' at all (§§ 13-19). The first question which we have therefore to ask is what is the 'case' (or 'state of affairs' of which religious knowledge is an 'awareness'. In other words, what is the 'referent' of religious knowledge. The other questions regarding the 'truth' and 'reasonableness' of religious knowledge will be asked later. But to raise and try to answer such a question, a previous question has to be raised and answered. In fact, some modern analytical philosophers maintain that in religious knowledge there is no 'referent' at all. So the question is whether religious knowledge 'refers' to anything at all. To put this in another way: has religious knowledge a 'cognitive function (or 'illocution', § 21). Some go as far as to say that religious language, having no 'cognitive' function at all, is made up of statements which are only seemingly so, that is of only seemingly propositions (but of no 'constative' function). And why? Because religious language, according to them is 'meaningless'. Hence, before we ask ourselves what the 'referent' of religious language is, we have to see whether religious language is 'meaningful' or not.

1. 'MEANING' AND RELIGIOUS LANGUAGE

§145. The history of the question of 'meaning' in language makes very interesting reading. It went through different phases, which for convenience's sake we call, the Logical Positivist stage and the Logical Empiricist stage.

a. 'Meaning' as 'Empirically Verifiability'

Logical positivists distinguish between 'analytical' and 'synthetical' propositions. By their very nature, the former are necessarily true but, being 'formal' they tell us nothing about reality. So while they are necessarily true (or 'tautologies') they are not informative about any state of affairs in the world, and in this sense, they are not 'cognitive, (§ 114). Only 'synthetical' propositions (in which something is affirmed or denied of a predicate) are informative or 'cognitive' and it is only of them that we can ask whether they are true or false. Hence, unlike 'analytical' propositions which are necessarily true, these are 'contingent', that is, they can be true or false. But how are we going to say whether a (synthetic) proposition is true or false? Well, we have got to see whether what is affirmed or denied can be verified by empirical means (sense-experience, observation, laboratory experiments, etc). If a proposition cannot be so verified (or falsified), in other words, it cannot be either proved – by empirical means – true or proved false, that proposition is 'meaningless'. Yes, it may be expressive of some kind of 'emotion' or other (like joy, appreciation, disgust, approval or disapproval, preference, etc.), but obviously of these expressions of emotion ("How good I feel today!"). I cannot simply go about trying to prove by empirical means whether that expression(or 'utterance') is true or false. It does not tell me –other than how you or I feel at the moment- about any state of affairs in the world. And hence such expressions of 'emotion' are not 'cognitive'; such expressions are 'meaningless'. Now according to Logical Positivists, religious language (and for that matter moral and metaphysical language too) are made up, or claim to be made up, of 'synthetic propositions' which however cannot be proved, by empirical means, to be either true or false. Hence, religious language (like moral and metaphysical language) is 'meaningless'. The so-called 'verification principle' underwent, through the course of time, certain modifications (e.g. for a proposition to be called 'meaningful' it has to be able to be proved, at least probably, even if not conclusively, either true or false; or at least it had to be so proved at least 'in principle', etc.) but the empirical nature of the means of proof remained unchanged.

§146. b. 'Meaning' as 'Function':

Logical Empiricists consider the Logical Positivists' understanding of the term 'meaning' and the 'verification principle' itself, even in its modified form, as too restrictive. The purpose of language is not simply to 'inform', it has many other purposes, or functions, too. Wittgenstein, for example, abandoning his earlier positivistic position, pointed out some of these functions (which he calls 'language games' such as reporting, telling a story, joking, asking questions, promising, thanking, congratulating, etc.). Hence if a proposition has a function, or use, no matter what this function is, it is to be called 'meaningful', otherwise not. – So far so good. But to apply this to religious language? Has it any function, and if it has, what is this function? Here, logical Empiricists all agree that religious language does have a function but not all agree what this function precisely is. Some see it as a means of expressing one's intention of acting in such and such a way. For example, when I say that 'God is love', I am simply expressing my intention of leading a loving way of life (Braithwaite), or stating that love is my ultimate moral norm in all aspects of my life (thus reducing religious language to moral language, thus Hepburn). More interesting still, others see the function of religious language to express the user's experience of reality as such and such, giving it a certain structure or pattern; a function, therefore, expressing one's outlook, view ('blik') of reality (thus respectively, J. Hick, Wisdom, Hare). Not all of these philosophers are 'empiricists' in the philosophical sense of the word on the contrary some, like Hick, are great religious believers. Still, to the extent, but only to the extent, that this function of religious meaning is seen to consist only in expressing the user's intention, conviction, experience, view, etc., of the world – without, that is, any other 'referent' than this – the understanding of religious language, implied by such an understanding of its function, can still be called 'empirical'. In fact, Logical Positivists will readily admit that religious language may have such a function. But then they will include this function as 'emotive'. If, and only if, it can be shown that religious language is informative about any factual state of affairs (other than the user's state of mind) that it can be said 'cognitive' and therefore meaningful.

§147. c. Critical Reflections

There are a lot of things to learn from this discussion regarding the nature and function of religious language.

1. To be 'cognitive', religious language must have a 'referent' other than the speaker's emotion, state of mind, etc. Religious believers themselves would insist that such is the case. Unless a religious believer knows that what is being affirmed or denied corresponds to actual state of affairs and not merely to his or others' emotions, whims and fancies, he will surely stop believing.

2. If religious language does have such a referent, not all religious propositions are analytical. If, and to the extent that, they are synthetical, they are subject to logical analysis, and to rules of logic and reason. If they are not they do not mean what they say. So one has to show not only what they mean but how it is that they are 'recalcitrant' to logic and reason. Do they have a kind of logic all by themselves, what kind of logic. This is a very important point. We have touched on this topic briefly already (§ 116-118).

§148. 3. If religious propositions are not verifiable by empirical means, they are not descriptive of empirical reality. Religious believers believe no argument, based on some empirical fact (e.g. evil), can disprove the truth of religion. If nothing can disprove, nothing can prove it either – by empirical means! This is a lesson which has practical consequences in one's religious life. Can 'answers to one's prayers' prove the truth of one's religious belief? What if one's prayers are not answered – would they then disprove it?

4. Religious language, like language in general, can have more than one function. It says of man (his emotions, convictions, etc.) as much as it says of any other possible 'referent'. We have seen that the same utterance (or 'locution' can have different kinds of 'illocutions'. This will lead us presently to distinguish between different kinds of 'illocutions' (§21). This will lead us presently to distinguish between different kinds of religious languages and different kinds of functions. This can be better appreciated if we stopped to consider that 'speech' ('discourse') as distinct from 'language' is a communication between persons. (we have spoken of 'knowledge' as a social phenomenon (§131ff); similarly, and for much the same reason, is 'speech'. It is one thing to consider language as an impersonal entity, so to say, like in Logic, Mathematics, or in its grammar, syntax, idiom, etc., it is another to consider language (or speech) as used in a particular social context. Often different contexts give the same word a different meaning.

§149. 5. But more indirectly we can learn other things as well. We have often spoken of EMPIRICISM in different contexts (§25, 34,67, 86, etc.). We have seen that as a theory it certainly cannot account for knowledge (e.g. in the formation of the concept, the drawing of a general scientific law, the apprehension of 'self-evident truths' etc.), and besides, and because of this, it is actually self-defeating, exercitively contradictory. And it is this theory which is presupposed both in Logical Positivism and – but to a lesser degree – in Logical Empiricism. An empirical stance in Philosophy is certainly incompatible with religious belief.

6. It has been shown that the 'verification principle' itself is not of much use in assessing the value of religious knowledge and language (indeed of knowledge in general). For if the principle ("whatever cannot be proved by empirical means true or false is meaningless") is understood as a definition, it has to be; a tautology (in the sense that every definition is one) and necessarily true. But then it is 'formally true' and would tell us nothing about any state of affairs, in our case, the nature and function of language. If, on the other hand, it is understood as a synthetic proposition, it has, like all synthetical propositions, to be able to be proved true or false by empirical means – which, obviously, it cannot be!

2. THE 'REFERENT' OF RELIGIOUS LANGUAGE

§150. So now we come to the first question we raised at the beginning of this chapter. We have first to distinguish between different kinds of religious languages.

a. Different Kinds of Religious Language

What we have in mind here is to distinguish these different kinds of language as far as the 'referent' is concerned. Suppose I said "Jesus Christ was the son of Mary, he was born in Bethlehem in Judea in such and such a year, he was crucified under Pontius Pilate, etc." Now, here the referent is, obviously, Jesus Christ. But all this can be historically verified (as much as historical events can). The kind of language used is not different than that used to refer to any person whether in the past or in the present. – But suppose I said, "Jesus Christ was the Son of God, the Second Person of the Blessed Trinity. He rose from the dead and is now seated at the right hand of God the Father, etc." This is a peculiar kind of language, which certainly cannot be verified or falsified by empirical means. (Whether it is true or false is another matter and is not our concern here at the moment). Here the 'referent' is still Jesus Christ but to the extent, that he is 'Son of God'.

Let us take another example. Suppose I said, "you are a man, subject to suffering, old age and death. If you detach yourself from all desires, from all attachment to worldly things and pleasures, you will find happiness." Again this may or may not be psychologically verified, it is not different from any other psychological discourse. The 'referent here is you. – But suppose I said, "you are Brahman, it is only because of 'maya' that you mistake the non-real for the real. And it is because of this that you are subject to pain, old age and suffering. If you realize what you really are, you attain moksa". Here, the referent is still you but you to the extent that you are "Brahman' and the usage of language is once again peculiar.

§151. This leads us to make a distinction between religious languages *first* from the point of view of whether 'religious' here is understood in a strict sense or in a loose sense. 'Religious' understood in a strict sense is when its 'referent' is strictly its own (as we are going to try and explain presently; understood in a loose sense, is language in a general sense (historical, psychological, geographical, etc.) but used in relation to, in connection with, religious language strictly so called.

Secondly, from the point of view of the 'referent' itself, that is when it is either referred to directly or indirectly. For example, suppose I said, "The church is the Body of Christ" – the direct referent would be 'The Church', but since this statement is to be understood in its own 'universe of discourse' (or 'linguistic field, § 94-95) and this 'universe of discourse' is religious, its indirect – or ultimate – referent is other than 'The Church'.

Thirdly, from the point of view of the 'purpose' for which the religious language is used. Often it is used to 'evoke' in the mind of the interlocutor its 'ultimate referent'. According to us this is the primary use of religious language. At times it is used to 'explain' it by means of clear statements (cf. 'dogma'), or, further still to show how a 'tenet of religious belief' is reasonable, coherent with its 'universe of discourse', unobjectionable, etc. this is the 'theo-logical' but secondary use of religious language. Hence our distinction between 'primary' or 'original' belief and 'secondary' or 'derived' belief.

§152. b. The 'ultimate referent' of religious language

It would have been simpler to say simply that this 'ultimate referent' of religious language is 'God' (or 'Brahman' or 'Allah', etc.). But apart from the fact that such words are so loaded with connotations that they can be, as in fact they often are, misunderstood, that would force us to dismiss e.g. Jain, Buddhist, Taoist language as non-religious. In these religious languages, the term 'God' either does not figure, or if it does, it has a different meaning than it has in Christianity. (Here we are touching on a very fundamental question: what is meant by the term 'religious' and 'religion' – a question with which we deal extensively in our *Philosophy of Religion*. Here, however, we are approaching the subject epistemologically and semantically). – At any rate, that would lead us to regard these languages as non-relevant to our purposes – which, in fact they are not.

So the best thing to do here is to go back to what we have already hinted in another context (§130). There we pointed out that great philosophers who were at the same time great religious men claim the possibility of a direct perception of supra-sensible Reality, of phenomenal reality itself but in its ultimate Significance, in its Ultimacy, or, to use a scholastic expression, it its 'Ultimate Causes' (i.e. in its ultimate meaning, origin, value and end). This is to say, that according to this claim, phenomenal reality not the be-all and end-all of reality, but, on the contrary, it can have its ultimate explanation in something 'other' (the word is here misleading!) than itself. For reasons we shall be giving lager, it will be seen why it is that it is so difficult to 'say' in no unambiguous words what this 'ultimate referent' of religious language precisely is. (And, by the way, the language we ourselves are using has the 'primary' function of which we have just spoken – i.e., to try and 'evoke' in the reader what we mean by this 'ultimate referent' of religious language!). In any case, we can, for simplicity's sake (!), say that this 'ultimate referent' of religious language is: Absolute Reality, Ultimate Value and Supreme Good of phenomenal reality itself. (Whether all this is 'true' or 'false', whether it is mere words, fiction of the imagination, etc., does not concern us here at the moment. We shall come to that later).

Hence, the distinction between the real (the empirical) and the really Real (the transcendental) in experience, knowledge, language and certitude! While this distinction between two 'levels', as it were, of experience, knowledge, language and certitude, can help us, in a way, to understand better what follows, it raises, in its turn, many interesting epistemological questions as we are going to see.

Chapter 2

RELIGIOUS LANGUAGE

§153. In this chapter we shall be dealing with *how* the 'ultimate referent' of religious language is precisely referred to. (In other words we shall be dealing with religious 'reference' itself). The two levels of which we have spoken at the end of the previous chapter already raises this epistemological issue. How can our empirical experience and the words we borrow, as it were, from it can be of any help to express our transcendental experience and speak at all – if speak we must – of any transcendental Reality?

St. Thomas, and Scholasticism in general, insists that our knowledge of 'God' originates from our sense-experience. And hence the concepts we form and the words we use to refer to Him are applicable first and foremost (in the way we are going to explain) to objects of our sense-experience. That is true is clear from an examination of the concepts and words we use. Even if we were to accept the theory (cf. Plato, Malebranche) that our 'ideas' are innate in us – which could make sense with regard, for example, of 'self-evident truths' – still, as far as the present question is concerned, the very fact that to express our ideas of this 'ultimate Reality' with the same words we use to express other realities of our sense-experience would create a difficulty. Consider, for example, words like 'Father', 'King', 'Lord', or '*Saccitananda*' ('being-consciousness-bliss'), or 'nirvana' ('blowing out'), etc., etc., – all these words can easily be applied to objects of our empirical experience. (Even the words we use to refer to the 'ultimate referent' alone are taken from our own human experience. For example, 'God' seems to be derived from the Teutonic, 'gudham' which meant 'to one to be invoked'; 'Brhaman' from the Sanskrit root 'brh' which means to grow, increase, etc.).

§154. In any case, this accounts, at least partially, for that 'ineffability' of 'God' which so many 'mystics' of many different religious traditions are wont to insist upon. And this seems to be a paradox. For 'mystics' are supposed to be those who are known to have had, or to have claimed to have, a 'direct perception' of this Ultimate Reality. If that is true, it means that, as St. Thomas says, the more a man understands God, the more he understands at the same time that God cannot be understood! (S.Th. II, IIae, 8, 7, c). Since, our knowledge and language about 'God' originates in our empirical experience, we can know and speak of Him only as experienced and not as He is in Himself. "Man is able to grap not what God is but what He is not and the relation of other things to Him" (C. G. 1, 30). St Thomas goes as far as to say that "the highest degree in our human knowledge of God is to know that we do not know God" (De Pot., 7, 5, ad 14) and in another place "the final degree of our knowledge of God is to know as unknown" (*De Trin.*, 1, 2 ad 1).

§155. This, of course raises the epistemological (i.e. regarding the knowledge) and the semantic (i.e. regarding the 'referent' of language) questions with which we are dealing here.

In the religious literature of the world we can discover three ways of 'referring' to what we have called (apart from 'God') the Absolute Reality, Ultimate Value and Supreme Good. We follow St. Thomas the way of 'remotion', the way of 'causality' and the way of 'eminence'. And we shall see that all of them find deep echos in his eastern counterpart, Sankara and others too. Needless to say that this part of our course has a great spiritual value. For it can serve to purify our knowledge and language of God. Many modern (as well as ancient) difficulties against religious belief stem, to a large extent, from a misuse of language – which, in its turn, stems from a superficial understanding of what is really meant by 'God'.

1. THE WAY OF REMOTION

§156. This way consists in saying what the 'referent' is <u>not</u> rather than what it is. It does so precisely by 'removing' from its idea all other ideas which are directly applicable to – since they are based on – objects of our empirical experience. It is also called the 'way of negation' because it denies rather than affirms, denies that whatever we can think and say about it does not really apply. Actually then it does not really say anything (apophatic) except to say that whatever we can think and say of it does not apply!

Hence either negations are used ("it is not this, it is not that") are negative terms are employed.[5] Negative terms are those with a negative prefix (like un-, in-, im-, dis-, non-). Certain seemingly positive terms are really negative (e.g. darkness = absence of light; spirit = non-matter; simple = non-composed of parts and parts, matter and form, substance and accidents; eternal = without beginning or end' etc.). Other negative terms are formed by adding a negative suffix (e.g. – less, as in beginningless). Thus 'God' is referred to as infinite, immortal, eternal, spirit,

5 S. Azzopardi, *Logic*, § 13.

simple, wilderness, (even nothingness, i.e. nothing that we can think and speak of!), etc.

§157. Still this way of remotion has got a great heuristic value. It is different from keeping completely silent. (Many mystics prefer to do just that!). Its heuristic value consists in, first, eliminating various other 'universes of discourse' (the cosmological, historical, ethical, etc.) which are not specifically the religious 'universe', thus narrowing down 'the range of reference' (Crombie); secondly, by purifying our ideas based on our empirical experience, it points to and tries to evoke in our innermost consciousness what it is that is therefore 'meant' by the referent of religious language. This it does 'asymptotically' (by ever approaching and approaching to the meaning of what is meant but never reaching it, so to say). But it is by so doing that it hopes to give rise to insight (in the wider sense of 'intuition').

§158. St. Thomas goes as far as to say that this is the 'principal way' in referring to God (C. G., 1, 14)! According to him all affirmations about Him are true only up to a certain extent (as we are going to show later), whereas negatives, in this respect, are simply true. This idea he takes from 'Dionysius' with the explanation, however, that affirmation *can* be made about 'God' but inappropriately as far as their way of referring to 'God' is concerned. This is an interesting point St Thomas makes (sent, XXII, 1, 2, 1 ad 1). When we speak of 'God' we have to use either abstract or concrete predicates. Now abstract predicates (e.g. 'existence', 'goodness', 'love') do not exist in themselves, whereas 'God' exists in Himself. Concrete predicates (e.g. 'exists', 'good', 'loving', 'wise') are more appropriately applied to objects of our sense-experience, whereas God is not such an object. Hence, the distinction between 'what' is meant by a word (its 'signification') and the 'way it is referred' ('way of signification'). Now for an affirmation to be simply (literally) true, it needs to be affirmed because of both what is meant by the predicate and the way it is referred. So no affirmation about 'God' can be simply true. But as for negation, it is sufficient that it is made because of either one or the other to be simply true. So only negations about 'God' can be simply true-since they deny that 'what' is meant by the predicate can be referred to 'God' in the way (concretely or abstractly) the predicate suggests (ibid). But even then, if an affirmation is true because of 'what' the predicate means (the signification), this, according to St. Thomas always "remain ununderstood and beyond human comprehension" (S. Th. I, 13, 5 in c.)!

§159. Here, St. Thomas follows long Christian 'apophatic' tradition beginning perhaps from Dionysius whom we mentioned already and continuing even today. Names like Nicholas of Cusa (who calls this way of knowing by unknowing, as it were, 'learned ignorance') and that of the author of 'The Cloud of Unknowing' stand out (18).

§160. In India, at least in some quarters, this tradition is even more strongly felt. Recall what we have already said about 'parisesa' as one of the 'pramanas' (§ 63) according to some Indian Schools. This is precisely a way to come to know by 'elimination'. Though there we already linked it with this way of 'remotion', two differences are to be noted: 'parisesa' is, at least principally, a way of cognition and of cognition of sense-perceptible things, whereas the Scholastic way of 'remotion' is a way of speaking and of speaking about 'God'.

§161. The 'apophaticism' of the Upanisads is indeed very pronounced. Its "neti… neti" (Brahman, Atman, is not this… is not that). This is the basis for the 'way of negation' (apavada) of Sankara.

According to Sankara, Brahman can only be known by Sruti and by no other pramana- and eventually by direct experience (anubhava). But even then Sruti serves us only to distinguish the really real ("the Self") from what is only apparently real ("the attributes superimposed on it") (G.B., 2. 18). Only through a direct perception, an immediate apprehension, (intuition, saksatkara) can Brahman be known. – Now, all our concepts, words and arguments are borrowed from this world of ignorance and cannot therefore be applied to Brahman. A concept, a word, necessarily limits and circumscribes the reality meant. And Brahman cannot be said to be limited in any way. No such limiting attributes can be predicated of Brahman – who is therefore 'without qualities' (nirguna). Not only positive attributes but also their contraries (e.g. 'being' and 'not being') do not apply to Him (G. B. 13, 12). So He is "unknown and beyond the unknown" (Ke. U. 1,3). This is, of course, from the empirical (vyavaharika) point of view. But from this point of view not even 'Brahman' (or 'Atman') can be predicated of Him! (B.U.B., `1, 4, 7). That is a man who has not attained the transcendental point of view (paramarthika) and uses such words does not really know what he is saying! – And so, according to Sankara, the constant negative terms used by Sruti to point to Brahman (e.g. 'unseen', 'unfelt', 'ungraspable', 'uninferable', 'unimaginable', 'indescribable', etc.).

§162. Notice, therefore, how for Sankara the heuristic value of such a way of speaking consists too in pointing to the Reality signified. And this it does by eliminating from what is signified the meaning suggested by concepts and words borrowed from the world of our sense-experience. The 'indeterminatedness' of the 'ultimate referent' of religious language is to be sharply distinguished from 'vagueness'. The former means that the reality signified is too rich in meaning to be able to let itself be limited or circumscribed by this or that concept or word – which are, moreover, sense-bound (the upadhis). The latter, on the contrary, means that there is no specific reality signified by the term – hence the ambiguity of the term used. In religious language, the claim is that words used – whether negative or positive - do signify a specific reality (and in this sense they are not 'vague' at all). But given the nature of the case, i.e., the nature of the reality signified itself and the inadequacy of the terms used to signify it, the terms can only become 'clear' on a higher (or deeper) level of experience and consciousness (as we are going to see later).

'Apophaticism' reaches its zenith in Sunyavada Budddhism. But here interpretations differ. Some interpret Nagarjuna's Logical Dialectic (about which we have spoken so much, §§117, 136) in the sense in which we are speaking of it here. Others, however, understand it to be a complete denial of the existence of any transcendental reality whatsoever. We, with many others, however, prefer to interpret it in the way we are interpreting 'apophaticism' here (19).

2. THE WAY OF CAUSALITY

§163. This way consists in saying what the 'referent' is and does not simply content itself, like the preceding, with saying what it is not. But if what we have just said about the 'way of remotion' is true, how is it at all possible to speak in a positive (kataphatic) way about it? The answer given by St. Thomas and others is this: since 'God' is the Creator of all things, there must some kind of 'similarity' between creatures and Him in as much as the effect somehow or other tells us something about their cause. To speak in our terms: the two levels of experience, consciousness, knowledge and language, which we have spoken of (§ 130, 152) are based on, due to, the two levels of Realty itself (the real and the 'really Real'). But these two levels of Reality are not mathematically two. We speak of 'two' a common and a progressively deeper stage of human experience and consciousness itself. But there is a continuum. 'Two' is taken only in a diagrammatical sense. (We could, if we liked, speak of three, four, five, etc. levels). Reality is one. The only thing, however, is that one can become aware that phenomenal reality – with its ontological limitedness, contingency, multiplicity, changeability – cannot be fully and ultimately intelligible in itself. It needs and 'over-plus' of being, reality, to make it so.[6] At any rate St. Thomas, using the Aristotelian terminology, speaks of 'God' as the ultimate origin and final end of all that is, i.e., in Christian terms, as the Creator. And the effects, especially spiritual beings, reflect their Maker. And from our knowledge of the former we can come somehow to know – and therefore to speak – of the latter. This way of speaking about 'God' is also called the 'way of analogy'. There are so many things to say about this way, that we go by points.

§164. 1. Scholasticism and analogy

a. Sometimes, we can use the same word to refer to two different referents in exactly the same meaning. E.g. I say 'man' referring both to John and Pradeep. When I do so, I am using the term '*univocally*'. Sometimes, however, we can use the same word to refer to two completely different referents, i.e., with a completely

6 This topic is fully discussed in Philosophical Theology.

different meaning. E.g. I say 'pole' referring to a Polish man and to a mast. When I do so, I am using the term '*equivocally*'. But sometimes, we can use terms to refer to two different referents with and without, so to say, the same meaning. E.g. I say 'head' to refer both to the upper part of my body and also to my father as the chief man in authority in the family. So when I say that my father is the 'head' of the family, I am using the word 'analogically'. There is a kind of 'similarity' between my 'head' and my father as the head of the family. Instead of 'similarity' in the usage of the term, one could speak of a kind of 'pointer-function' in the use the term 'head' when it is thus analogically used to refer to my father as the 'head' of the family. The term serves as a pointer, or as sign, of what is really signified by the term. Think of the following examples: "The lion is the king of the jungle", "I have set my heart in my job", "the teacher shepherded the youngsters across the street", "they were the pillars of their society", etc. So analogy, or the analogical use of a term, stands mid-way, so to say, between equivocity (or the equivocal use of a term) and univocity (or the univocal use of a term).

§165. b. There are, however, two ways of understanding analogy. One way is to see the meaning of the term is strictly speaking applicable only to one referent and by some kind of derivation applicable (but not strictly) to another. E.g. 'healthy' applies strictly speaking to, and only to man. But when I say that the medicine is healthy, I am using 'healthy' here in the sense that it causes health. But the medicine in itself is not healthy. Similarly, when I say that the room is healthy (I mean that it is bright and airy and so conducive to man's health). This way of understanding analogy is called analogy of *attribution*. The other way of understanding analogy is this; the term is applicable, strictly speaking, to both referents but only in a proportionate way. To stick to the same example. Suppose I said that "he has got the healthy habit of doing serious reading." Now, here there is no question of health in a physical sense. I am using 'healthy' here in the sense that as medicine is healthy to the physical condition of man, so the habit of serious reading is healthy to the spiritual condition of a man. To put it mathematically (but, of course, crudely) one is to two, as two is to four!) This way of understanding analogy is called the analogy of *proportionality*.

§166. c. Now when Scholastics apply all this to religious language, they all hold in common all words used to refer to 'God' are neither univocally used nor equivocally used – but analogically! They also agree on this further distinction between 'intrinsic' and 'extrinsic' analogy, based on the kind of terms used to refer to 'God'. Suppose I said, "God is good". The word 'good' here is used analogically (whether by 'attribution' or by 'proportionality' does not matter here). But surely I do not mean "God is, as if were, good", or "it is as if God was good". I mean literally, simply, what I say even if analogically. But suppose I said, "God is my rock, the word 'rock' is used analogically also, but surely I do mean that God is, as if it were, my rock, it is as if God was my rock. Here I do not mean it literally, simply. So when a term is used to signify a quality ('perfection') which does not imply materiality, and especially if, besides, it is used to signify a quality which is better than its opposite ('goodness' is better than 'badness'; 'wisdom' is better than 'stupidity', l 'love' is better than 'hate', etc.), this term can be said to apply to 'God' by an '*intrinsic analogy*'. Otherwise the term is said to apply to Him by an '*extrinsic analogy*'. The former is applied in a literal sense, the latter in a 'metaphorical' sense. So Scholastics agree that these no-material perfections (simple perfections) can be applied to 'God' by an 'intrinsic analogy', the others by the 'extrinsic analogy' (or 'metaphorically').

§167. d. But where Scholastics disagree is here. For some (e.g. Cajetan) for an analogy to be intrinsic, it has to be an analogy by proportionality; for others, on the contrary (e.g. Suarez), for an analogy to be intrinsic, it has to be an analogy by attribution! We need not go into all this. Suffice it here to note the difficulty inherent in the very concept of 'analogy' itself! If the 'sameness' of meaning between the two terms (e.g. 'good' as applied to man, and 'good' as applied to 'God') is insisted upon, analogy tends towards univocity; if the 'difference' of the two terms is insisted upon, it tends towards equivocity. Analogy has to stir midway without going to either extreme. (This discussion has its spiritual value: how carefully and reverently have we got to speak about 'God' who is the 'adorable and incomprehensible Mystery!).

§168. 2. Advaita and 'laksana' (20)

a. *Comparison* (upamana, § 46-47). Sankara recognizes the value of the comparisons Sruti makes between the unthinkable and indescribable Brahman and objects taken from our sense-experience (e.g. Brahman is likened to the sun reflected in the water, to the sea with many waves, to space contained in many recipients, to consciousness expressed in many ideas, to the spider shedding and reabsorbing its web, to fire emitting sparks, B.S.B., 3, 2, 18). These comparisons are, of course, to be understood metaphorically, particularly to give some idea that in spite of the apparent multiplicity (prapanca) and conditions (upadhis) of empirical reality – which completely depends on Brahman for its existence – Brahman is yet undifferentiated. Such comparisons have only, according to Sankara, a pedagogical value.

b. The *'Laksana' Theory* (1) More interestingly still, however, Sankara makes ample use of the various meanings of words already prevalent in his days (but which came to be systematized and better explained after him). First of all a distinction is drawn between the literal or principle (mukhya) meaning a word, as found by itself independently of a context, and the implied or indicated (laksya) meaning, as gathered and understood from the context. – There are three types of direct 'implications' (laksana). The first is when the primary meaning is not excluded, nor is it substantially changed but only specified by the context; the second when the primary meaning is so excluded; the third is when the primary meaning is both excluded and included (jahadajahalaksana). Indirect implication is when the implied meaning is, in its turn, already implied in a first implication (e.g. 'you are a lion among men! means you are courageous – 'courageous' is implied in 'lionness' which is implied in 'lion'). This indirect implication is clearly figurative (gauna) or metaphorical.

§169. It has been shown that these three types of direct implication correspond to the univocal, equivocal and analogical uses of the term respectively and how Sankara makes use of the last in his interpretation of the words of Sruti. But the important thing to remember is that for Sankara too this is possible because of the suggestive (as distinct from the denotative) power of words and sentences to direct thought beyond their literal meaning and thus extend their normal referential range. Even in his interpretation of what can be said of Brahman alone (svarupalaksana), e.g., Truth, Consciousness, Bliss, Purity, Freedom, and of the 'chief sayings' of Sruti (mahavakyas), e.g. "I am Brahman", "you are That", Sankara is aware of the sense bound nature of words and sentences and the mere pedagogical value of human language when it comes to speak in a positive way about the Absolute.

§170. 3. Symbolic Language and Analogy

We have seen how both Scholasticism and Advaita, both in their respective way; distinguish analogy from figurative, or metaphorical, language. Still there is a close similarity of function between the two, namely, their power to point to beyond the literal meaning of the word and to indicate (even if not to express) what otherwise would remain impossible to be said at all. This means that if this true, thought and language are not commensurate, i.e., the former exceeds the other. And this is particularly true as man progressively becomes more and more aware of the 'total' meaning of Reality. In any case, as far as religious language is concerned, figurative or metaphorical ('extrinsic analogy') – or *symbolical language* – is today, more than ever before, appreciated for its powerful evocative power. St. Thomas himself, and in this he follows again 'Dionysius', not only recognizes the necessity and usefulness of the use of symbolical language in speaking about God, but the clearer the metaphor is a metaphor, the less likely it is that it be taken literally and hence the more fitting it is to be used in religious language (S. Th. I, 1, 9). Today we would have no hesitancy in saying that ultimately all religious language is 'symbolical' (in the wide meaning of the term as distinguished from 'literal'). And a proper understanding of 'analogy' is at the basis of all symbolical language.

171. a. Signs and Symbols

A symbol is distinguished from a sign in that while the latter is simply a pointer to a reality, chosen conventionally, in a one-to one relationship, the former is a representation of a reality (i.e. it makes it somehow 'present'), somehow partakes of its nature, in one-to-many relationship with a great intellectual, evaluative and emotional power. Consider the difference between a sign of the cross (on the street simply to point to a Christian Church) and the symbol of the Cross (on the altar to 'represent' Jesus Christ)! When the president of a country is on an official visit somewhere, he does not merely points to his country, he is somehow his country, he is therefore a symbol of his country. Symbols, unlike signs, are not arbitrarily or conventionally chosen. The sun, water, darkness, fire, water, the sea, the mountain, the serpent, are 'natural' symbols. (C. Jung has been able to speak of man's 'collective unconscious' made up of these natural symbols, or 'archetypes', common to all men). Notice the power inherent in the symbols to evoke insight, emotion, evaluation about life symbolized 'water' (its creative and reproductive power, its dreadful and destructive power, its soothing and healing power, its refreshing and cleansing power, etc). – When we say that religious language is symbolic, this does not mean that we choose to express ourselves in symbols. It means that first, we cannot do otherwise, but secondly, that given the nature of symbols, religious language becomes appropriate by using them to 'intuit' the Reality symbolized – the 'referent' of religious discourse. No question here then of description of this Reality but of evocation! One can only properly describe what belongs to the realm of sense-experience and empirical reality.

172. A few other remarks about the 'symbol'. We have distinguished between a sign and a symbol. But notice a sign, by usage or other circumstances, may assume gradually that intellectual, emotive and evaluative power which is proper to the symbol. And thus it may become a symbol, while retaining its nature of a sign too. For example, an ideogram like a three-sided figure used as a sign for a triangle became for Christians the symbol of the Trinity, the circle the symbol of eternity. – Vice-versa, by usage and other circumstances, a symbol may lose its original power and becomes a mere sign. It is the case too that though symbols are 'natural' some are more evocative to some people and less to others according to differences of culture. Surely the elephant used as a symbol for Ganesh has much more symbolic power to worshipers of Ganesh than to others! – Referential words (the syncategorematic) as such are signs of their referent (and so are logical, mathematical, musical notations); it is only when the referent is used as a symbol that the word becomes a conceptual symbol. But the symbol as such is not so much the word but its referent. Suppose I said, 'the other shore', this phrase just means what it says. It is only when I use 'the other shore' as a symbol for 'heave' (or as the Buddhist do for 'nirvana') that 'shore' becomes for the user a symbol. – The ancient Indian grammarians (the Alankarikas) developed a whole theory about this insightful and emotive power of the symbol – a power which they called 'dhvani'.

§173. b. Similes and Metaphors

A simile is an overt comparison. We have already referred to it when we spoke of 'extrinsic analogy'. The assidion of words such as 'like', 'can be likened', 'as it were' (e.g. "the kingdom of Heaven is like...) makes it clear that the two terms of comparison are being simply compared. A metaphor, on the other hand is a hidden comparison. The absence of the additional words just mentioned conceals, veils, the comparison as a comparison and makes it look like a statement of identity. Notice the difference: "God is king of the earth" (metaphor); "God is like a King of the earth" (simile). But notice how more powerful the metaphor is than the simile. In poetic usage, in fact, similes would blunt the insight and the emotion which the words intend to convey. Hence the preference for the metaphor is poetry. Again, compare and contrast the following two verses: "the ploughman homeward plods his weary way and leaves the world to darkness and to me"; "the ploughman returns home tired in the evening and leaves alone in the dark". Do the sentences 'mean' the same? – The constant use of metaphors (rather than that of similes) in religious language can lead, however, as very often in fact it does, to gross misunderstandings. When a metaphor, especially when extended into an 'allegory' (as we are going to see) is mistaken for its literal meaning, then the metaphor, and religious language, is 'reified' and taken to refer to a historical, physical, chemical, biological, etc., fact of sense-experience. Many disputes arose in Christianity with regard to the 'historicity' of the Resurrection, the 'physical' nature of the transubstantiated Eucharistic bread and wine, the biological status of the resurrected body, etc. In Hinduism, the truth of 'karman' and 'sansara' has been taken to be subject to proof by experience and arguments as if they were physical laws of causality! The thing is that the metaphor, like the symbol, of whose nature it partakes, both reveal and conceal the referent! That is why, St. Thomas (§170) says that the clearer it is that the metaphor is a metaphor – the more outrageous and odd it is – the less likely it would be that it be taken for its literal meaning. Needless to say that science too makes great use of metaphors to indicate what otherwise would be difficult, if impossible, to express. (E.g. 'wave-lengths', atomic 'nucleus', the retina as a 'photographic lens').

§174. c. Parables and Allegories

A simile extended into a narrative is a parable, a metaphor similarly extended into a narrative is an allegory (some authors, like Fawcett, invert the order). Recall the parables of Jesus: "The Kingdom of Heaven is like ... a sower who went to sow good seed in his field, etc. Very often parables have more religious praxis in a mind than speculation (e.g. conversion, realization of what or who one is, moral virtues) and in such cases, it would be beside the point to try and find a symbolic meaning in every detail. On the contrary, in the allegory, each detail may have a symbolic meaning (a good example of this is the Jain allegory of the 'Man in the well'). – In the religious literature of the world we often come across narratives of supposedly historical events whose true meaning would seem to be more of parables (or allegories) in action. In such cases, we can speak of parables-in-action, or of actions with a symbolic meaning, or simply of symbolical actions. (A good example in the New Testament seems to be Jesus' putting the fig-tree under a curse). It is clear that very often it is difficult to say whether the narrative refers to a historical event at all (i.e. whether it is narrated merely as a parable- allegory or as a historical event with symbolical meaning). In any case, if the narrative is to be counted as religious language, the religious meaning of the narrative should always be borne in mind. – Finally, we cannot insist enough on the importance of distinguishing between the literal and the allegorical meaning of religious language.

§175. d. Diagrams and Models

The distinction between these two is not so sharp – what is sharp, however is the distinction between their literal and symbolic function which is not always very clear to everybody! By 'diagram' we understand a graphic (pictorial, visual) representation, in spatial dimensions, of a non-spatial reality. Unlike a picture or image (of a saint, for example, which is a sign) it tries to represent relations – of man to the environing world, of the phenomenal to the transcendental, i.e., it is a 'picture of the world' (*Welt-bild*). Think, for example, of the nature, symbolic nature and religious and spiritual function of the 'mandala'. – If I represent time (which is not spatial) in spatial dimensions (as linear, for example, with a beginning, present and end, or as circular without beginning and end, or as spiral which is a combination of the linear and the circular), I am using a diagram, as it were. If I represent man's consciousness (which, again, is not spatial) as a composite of higher, middle and lower strata (e.g. Freud's super-ego, ego, and id), or if I represent man's experience of himself as a two or three layer entity (body and soul, or body, soul and spirit), etc., again I am using a diagram. Recall that when we ourselves spoke of 'two' levels of Reality and of experience, we said explicitly that 'two' should be understood in a 'diagrammatical' sense (§ 163). – A 'model' is a conceptual diagram. It is not visual but imaginative. It is used not only to represent in spatial dimensions what is non-spatial, but also to represent in temporal dimensions what is non-temporal. Hence, in our understanding of the term, a model is more comprehensive and more far reaching. Its symbolic meaning and function is correspondingly more powerful. Thus for example, mystics speak of man's spiritual progress as succeeding 'stages' on some kind of 'ascent', or of different 'mansions' of a palace. We ourselves use models to try and understand the phenomenon of religious pluralism (in our *Philosophy of Religion*) – its origin from a single point and lines flowing down from it, each line representing a different originary religious experience, etc. When Hegel represented the course of history as a dialectical theses, antitheses and synthesis, he used a model. Notice that many religious words are by themselves understandable in a model, e.g. descent, ascent, pilgrim Church, stages of consciousness, origin and end of the world, alpha and omega, ying-yang, purusa-prakrti, etc. The importance of all this is again to bring out in bold relief the symbolical nature of religious language!

§176. e. Stories and Myths

The story belongs to the category of the simile and the parable; the myth belongs to the category of the metaphor and the allegory. But in our understanding of the term, myth has an added particular meaning. – A story is a piece of narrative, a tale. Parables are not always told as a story (e.g. "which of you who has got a hundred sheep and loses one, etc."). Very often a story is clearly discernible as a mere story to entertain, even sometimes with a moral, etc. (A legend is a story popularly regarded as a historical). As is clear, the story has its place in religious language for pedagogical purposes.

It is only relatively recently that the nature and function of myth in religious consciousness and literature have been re-discovered (thanks to such historians of religions as Mircea Eliade among many others). We have to distinguish carefully between the popular (and even the dictionary) meaning of the term, i.e., a legend, purely fictitious narrative, a tale born out of a fanciful imagination, and the technical term in usage today in academic circles. In our understanding of the term, a myth is a story which tries to express religious truth in a way which appeals to the feeling and imagination rather than to reason and logic. Here again, like in the metaphor and the allegory, we have to discern, as much as possible, 'what is signified' from 'the way it is being signified'!

§177. Of course this is not always very easy. Many cultures have their myths, but ancient myths, embedded as they were in their time and place, may be too difficult to 'decipher' today. But the renewed interest in the study of ancient religions (and of the origins of the present ones) can help. The rest is left to the scholar's religious perceptivity. But it is becoming more and more now that the myth tries to view, picture, reality as holistic' (everything related to the rest), personalistic (god and goddesses as 'personifications' of the elements of nature itself) and ultimately meaningful (its significance to man), thus its 'numinous' character (its awe-inspiring and yet dreadful nature) is brought out. Particular myth could be better understood against the general belief-system ('mythos') of a people. This 'mythos' is as such pre-reflective, unformulated awareness, but it is it which makes the particular myths intelligible and credible. Still, since the myth, as we have said appeals to feeling and imagination rather than to reason and logic, it would be beside the point to look for any 'proof' for what the myth says. Much more would it be beside the point to look for any 'logical' connection between the myths even of one culture. (Sometimes, a god appears as the 'Father of all the gods', sometimes he appears as originating from still a higher god. Sometimes, he appears as a benevolent god, at other times as malevolent. (Would it be to the point to see an illogicality if a Hollywood actor assumes one character in one film and a completely different one in another film? Again, it would be beside the point to judge the 'morality' of the characters figuring in the myth. The myth is not a 'morality play'!).

§178. One noteworthy about the myths is that they cannot be traced to any historical origin or author. (Recall the 'authorlessness'of the Vedas according to the Mimamsikas!) The 'collective unconscious' unearthed by Jung (§ 171) may throw some light in this respect as also on the fact that so many elements are common, or similar, in so many myths of many different cultures. They mirror, as it were, man's common experience and 'interpretation' of reality, man's universal religious experience. Some like to think that the myth originates from the ritual, others that the ritual originates from the myth. We ourselves are inclined to think that given the fact that religion is both 'theoria' and 'praxis'(understanding and interpretation of reality existentially expressed in certain actions and everyday life), the myth and the ritual have been and still are mutually influenced. Myth may have been spontaneously arisen, handed down from one generation to another. They may have gone through changes in as much as man's experience of reality changes. And whether they persist today –or, more importantly, whether some are spontaneously being replaced by others, for we ourselves have today our own myths without realizing it, they are not to be understood as 'pre-scientific thinking'(although ancient myths are scientific!). But in terms of the symbol about which we have been talking all along.

§179. We have said that in our own understanding of the term, myth has an added particular meaning. By 'myth' – in a wider or looser sense – we mean expression of religious truth believed in literally (i.e. in accordance with the literal meaning of the words in which it is expressed). It is, in another words, the mistaking of the symbol for the symbolized, the expression for the Reality expressed, the way of signification for the signified, the metaphor for the simile, the analogy for the univocal! In such a case one is not aware – and most people are not – of the fact that a myth <u>is</u> a myth. Once one becomes aware that the myth is a myth, i.e., when one de-mythologizes it (or as we prefer to say mythologizes it), one passes from a 'mythic' to a 'mytho-logical' stage of religious awareness (We shall return to this topic later).

What does this mean? It simply means that by his intuition, perceptivity, (logos), one begins to see through, as it were, the myth. One understands it for what it is and also, up to a certain extent, its meaning. This meaning, of course, can perhaps never be exhausted. As we have said, the symbol does not stand to one-to-man relation to reality (i.e. having only one meaning). The symbol is polyvalent, standing in a one-to-many relation to reality. And so is the myth which is essentially symbolical. And it is for this reason that we prefer to speak of 'mytho-logization' rather than of 'de-mythogoziation'. For one thing, as we are saying, the meaning of the myth can never be exhausted, secondly, and more importantly, one never knows whether, and to what extent, one is fully aware that one is not believing literally in what should be believed only symbolically. Can one, in other words, fully demythologize oneself?

§ 180. This process of 'mytho-logization', let it be said in passing takes place not only on the level of 'belief' (§§ 2, 128) but also on the level of 'practice', comprising both those certain actions to be performed at certain times, in certain places, and also one's everyday life. We treat of all this in our Philosophy of Religion and it would take us too much off our way to go into detail here. Suffice it to say here that the understanding of 'cult' and general religious praxis can go through the same mytho-logization process as religious belief in general and dependently on it. In fact, it is impossible that one would have seen through the sign the signified (progressively, gradually) without this having its repercussions on his affective response ('cult') and his general everyday practice (volitional response).

§181. The most important thing to retain from our remarks on the myth is precisely that it belongs to the category of the symbol – and that consequently it has to be understood accordingly. This is definitely not to say that one has necessarily to revive dead myths or even that one has to continue clinging to one's own once he has mytho-logized oneself. But it does mean that, first, one could find it profitable if one were to try and see through ancient and present myths. One's religious perceptivity could thus be sharpened, Secondly, it means that a better understanding of the nature and function of the myth could make one more attuned to religious beliefs different from one's own – and thus one could become more open to religious truth in the many ways it is expressed, and consequently less closed in in one's own 'mythos'. Thirdly, and perhaps more importantly, such an understanding could purify one's religious belief more and more by both becoming more and more receptive of religious truth, more in empathy with religious beliefs other than his own, and more and more aware of the symbolic nature of his and any other religious language.

§182. 4. Analogy and Some Modern Difficulties

Modern objections against the usefulness of having recourse to analogy to account for the possibility of talking about 'God' stem from two different sources and are concerned with two different questions. The two sources are: some analytical philosophers and, to the opposite extreme, some Christian Protestant Theologians (e.g. Barth, Baillie). The two questions are: the usefulness of analogy to 'prove' the existence of 'God' and the usefulness of analogy to speak about 'God' at all. Needless to say that the reasons emanating from the two sources are of a completely different kind. We have spoken enough of the general position of the former (§§ esp.145 ff.) A word about the latter. According to these, 'God' is so beyond human thought and speaking that He can neither be known, much less spoken of, except by means of 'Revelation' and through the words used in Scripture. It is clear that by 'Revelation' they mean the Christian Revelation, and by 'Scripture' they mean the Christian Scriptures. Of course, to discuss this issue goes much beyond the scope of this Course. But suffice it here to say that such an exclusivistic position can be seriously debated both on theological and philosophical grounds. (We discuss this topic in our *Theology of Religions* and in fact it is increasingly abandoned by many Christian Theologians today).

§183. But what concerns us here more immediately is the epistemological and semantic difficulties against analogy. We need not go into the different kinds of arguments brought forward to discredit, as it were, the use of analogy in religious discourse. For, in fact, they boil down to two or three main ones. And if we keep in mind the following summary of what we have said about analogy, these difficulties will not seem to be so decisive:

1.Analogy is used not so much to 'prove' the existence of 'God' but to account for the possibility of talking about what is not directly an object of sense-perception and of our empirical experience.

2. Analogy makes sense only if the existence of 'God' is already, therefore, somehow posited – by whatever means (e.g. argument, insight, Scripture). It would make even more sense if 'God' is understood as the 'ultimate Cause' (or 'ultimate intelligibility') of all Reality.

§184. No matter how useful, analogy never pretends to describe 'God' as He is in Himself, as it were, but only to have the power of evoking insight thus widening the referential range of normally sense- bound images, words and concepts. God remains, therefore, the ultimate 'unknowable' Mystery. The way of 'remotion' can never be divorced from the way "of 'analogy'. This will become even clearer presently.

4. Particularly with regard to the analogy of proportionality, the proportion in question should not be taken mathematically but as a pointer. Even then, it would be incorrect to say that it implies two unknowns (e.g. goodness is to man as 'goodness'(?) is to 'God'(?). 'God' remains, as we have just said as 'unknowable Mystery' in Himself but not totally unknowable in His effects if what we have said about Cause as Ultimate Intelligibility' is properly understood.

§185. 5. Analogy is at the basis of symbolical language. If its cognitive function is denied, symbolical language has to be denied its cognitive function too. What would remain would be purely its emotive function. But surely this does not mean that 'cognitive' should necessarily mean the same in all fields of knowledge. Given the nature of the case, in religious language 'cognitive' has its own particular field of application. This will become clearer when we discuss 'religious truth and certitude.

6. Far from being the last word on the subject, the theory of analogy shows, if anything, that human language is inadequate to speak about the own 'ultimate referent' of religion. The intrinsic difficulties inherent in its very concept – which we have discussed – show this even more plainly.

3. THE WAY OF TRANSCENDANCE

§186. Also called the 'way of eminence'. St Thomas mentions it frequently but as far as we know never treats it as fully as he does the 'way of causality' or analogy. To understand this 'way', it is necessary to keep in mind what we have said about the negative (apophatic) and the positive way (kataphatic) and about their essential complementarity. Now this way of transcendence tries to express both at one go, as it were.

This is done in several manners, (a) by the use of superlatives like 'super' ('God' is super-being, super-consciousness) or 'most', 'highest', 'supreme', 'absolute', 'ultimate', 'transcendent', etc. Notice what is toting done. By saying, for example, that 'God' is 'First Cause', on one hand I am saying positively that He is 'Cause' but on the other hand, I am denying that He is 'Cause' in the same sense that anything else can be called 'Cause'. Again, suppose I said 'infinite being'. By saying 'Being' I am affirming that 'God' is Being but at the same time I am denying that he is 'being' in the same sense that anything else can be called 'being'. I am saying that 'God', yes, He is Being but without the essential limitations which I experience in myself as being and in every-thing else which I can call being. Still, this does not mean that I am stretching to infinity, as it were, the quality 'being' to 'God'. I am rather saying that 'God' is the 'Cause' (the 'ultimate intelligibility') of all beings, its 'Source'. I am saying, therefore, that by 'God' I do not mean a being among other beings, not even the most eminent of them all, the first in rank in a series of beings. But that He is being in a sense, and "He is more than being in another sense! This applies to everything else I can say of 'God'. (When we spoke of the 'ultimate referent' of religious language as: Absolute Reality, Ultimate Value and Supreme Good (§ 152), we used this way of speaking!). This is the 'way of transcendence' because it unites and goes *beyond* both the affirmative and the negative-way.

§187. But (b) another manner to express this would simply be to unite an affirmative and a negative proposition, e.g., "'God' is kind and 'God' is not kind." Or simply "God is and is not kind." This can be understood in the same sense as above. Of course, this applies even to the 'simple perfections' of which we spoke already – even though, to most ears, it may sound more jarring: e.g. "'God' exists and does not exist!" "God is good and He is not good." But if understood properly, this should not afford difficulty. Notice that the terms 'exists' and 'good' are not used in exactly the same sense (univocally) in the affirmative and in the negative propositions. Even though they are not used in a totally different sense (equivocally), they are used 'analogically'. This explains on the one hand how the famous Buddhist madhyamika dialectics of which we have spoken so much (§§ 117, 136) does not really contradict the Principle of Non-contradiction, but, on the other hand, that the principles of Logic cannot be used in religious language as they are in other kinds of language. If analogy is denied or if it is not properly understood, one has to say either that religious language is logically contradictory and hence meaningless, or that religious language has a logic which is completely its own. Neither of these two positions is according to us satisfactory.

§188. A third (c) manner of expressing 'transcendence' would be to use *paradox*. Actually in a sense such expressionsas 'infinite Being', etc., are already paradoxical, and so are – and much more clearly- the simultaneous affirmations and negations. Only when explained, can they be seen that they are not really so. A paradox is, in fact, a real or apparent contradiction. But the paradox can be expressed in different ways such as in phrases like 'luminous darkness', 'dark light', 'full emptiness', 'an empty fullness', 'fertile wilderness', 'immanently transcend', 'transcendentally immanent' 'greatest than the greatest and smaller than he smallest". Such seemingly paradoxes fill the pages of all religious, especially mystical, literature. They are seemingly paradoxes because, it is clear, they are symbolical and not logical phrases or propositions. But their semantic value is immense in that by uniting positive and negative language, they drive thought beyond discursivity, by a "united power of intuition and reason" (St. Thomas), to apperceive what can be only conceived and spoken of ... in silence!

Chapter 3

RELIGIOUS TRUTH AND RELIGIOUS CERTITUDE

§189. In Section One it should have become clear that Epistemology, especially in the way we have gone about presenting the various issues is one whole problematic (i.e. a series of closely related problems). We started by defining knowledge as 'an awareness' that such and such is, or is not, the case (§§12-13). This led us to see that 'to know' implies that knowledge, to be really called 'knowledge', must be necessarily true and reasonable (§§ 15-19). This led us, in its turn, on the means of knowledge (§§ 25-63) and especially on the concept of 'truth' (§§ 76-100). Which led us, in its turn, to the concept of 'certitude' (§§ 109-130).

In Section Two we started applying all this to religious knowledge. We began by asking, first of all, whether religious knowledge can be really called knowledge. To answer this question we had to see whether the general definition of knowledge as given in the first Section applies to religious knowledge. And for this we had to see whether there was anything at all (the 'case') which religious knowledge could be said to say that it is or that is not. In other words we had to see what the 'referent' of religious knowledge is (§§ esp. 150-152). This led us to see how this referent is indicated in religious language and therefore to reflect on the nature and function of religious language (§§ 153-185). As in the first Section, the problem of knowledge has now led us to raise the question of the truth and certitude – here of religious knowledge.

1. RELIGIOUS TRUTH

§190. In the first Section, we defined truth as 'the correspondence between what is affirmed or denied to what really is the case' (§ 75 ff). Though this agrees with the 'correspondence theory of truth' we have enriched this definition with precious insights from other competing theories (§§ 80-101). We remarked that though religious language has other important functions or 'illocutions', unless and until it can be shown that religious language has *also* an informative or 'constative' illocution, religious knowledge as expressed in such a religious language cannot be said to be 'true' and hence really knowledge. We have taken pains to show that religious language is essentially and necessarily 'analogical' or 'symbolical' (§§ 163-185) in its assertions. But if one were to take refuge in its symbolical character to avoid the question regarding its cognitive dimension, one would be simply avoiding the question regarding religious truth. So we shall try to face this question squarely. Recall that not even Logical Positivists would deny that religious language may have an 'emotive' function; the question is to see whether religious language does anything more than express the speaker's emotions, attitudes, choices, preferences, way of looking at things, etc.

§191. If 'knowledge' is intimately related to 'truth', 'truth' *and* certitude, as we have seen (§ 77) are intimately related to 'evidence'. I know that what I am affirming is true because I am certain of the evidence. The kind of evidence required and sufficient in any particular case determines the kind of certitude I can have and expect to have on that particular matter (§§ 109 ff.) Keeping all this in mind we can now proceed to sort things out in this admittedly complicated question regarding religious truth in the following manner.

1. The question of interpretation. This is a hermeneutical question. (Hermeneutics is the science of interpretation especially of Scripture. In a broad sense, it can mean any kind of interpretation, e.g. of facts, of one's experience, etc.). What we mean here is simply to try and determine whether the religious statement whose 'truth' is in question is (a) 'religious' in a 'loose' or 'strict' sense, that is to what type of religious language it belongs (§ 151); (b) if 'religious' in the strict sense of the term, to try and determine its 'universe of discourse'. We have seen that a religious statement (like, for that matter, many other kinds of statements) cannot be understood in isolation. It is its 'coherence' in its linguistic field gives its the meaning it has (§§ 94-95, 151); (c) to try and determine whether I can discover, as it were, the way in which the 'ultimate referent' of this universe of discourse has been expressed in its 'primary' beliefs (§ 151). But as if this were not already enough, one would have to go a step further – and herein lies the whole difficulty, apart from the added fact regarding their 'symbolic' nature.

§192. **2. Original Belief and Originary Experience.** Primary or original beliefs, actually, are not hard to discover. If you are a Christian and I asked you to 'put in a nutshell' your Christian belief, you would not find it too hard to answer me. Anybody, well familiar with his religious tradition would be able to do the same. Now suppose 1 asked again whether you could discover in the Scriptures statements which would bring out what you said more forcibly, more succinctly, if you are reasonably versed in your Scriptures, you would not find it too difficult to do so either. Now, by 'original' or 'primary' belief, we mean this body of tenets of belief which would seem to be the source of the other 'derived' or 'secondary' beliefs. – Now by a phenomenological analysis of human consciousness and a historical study of the religions of the world, one could make a reasonable hypothesis (a hypothesis at least !) that the world religions originated, yes, indirectly from man's general experience of reality, but more directly, from particular experiences of the persons to whose teachings these religions can be respectively traced.[7] These experiences giving rise to the 'original belief' we are calling 'originary experiences'. So a particular religious statement (or a tenet of belief) has to be understood in its universe of discourse whose ultimate referent has been more directly expressed in its original belief – which is, in its turn, the expression of' an originary experience! Can one 'recapture' this originary experience as easily as one can 'discover' the original belief? How can one unless one makes the same experience for oneself? And if cannot or until one does it, how can one really, understand – to start with – and to raise the question of its 'truth'? That is the whole question!

§193. **3. Belief and Faith.** Our hypothesis, just referred to, also says that these originary experiences are different experiences. (It would take us too long to try and show here the appropriateness of our hypothesis in this respect. And even then that would not be directly relevant to the question at issue here). Different experiences of the 'ultimate referent' of religious language (§ 152). That the original beliefs of the religions of the world are different is a phenomenological fact; that these express different originary experiences, and that they are different precisely because they express different originary experiences, is our hypothesis. Now in this respect we have therefore to distinguish between 'belief' and 'faith'. Notice however that these terms are fluid. So we are giving them our own meaning.

§194. We have already given one meaning to 'belief' in the very beginning of our Course, namely knowledge based on witness (§ 42). But as we went along we used the term in other meanings made clear by the context. In fact, the term has other meanings, e.g. the act of trusting the reliability of the witness, the usefulness of something ('I believe in a good night's sleep as a remedy for all ills"), the competence of somebody ("I believe in my doctor"), etc. But as far as we are concerned here, the two more important meanings are: the actual knowledge believed on truth – of the witness, of Scripture, etc., ("l believe that") and the act of trust itself ("I believe in"). Now *'faith'* is often used with the same meaning of belief- indeed since in English it cannot be used as a verb, its verb form is to believe' (or 'to have faith'). But even in contemporary Christian Theology, belief is distinguished from faith. Faith, as so distinguished from beliefs, is taken to stand for that openness of heart and mind to what is true, good and beautiful. There is a logical (but not chronological) priority of faith to belief. As such faith is just an attitude of soul, a readiness to listen and learn, it is a loving devotion to what is true, it is 'sraddha'.

Now what we more particularly mean by faith is this attitude of soul which is both an imperative (man cannot refuse to be open to the truth whatever this is!) and at

7 We treat this topic at some length in our *Phenomenology and Philosophy of Religion.*

the same time an invitation (he can in fact refuse to respond to its appeal) present very early in life in a pre-reflective stage and liable to grow in intensity and depth. If responded to, it can be a life-process (cf. such expressions as 'the life of faith'). These stages of this faith-process we can describe as follows:

§195. **4. The Mythic, Mytho-Logical and Mystical.** We have already spoken of the mythic and the mythological stages of religious awareness (§ 179). (And in fact faith, in our understanding of the term, can be identified with this religious awareness – except that 'awareness' already implies a certain explicitness whereas faith is at first always present in a pre-reflective stage). But here we have to add the mystical stage. And by this we mean basing ourselves on our study of the subject (in our Mysticism) 'a direct' (as distinct from 'based on other people's witness'), *progressively immediate* (as distinct from knowledge mediated through sense-perception, the imagination, the concept, inference and other pramanas, but 'progressively' for this stage admits of degrees of intensity and depth too), *intuitive* (as distinct from discursive, §§ 65 ff), *life-transforming* (spiritually, morally) *consciousness of the 'ultimate referent'* of religious language. – Needless to say that these stages are said to be 'three' in a diagrammatical sense (§ 175), but we think the diagramme pictures well the growth in religious awareness attested to by many religious philosophers and mystics – a growth which is after all a fact experienced by many. One could say, simplifying a lot though, that the first stage corresponds to uncritical belief, the second to personal conviction (and therefore a certain kind of certitude, at least moral certitude in the 'third' and 'fourth' senses spoken of in §§ 123-124), and the third to personal experience, the immediate perception of the Truth' (St Thomas), the paramarthika perception spoken of in Jainism, Buddhism and Hinduism generally (see also § 30)! An 'originary (religious) experience is this stage of religious awareness but giving origin, in its turn, to a whole religious tradition. We have spoken, in another context, of the 'continuum' of religious awareness.

§196. **5. The Evidence of Religious Truth.** We have to retrace our steps a bit here. We have indicated the difficulty of this topic in § 192. But in the light of what we have just said in the meantime, we have to approach the topic on different levels. Throughout the history of religion, the topic was expressed in such questions as: can man come to know God by reason, can he prove his existence by argument (i.e. independently of the witness of Scripture)? 'God' or 'Brahman' or the 'ultimate referent' of religious language, no matter the way in which it has been expressed.

So the difficulty is not the reasonableness of belief as trust. It can easily be seen that sufficiently good reasons makes my religious belief, understood as trust, reasonable and I can be morally certain of its truth-like, for that matter, any other belief in different fields of knowledge (§§ 110 ff.) Nor is the difficulty in the evidence of religious statements loosely so-called – the evidence is of the same nature as other non-religious statements (§ 151). Nor, again is the difficulty in the understanding of particular religious statements, strictly so-called, these have to be understood in their universe of discourse as we have just repeated once again. The difficulty lies in what regards the evidence for the primary religious statements directly touching on the 'ultimate referent' itself! And the difficulty varies precisely, in accordance with the way this 'ultimate referent' is conceived and spoken of in the respective religious traditions. It is one thing to ask: does 'God' really exist (what is the evidence for asserting that He does independently of blind trust? Can one prove by reason and argument that He does?). It is another thing to ask: what is the evidence for asserting that 'nirvana' is really man's self-realization – again independently of blind trust?), etc. On the 'mystical' level, it is obvious that there can be no question of blind trust. It is direct perception, as said, and thus on this level, religious truth is its own evidence – or so, it is claimed by mystics. So, the difficulty is in the possibility of providing rational evidence in what regards the religious 'ultimate referent' by or to those who make no claim to have had any 'mystical' experience.

§197. The epistemological, indeed the religious, importance of such a question cannot be minimized. In fact, if one says that only evidence which is possible for asserting the truth of 'the ultimate referent' (e.g. that God exists, that 'Brahman' is) is scriptural witness, great difficulty can arise both on philosophical and theological grounds. (Isn't 'revelation', Sruti, already the result of man's own experience of reality and not simply 'God's word' spoken to man? What could a revelation without a revealer possibly mean-as in Mimamsa? If 'Revelation' is the result of man's experience, is not the written word as 'historically conditioned' as any other human writing? If so, what would be the evidence for a man living in the 20th century believe in what the human author of scripture, the 'seer', claims to be the truth?, etc.). Christianity always rejected 'fideism' (the doctrine which says that man has to believe just because he has to believe without any human motives of credibility and credentity) as incompatible with its basic attitude. – If, on the hand, one says that there is ample evidence based on reason and argument, for asserting the truth of the 'ultimate referent', no smaller difficulties can arise, again both on philosophical and theological grounds. (If this so, how is that many people, including great minds, or unbelievers? Is it that they are blind or insincere in their unbelief? Can 'God' who is essentially the 'wholly other', the all comprehensive Mystery be an 'object' of proof or disproof by logical argumentation? Besides, even if such evidences are possible, where would 'faith', understood as complete trust in the 'self-revealing God' come in? etc. – We cannot, of course, go into so many details here (This will be done, to a great extent, in philosophical Theology). But what we have to do is to take the famous question regarding the possibility of 'proving' the existence of 'God' as a *paradigm* of such questions regarding the possibility of rational evidence for asserting the truth of the 'ultimate referent' of religious language, thus underling some of its semantic and epistemological implications.

§198. 6. 'Proving' the Existence of 'God'

Naturally two clear-cut position can be taken: an unequivocal denial that the existence of 'God' can be rationally proved, and an unequivocal affirmation that it can be.

In this context, we shall have to leave out of consideration that denial which is based not on epistemological but other reasons (The question of 'atheism' will be adequately dealt with philosophical Theology). The denial which concerns us more directly is that based on an empirical or subjectivistic stance in the whole philosophical question regarding human knowledge. We have touched on these stances in several contexts of our first section. The affirmation, on the other hand, is based on rationalistic or an idealistic stance. We have touched on these stances also in several contexts of our first section. We need only refer to them (see Index for an easy way to look the relevant paragraph).

§199. Within the framework of two Extremes, we would like to place both scholasticism (esp. St Thomas) and Advaita (esp. Sankara) and then make more reflections.

Recall what we have said about the 'apophaticism' of St Thomas (§158). God for St. Thomas always remain, in himself, the supreme 'Unknown'. That is why the 'principal way' to speak about Himat all is the 'negative way'. But it is because St. Thomas sees God as the 'ultimate cause' of all that is, that he maintains that man can also speak of God in a positive way – which however is 'analogical'. And what is signified always remain beyond the meaning of the word which tries to signify anything conceived and spoken of God. Now it is the same reason which convinces St Thomas that man can argue for the existence of God. It is interesting to see how St Thomas does not call the arguments he puts forward 'proofs' but 'ways of approach' (viae) – although in the question he arises he does use the term 'proof' ("whether it can be proved that God exist" S. Th. I, 2, 3). At any rate, St Thomas is convinced, as we already said in another context, that the world of things and of men, in its mutability, very existence, contingency, imperfection, cannot be its own explanation. It can only be 'ultimately intelligible' by positing "what we mean by God". Now notice that this world has to be intelligible, St Thomas never tries to prove. This is, we think, because it is for St. Thomas, a principle of reason intuitively grasped – an insight in the sense already explained (SS65 ff). This means that reason in the sense of discursivity alone, divorced from insight, would not be enough to 'prove' the existence of God. Notice, secondly, that the idea of 'God' is already pre-supposed. St Thomas does not believe man has an 'innate idea' of God. St Thomas does maintain that there is "a certain kind of common and vague knowledge of God, which is, as it were (quasi), present in all men". Without excluding the possibility that God could be known by some kind of 'internal evidence', he holds it more likely that this common and vague knowledge is the very possibility of easily arriving at positing a transcendent Cause (C. G. III, 38).

§200. Further still, St Thomas sees different habits or powers (virtues) which can perfect this mind. We have already mentioned and explained in some detail the distinction between 'reason' and 'intellect' according to St. Thomas. But in this context, 'intellect' adding two St Thomas (SS 67-69). But in this context 'intellect' is often translated as understanding-i.e., the power, the habit perfecting the 'intellect' to see into the 'first principles'. Again, 'scientia' we could translate as 'scientific knowledge'.- i.e., the power to reason things out, the 'reason' as distinguished from 'intellect'. This brings us to the point which is more relevant here. Apart from 'understanding' and 'scientific knowledge', St. Thomas sees wisdom (*Sapientia*) as the power or habit of the mind to see into, consider, contemplate the "highest and deepest cause (*causam altissimam*) in the light of which it can pass a most certain judgement on all other causes and order every knowledge (S. Th. II IIae, 45; I II ae, 57, 2).

§201. Again, St. Thomas links contemplation-which he calls 'true and certain intuition of the soul' (after St Bernard) – with the 'intellect' as meditation he links with reason (Sent. 34, 1, 2, 2). Contemplation is a kind of 'vision' by which man is 'more than a man' (ibid, ad, 1). And moreover though contemplation requires meditation (the discursivity of reason) as a means, at a certain point this discursivity becomes an impediment from which the 'intellect' in which contemplation essentially consists has to get rid of two deformities, namely the consideration of the multiplicity of sense-perceptible objects and the discursivity of reason itself (S. Th. II IIae,180, 6 ad 2)!

§202. Finally - and this will be our final remark –for St Thomas contemplation, as here understood, is no mere academic quest. It needs that one's whole be geared to contemplation and predisposed by the love of God and neighbour and the other virtues for the passions hinder the purity of reason and concupiscence darken its light (cf. S. Th. II IIae, 180, 3).

§203. As for Sankara recall what we have already said about him already (esp. with regard to the apovada and his theory of laksana, § 161-162, 168-169). Now it is true that according to Sankara, 'Brahman' can neither be known nor be proved by any other pramana, the sabda (Sruti). But this is because he is convinced that Sruti is the record of experience and of high spiritual intuition (samyagjnana) by means of which alone can Brahman be known. As a matter all men can, and should, attain to this high spiritual intuitive knowledge in which moksa precisely consists. Discursive knowledge has still its role to play in the meantime. As a matter of fact, Sankara describes the process of the study of Vedanta as consisting of three steps: listening to the instructions of the Vedas as explained to him by the guru who has himself realized Brahman (Sravana), understanding the instructions precisely by means of reasoning till all doubts are dissipated and personal convictions are born (manana) and finally persevering meditation on such convictions till the truth is realized (nididhyasana) (B. S. B. 1.1.1 ff).

§204. As is clear, Sankara, like any philosopher does not fail to use reason (discursive knowledge) not only to refute on logical grounds competing theories but also to give a kind of rational basis for the teaching of Sruti. For the latter purpose, he reflects on our common experience of the changeability of objects of sense-perception and on the possibility of our knowledge based on them to be eventually contradicted, to posit Being as the unchanging and absolutely true ground of all things. Similarly with our ideas and changeable states of consciousness. He shows by argument how therefore sense objects, immediate states of one's own consciousness, are only real as appearances of what is really, indeed the only Real. And this he identifies with the Brahman of Sruti (B. S. B., passim, C.U.B. passim, etc.). Being cannot be denied in as much any affirmation and every negation presuppose it, but it cannot be inferred either precisely for the same reason; all the other pramanas are founded on Being (S.B. passim). Of course, Sanakara could not proceed in the same way as St. Thomas by 'way of causality'. The 'universe of discourse' – and the original beliefs of both – are different (and hence too the originary experiences which gave rise to them). Though, for Sankara, Brahman is in a sense the material and efficient Cause of phenomenal reality- and as such Brahman will be spoken then in terms of Isvara the Creator – creation belongs to the order of appearances and is not really real. Hence, the distinction itself between phenomenal reality and Brahman, the conception of Isvara itself and of creation, are not really real. Only Brahman is (sat).

205. All that was simply to bring out the place Sankara allots to discursive knowledge (reason, manana) in the process of realising Brahmin and it is ancillary but essential link to intuition, the direct apperception of truth. Here again, this is no mere academic quest. Sankara, even more than St Thomas, demands a spiritual ascesis (or asceticism) for the study of Vedanta. This consists in a purification of the mind enabling the seeker to discriminate between the eternal and the non-eternal; of the heart enabling him to renounce to all search after pleasure either here or hereafter; of the emotion enabling him to control his mind and his affections and increase his power of concentration; and finally of his will enabling him to ardently desire liberation (mumuksutva). This is in sum the ardent search after Brahman (Brahmajijnasa) (B. S. B., 1, 1, 1 f f).

§206. So a few remarks by way of conclusion on this thorny problem. Can the existence of 'God' be proved by rational argument? Notice that this problem is also discussed within Christianity itself.

Those who (among the believers) maintain that 'God' cannot be proved by rational argument insist on the ineffable transcendence of 'God', who is not an 'object' to be spoken of and whose existence is not of the order of the problems, but the subject par excellence, encountered only in intimate experience, on the level of 'Mystery' of the 'meta-problematic' (cf. Gabriel Marcel). To try and 'prove' His existence already presupposes that one has already received his notion of God from elsewhere (i.e. from his personal experience) and presupposes, at the same time, and openness of heart and mind on the part of him to whom this proof is being addressed – and openness which cannot be merely an academic curiosity but an existential attitude in trust and Faith. – On the other hand, those (among the believers) who maintain that 'God' can be proved by a rational argument insist on the power of the human mind to come to know, both spontaneously and by reflection, the cause from the effect, indeed the Being "in whom we live, move and have our being" present, as it were, already in the heart and mind of all men. By 'reason' and 'rational', they certainly do not mean to limit the power of the mind to discursive knowledge. On the contrary, 'reason' and 'intellect' go hand-in-hand. And if the 'intellect' is the seat, as it were, of 'self-evident truths' it is because it is, as it were, "a kind of participation in the Divine Wisdom itself" (St Thomas).

§207. Again, the former do not mean to say that rational arguments in this respect are completely useless. Rather that they can serve as rational justification for their already established convictions, but not as apodictically binding (like logical, mathematical or even scientific proofs). They can serve to indicate the reasonability of their 'faith', when and to the extent that this is needed in face of doubt on their own part or of challenge coming from others.– The latter do not mean to say that the rational argument, independently of the attitude of one's whole being, is enough. The theory of the 'free attitude', in this respect, is proof enough that the latter (mostly scholastic) realize then in certain cases, though the argument may be logically irrefutable, it is not enough by itself to move the assent of the will if this is not 'moved' by extra-logical motivation. And it can only be so moved if it is open and ready morally and spiritually.

2. RELIGIOUS CERTITIDE

§208. We have already touched on this topic on our first Section (§§ 126-130) but only by way of anticipation. We had to lest, as we said, after having dealt with certitude in general,we should have left this important aspect of certitude hanging in the air. But now, we hope that what we said there by way of anticipation can be better appreciated now that we have gone through the whole discussion of the nature of religious knowledge, religious language and religious truth.

So recall first of all what we have said about certitude in general. We have defined certitude as 'the conviction that such and such is (or is not the case' (§109). We have contrasted conviction with other possible states of mind like doubt and opinion (§110), the difference between the one and the others consisting in the kind of 'evidence' necessary and sufficient. So we examined the different kinds of certitude itself in accordance with the different kinds of fields of knowledge and therefore of the possible and necessary evidence available therein and the way we go about obtaining that evidence (§§ 112ff). As for 'evidence' we defined it as 'the clarity – obviousness, conspicuity – serving to indicate the truth of the judgement' (§77). Certitude, like truth, is, properly speaking, an affair of the judgement.

§209. Once certitude is differentiated on the basis on the different fields of knowledge (as well as on the evidence possible and necessary), enough has been said already to show that religious certitude cannot be either logical, ontological, or physical (§§ 114 ff). We have seen – at least glimpsed at – how religious knowledge is specified by its 'ultimate referent', how this is conceived and spoken of in a language which is distinctly its own (negatively, analogically, transcendentally). But we have seen too that religious knowledge claims to be cognitive and true and therefore 'knowledge' in the genuine sense of the term. It remains to be seen what evidence is possible and to be expected and hence what kind of certitude is possible and to be expected in religious knowledge.

§210. We have distinguished between the mythic, mytho-logical and mystical stages of religious awareness (And recall that we had defined knowledge as 'awareness that such and such is, or is not the case', §13). Roughly this, we said, corresponds to belief, personal conviction, and direct apperception of religious truth (§195). – Hence, on the level of 'belief', religious certitude can be, we think, no different, in this respect, from any other kind of certitude based on witness. It is neither more nor less reasonable than the latter. But we have seen (§128) how most of our knowledge in most fields of knowledge is based on the word, authority, competence of others. Notice that in such cases, we do not even reflect on 'evidence' at all. We take it spontaneously for granted. And it is the case too with most believers in their religious knowledge. There is a kind of 'pre-reflective' awareness of it. And it is this which makes it reasonable and quite distinct from mere credulity – though, needless to say, much of what passes as knowledge – whether in the religious or any other field of knowledge – is credulity, i.e., belief without even the semblance of reasonableness. – On the level of personal conviction, religious certitude can be no different from any other kind of certitude based on 'good reasons'. As we said before (§ 129) it is only when one starts thinking things out for oneself that mere belief passes on to personal conviction. One 'good reason' can certainly be the reliability or competence of the witness. But if that is the only reason, then in that case certitude remains on the level of belief. But if added to that, there are other 'good reasons' by which the truth is made more manifest, then these serve as motivations for his assent to the religious truth. It is in this sense that St. Thomas says that "man would not believe if he did not see that he has to believe". This is what makes the act of belief even more human, what makes it the "reasonable obedience" of which St Paul speaks.

§211. On the level of belief and on that of personal conviction religious certitude is moral certitude in the different senses of the term explained in the first section (third and fourth senses respectively, §§ 123-124). It is only on the level of direct apperception of religious truth (the 'mystical' stage) that religious certitude is, from the point of view of 'evidence' specifically itself. It is comparable to 'ontological certitude' in that it is a kind of insight into what for the mystic becomes 'self-evidently true', indeed the ground of all immediate or mediate truths. But it differs from ontological truth in that the field of knowledge here is different – or at least not quite the same. Here it is no question of the knowledge of beings, of their first principles as principles, it is not even a question of 'Being' in the sense that all beings are beings. It is question of the 'ultimate referent' of religious language which we have seen at some length could even be indicated as 'Non-Being' or the 'Super-Being'. It is not Being as the first link in the whole chain of beings, it is not being besides other beings, it is the Source, Support, Ground of All Beings. Hence this knowledge, at this level, is a kind of super- knowledge, the awareness or consciousness in which this super-knowledge consists is a kind of super-awareness (or as it is often spoken of in mystical literature as Super-consciousness). It is the level of 'Wisdom' (St Thomas), the paramarthika drsti (Sankara). It is not knowledge in the common sense of the word because it is not a knowledge which is mediated by concepts and logical arguments (§ 195) though these would have served their purpose as a stepping stone, as a stage on the path. It is the mystic's claim, wherein Truth is most evident and where certitude, consequently, is most firmly established.

§212. But, one could ask, after having spoken of St Thomas and Sankara, could we still maintain that even on the mystical level there is no contradictoriness of conviction' and therefore of incompatibility of even the highest religious experiences? What becomes of certitude then if such is the case? Recall that in our hypothesis originary religious experiences are different – of the same 'ultimate referent'. Before one decided about contradictoriness and incompatibility one has to place oneself – at least by a kind of mystical 'sense' – on that level. But more than that one can see without too great a difficulty that what on the level of belief (concepts, words, and statements,- explanation) can be contradictory can 'converge' harmoniously on the mystical level. We have said that a statement (tenet of belief) has to be understood in its universe of discourse which in its turn has to be understood, as much as possible, in the light of the originary (mystical) experience which gave it rise (§ 192). So what on the level of belief can be 'opposite' statements, on the level of direct apperception can be seen to coincide. (Take for example, the notions of 'transcendence' and 'immanence' – for this 'opposition' can and in fact is found even within one given religious tradition. Logically they are opposites, mystically they coincide!). This is the famous 'coincidentia oppositorum' of which Nicholas of Cusa and in his wake many contemporary authors on mysticism speak. It is an instance of the 'paradoxical' (§ 188) usage of religious language. It is where language has to die to give birth to ecstasy!

3. CONCLUDING REMARKS

§213. It would be a good thing if the student went over the Introduction again now that the Course is over and try to check the responses he is now prepared to give to the perplexities which we have tried to make him aware of at the beginning of the course. It is not that we expect him to try and give a full and sure answer. After all, this Course with that of Logic was meant only to lay the foundation for a philosophical programme of studies. Many questions barely touched upon here will be taken up and discussed in greater depth in the various treatises. But can the student 'recognize' the perplexity for what it is – understand why it is a perplexity, what the question or questions involved are, how it was handled throughout the history of Philosophy, in the East and in the West and what possible answers have been given, and especially what the student's own reaction to it now is.

§214. Can the student now see the importance of the study of Epistemology and particularly its relevance to his future ministry as a priest? Of course depending on the intellectual level of the people with whom he will have to deal, he will have to adapt and 'translate', as it were, what he has learnt and reflected upon. But whether in more technical terms or in simpler language will have to answer the question: How do we know? How can we be certain? – This Course, we ardently hope, would have made the student aware of what it is to know, what it is to be certain. Which means on the one hand the wonderful power of the human mind to come to know and to be certain and, on the other hand, the never-ending process of growth in knowledge and certitude. Diffidence on one side and presumption on the other are the Scylla and Charybdis of thinking man. Or to change the metaphor, light and darkness, darkness and light, are the dialectical poles of human knowledge and certitude in his search for the Truth. "We look to find, we find to look again" (St Augustine). – In our search for 'God', presuming to know too much and to be certain more than is reasonably expected can be as harmful to one's faith as despairing of knowing anything at all and to being certain in any way. Love for the Truth implies both boldness and humility. Truth is never something which we can possess but something which can possess us. And "to be in the Truth is to let oneself to be open to its light" (G. Marcel).

§215. We might as well end up with this beautiful prayer of St Anselm:

Let me seek Thee in longing,
and long for Thee in seeking;
let me find Thee in loving,
and love Thee in finding.
Truly I see Thine light
not because it is too bright for me
but because whatever I see,
I see in Thine light.

PART THREE

PHENOMENOLOGY OF RELIGIONS

"Religion is the vision of something which stands beyond, behind and within the passing flux of immediate things; something which is real, and yet waiting to be realized; something which is a remote possibility, and yet the greatest of present facts; something that gives meaning to all that passes, and yet eludes apprehension; something whose possession is the final good, and yet is beyond all reach; something which is the ultimate ideal, and the hopeless quest." (A. N. Whitehead, *Science and the Modern World*, 1933 ed., p. 228)

GENERAL INTRODUCTION

§1.We are witnessing today, perhaps more than ever before, a curious phenomenon: on the one hand, a widespread atheism, a religious indifference, dissatisfaction with 'organized' religion; on the other hand, a no less widespread search for authentic religious values, a growing need for personal religious experience and an interest in the world's religious pluralism.

One could point out many reasons for this phenomenon, indeed for this double phenomenon. Religion, in fact, often stirs up in man a feeling of repulsion and at the same time a feeling of attraction; a feeling of repulsion because of its other-worldly concern, its unprovable beliefs, its apparent superstitions, its rigid pattern of behavior and customs - all of which goes counter to the increasing secular, rational and empirical spirit of man – and a feeling of attraction because of its sense of mystery, of the human and spiritual values it promotes, of its offer of inward peace and happiness.

§2. Interest in the world's religious pluralism, in particular, has been aroused not only by such sciences as anthropology, psychology and sociology and by the coming closer together of people professing different religions and by the need for political and economic co-operation on an international level, but also, and perhaps especially, by the growing awareness on the part of many religious people of the inherent significance and import of religious pluralism as such.

This growing awareness has had its repercussions, as it could be expected, on the Catholic Church. A sign of this is the three documents of Vatican II: *Gaudium et Spes* (On the position of the Church in the modern world), *Nostra Aetate* (On the relationship of Christianity to the other world's religions) and *Ad Gentes* (On the meaning of the Church's missionary activity).

It would not be mere rethoric to say that the significance and import of the world's religious pluralism is being to the Church a kind of 'discovery' comparable, in many respects, to the discover of Aristotle in the Middle Ages.

§3. The over-all aim of our study is to attempt and understand what 'religion' ultimately and fundamentally is and what 'religious pluralism' can signify.

Needless to point out that the perusal of our aim is not born out of a mere academic interest. Our study can help us understand better our 'religiosity' and prepare us to face, as future priests, one of the greatest challenges which face the Christian, and the Catholic Church as a whole, especially in a country like India, the 'cradle of many world religions'.

§4. Our study will be divided into four main parts. Each part will be presented as a self-standing unit but serves actually as a basis for the succeeding part. This explains the method we intend to follow:

The first part will be a *Phenomenology of Religion*. Whatever 'religion' is – something which we shall have to settle in the second part of our study – it is something which is, at least ordinarily, expressed also outwardly, that is, in creeds, ritual, moral behavior, feasts and festivals, temples and places of pilgrimage, art and literature, etc. All these are visible things ("phenomena"), subject to observation and study and often historically traceable to their origin. It is this kind of study which we mean by Phenomenology of religion.

One can take different approaches to such a study. What one is looking for determines, to a great extent, one's method of approach. Hence, if one is looking for how religions originated and developed, their possible branching out from a primeval form of religion and their subsequent vicissitudes, the method more indicated will be the historical one. If one is looking for common phenomena, common structures and patterns whether in religious belief or practice, the method most suited would be the comparative or homologous method. Needless to say, all methods not only have advantages and disadvantages but also can hardly escape a certain kind of subjective interpretation of facts- an interpretation which often misrepresents and hence distorts the objective reality.

§5. We like to call our method *historico-existential.* What we shall 'be looking for is how the different world religions arose historically and how they are lived existentially. This is the reason why we prefer to limit ourselves to the more widely spread religions and to treat them separately, each one on its own count. We believe that a religion can be better understood if it is compared and contrasted with other religions only *after* it has been understood in itself. Similarly, one tenet of belief or practice of one religion can only be compared and contrasted with a similar, or apparently similar, tenet of belief or practice after it has been understood in the *context* of the religion to which it belongs. These remarks will be justified in the second part of our study.

§6. Any phenomenological study of religion aims to be as objective as possible and to refrain from passing value-judgments. Its aim is to understand what religion or religions are. This is, of course, a particularly difficult task because to understand a certain insight is required. And this insight penetrates, or seeks to penetrate, into the reality of which the phenomena are but its outward expressions. Any 'observation' can easily become an 'interpretation' for it is not easy for the observer

– whether he is a religious man or not (indeed much more if he is not!) – so to 'suspend his judgment' (to practice the 'epoche') as not to interpret what he observes in the light of his own religious belief or disbelief! On the other hand, if it is not normative, a phenomenology of religion, as we conceive it, is not purely descriptive either, for it tries, as we have said, to understand – as objectively as possible – the reality of which the phenomena are the outward expressions or manifestations.

§7. The second part will be a *Philosophy of Religion*. Here we shall attempt to reflect philosophically on the meaning of religion in general and the significance of religious pluralism – always basing ourselves on the data gathered in the first part but aided, this time, by certain philosophical principles.

Here one can raise two objections against our attempt. One objection is to ask on what basis are we to justify our choice of the philosophical principles to aid us in our attempt. There are different philosophical systems, each one of which works with different philosophical principles. Would not our choice then be arbitrary unless it is first grounded on reasonable arguments, and are such arguments possible? We readily admit that such different philosophical systems are possible, but if they are true, they cannot be contradictory to one another. If 'we prefer to look at them as different approaches to an understanding of reality, each approach must admit its limitations, its one-sidedness, but not necessarily it's falsity. In point of fact, we shall not claim that our understanding of religion and of religious pluralism is exhaustive or the only possible one. Our understanding will be a kind of a *model,* one among many possible ones, which, we believe, can help one understand religious reality. Or if one prefers, we shall attempt to form a *hypothesis*, and like any hypothesis, it can legitimately be deemed valuable if, and only if, it will be reasonability grounded, explains the facts in question as satisfactorily as possible, and answers objections as consistently and as fully as possible.

The other objection is to ask whether religion can at all be understood by a mere philosophical (and hence rational) enquiry. This is indeed a more serious objection for all religious people, and more emphatically the mystics, will tell you that religion can only be understood by a certain kind of 'religious experience'. There is nothing worse to understand religion than a kind of impersonal, detached and uncommitted study. But this objection presumes that any philosophical enquiry is necessarily rationalistic, impersonal, detached and uncommitted. Our understanding of philosophy is different...

§8. Notice that the term 'Philosophy of Religion' is still used today in senses different from the one we are using it here. In fact, it is used to sometimes to mean that philosophical study of the a-priori conditions of possibility of the relationship between man and God or the Absolute (as in Hegel, Fichte, and Schelling). It is also sometimes used in the sense of a rational critique of a given religion (as the one Dumery makes of Christianity). Most Often, it is used in the same meaning as Natural Theology (that is a philosophical study into the existence of God, the meaning of religious language, man's relation, to God, etc).

§9. The third part of our study will be a *Theology of Religion*. Here, our task will be to reflect on the conclusions of our phenomenologically— bused philosophy of religion in the light of the Christian Revelation. More concretely we shall reflect on what Christian Theology says, or *can* say, 'about religion and religious pluralism.

It is our belief that any given religious tradition, once it is understood in itself, on its own count, can be even better understood in the light of the whole religious experience of mankind. This applies equally well to Christianity as to any other religious tradition. This field of enquiry is a relatively new one. Our conclusions here will be therefore provisional and tentative. But such questions will be raised as the religious significance of the world religions in the economy of salvation, the specificity of the Christian religious experience, the 'meaningfulness' of Jesus Christ, the nature of the Church and the purpose of its missionary activity, the fruitfulness to be expected from a sincere inter-religious cross-fertilization, etc.

§10. The fourth and final part of our study will be a *Mysticism of Religion*. It is not difficult to see that religion originates from and leads us to mysticism. Here, we shall attempt to describe the essential nature and chief characteristics of mystical consciousness, corroborating our analysis by the experiences and teachings of mystics of as many religions as possible. This part of our study will be both theoretical and practical.

Religion, in fact, and much more mysticism, is not, and simply cannot be, a mere subject-matter for academic study. We have just answered the objection against our attempt at a philosophical study of religion and we have given our answer. The objection will be a valid one if by a philosophical study (or, for that matter, any study whatsoever) one were to understand, to use the same expressions we have just used, an impersonal, detached and uncommitted enquiry. Unless a study of religion is motivated by a sincere quest for the truth, the absolute Truth, it is bound to remain sterile. And such a sincere quest for the Truth is already a 'deep human experience which cannot fail to attain its end.

INTRODUCTORY REMARK ON STUDY OF RELIGION

§11. In our General Introduction, we explained what we mean by Phenomenology of Religion, its place in the over-all plan of our study, how we intend it to serve as a basis for a Philosophy of Religion, our approach to it and the method we mean to follow. But here we wish to pass a further remark.

If our overall aim is to try and understand what 'religion' is (and what 'religious pluralism' can signify), we shall have to leave it till at least, the second part of our study (the philosophical part) to come out with our definition, or at least description, of 'religion'. But then we are immediately faced with the question what 'phenomena' are we to consider as 'religious'. For this already implies that we have made a pre-judgment what 'religion' is, or, to put it in other words, that we have made a criterion by which to judge what 'phenomena' are 'religious' and what 'phenomena' are not. Our answer to this question is that at this initial stage of our enquiry, we shall have to content ourselves with a phenomenological study of what are generally considered to be *religions*. Our criterion is therefore simply ordinary language.

§12. Notice, however, that at this stage we take this criterion uncritically. This means that at this stage we do not pre-judge the issue whether 'religion' and 'religious phenomena' are co-extensive with 'religions' and the data these, and only these, provide us with. This issue has to be discussed in our second part. This means too that ideally we should study *all* the religions – or what, in ordinary language, are called 'religions' – of the world: those which existed in antiquity but which are now dead (e.g. Egyptian, Mesopotamian, Syrian, Iranian, Greek, Roman, Hellenistic, Germanic, Celtic, Mexican, Peruvian, Oceanic, etc.); the hundreds of religions professed and practiced by ethnic groups all over the world today (particularly in Africa, but also in Australia, India and North as well as South America), and the world-wide contemporary religions. If we shall limit ourselves to these latter, we do so for pragmatic reasons. As for the dead religions, they are obviously of much less existential relevance to us today. As for ethnic religions they are too many to study them in a way which does full justice to them and without the risk of making over-simplified generalizations.

§13. Even then, our treatment of the main contemporary religions is simply meant to bring out certain features of each religion more directly relevant to our later philosophical reflection. On each religion one can write whole volumes, and in fact whole volumes have been written. What we shall have to say about each religion can only serve as a kind of first *introduction* to it.

We shall first try to bring out certain phenomena common, from a historical point of view, to all these religions. Then we shall try to treat of each religion in particular.

Chapter 1

SOME COMMON PHENOMENA, IN THE HISTORY OF THE WORLD'S MAIN RELIGIONS

§14. Sometimes, historians of religion distinguish between 'prophetic religions' (by which is meant Judaism, Zoroastrianism, Christianity and Islam) and 'mystic religions' (particularly Hinduism, Buddhism, Taoism, Jainism). This distinction has certainly some value in that it serves to distinguish certain emphases. The so-called' 'prophetic religions' certainly emphasize the necessity of accepting in religious faith the experience and teachings of the prophet or prophets (without, however, diminishing the importance of one's making one's personal religious experience); the so-called 'mystic religions' certainly emphasize the necessity of making one's personal religious experience (without, however, diminishing the importance of accepting in religious faith the teachings of their Sacred Scriptures).

From a historical point of view, however, such a distinction can be misleading. In fact, a common phenomenon in the history of the worldwide religions is the fact that these religions owe, or at least claim to owe, or at least claim to owe their origin to a person or persons! It was their kind of experience and their teachings which gave rise to these religions – whether this experience was the result of a 'divine revelation' or of their own effort and whether their teachings were 'divinely inspired' or not.

§15. This is no less true of Hinduism and Shintoism. Hindus love to call Hinduism the 'eternal religion' (sanatana dharma), but as Vivekananda explains, when the Vedas are said to be without beginning and without end, by Vedas no books are meant but spiritual laws. These laws as laws are without beginning and end but they have been discovered by the rishis – discovered, that is, in time. The origin of Shintoism is perhaps even more wrapped in the mists of time, but Shinto's trace their religion to their ancestors.

§16. These persons can rightly be called initiators of religious movements. More than 'founders' of religions, they are reformers, charismatic teachers and, above all, persons of deep religious experience. With the exception of the Vedic rishis, and perhaps Zoroaster and Confucius, none of them put their teachings in writing. Whether they were later believed to be 'divinely inspired' or not, they ended up by being given a deep religious veneration and their teachings were given a kind of authoritative bindingness. Indeed, their very birth, and their whole life was 'apotheized'.

§17. It was left to immediate disciples to put down in writing the teachings of these initiators of religious movements. Thus gradually grew the *Scriptures*. Believed to be the record of their teachings, they gradually ended up by being considered 'sacred' – not to be tampered with but left intact and handed down faithfully and in their integrity from generation to generation. In monotheistic religions, the Scriptures are sacred, especially because they are the 'word of God' itself. In Islam, the belief in the 'pre-existent Quran' reminds us of the Hindu 'Santana dharma' on the one hand, of the 'pre-existent Christ' on the other.

In all the Scriptures, however, we find different 'genres' or literary forms, such as, historical narratives, prayers and hymns, moral and spiritual exhortations, theological treatises, stories about deities and spirits, maxims and rules of conduct, prescriptions for religious cult, etc.

In Shintoism – which in many ways, as we shall see, resembles ethnic religions which have no Scriptures – Scriptures were compiled as late as the eight century A.D. Before that time, as well as in ethnic religions up to today, oral tradition which is as 'sacred' and as faithfully and as integrally guarded, played the role of the Sacred Scriptures.

§18. During the course of time, another body of literature arose whose function it was to interpret the Scriptures, apply their teachings to daily life and its problems. This body of literature which we shall call 'Tradition' (Hadith, Smrti, Talmud, etc.) is subordinate to the Sacred Scriptures and derives its authoritativeness from it. Hence the earlier it is, the greater its authority.

Later still, saintly men and thinkers wrote Commentaries, Summas, etc., for didactic and apologetical purposes. The authority of this body of literature is obviously much smaller than that of the Sacred Scriptures and of Tradition proper. To distinguish between the absolute authoritativeness of the Sacred Scriptures from the relative one of the rest of the religious literature, a 'canon' of Sacred Scriptures was in time to be drawn up, either spontaneously or officially.

§19. From as far back as we can trace these world-wide religions – and this applies equally well to ethnic religions – we notice that sooner or later these religions assumed a social character. A first group of disciples soon swelled into a bigger and bigger community bound together by the same beliefs and consequently by the same religious spirit and by the same religious practices.

However, we notice that this community is variously organized. But whether loosely or more rigidly organized, there is in the community a sense of belonging, a sense of identification.

While we notice the beneficial role the community plays not only in the life of the individual member as providing him with a religious 'milieu' to grow in and strengthen his religious faith but also in the religious history of the world as providing mankind with Sacred Scriptures, preserving him in their originality and handing them down in their integrity from one generation to another, etc., we cannot help noticing at the same time regrettable results. In fact, a sense of belonging to and identification with one community seems to cut one from and put one in contrast to the rest of his fellow-men. This seems to have been at least one of the deepest reasons for *doctrinal exclusivism, communal rivalry and religious antagonism*. It is understandable but regrettable (as we shall try to show in our second part) that when one thinks that his religion is the 'true', and the only true, one, one is spontaneously led to believe that all other religions are necessarily 'false' and hence opponents to one's own.

§20. A particularly interesting phenomenon in the history of these worldwide religions is the fact of religious splits. We can distinguish different kinds of splits. A 'sectarian' split is caused when a group of persons, without cutting themselves from the main religion, so emphasize one or other aspect of its beliefs or practices, that they end up by assuming a clearly distinctive character. It may happen that, along with the originary Sacred Scriptures, they adopt other texts as their own specific Scripture. (In Hinduism, Vaishnavism, Saivism and Tantricism can be considered to be 'splits' in this sense). An 'apostasy' is a rejection of the originary Sacred Scriptures. In a pejorative sense, it means a complete loss of religious faith. But it can mean too a complete branching off of a religious movement from the original one due to some authentic religious experience of a person or persons. In the latter sense, Buddhism and Jainism are 'apostasies' from Hinduism. Both rejected, the Vedic Sacred Scriptures and gave rise to their own. A 'schism' is a rejection of religious disciplinary authority but not of the originary Sacred Scriptures. It is clear that the more 'institutionalized' this religious authority is, the more passible schisms become (The Catholic Church always looked on Eastern Orthodoxy as a 'schism' but never as an 'apostasy' and not even as a 'heresy').

§21. But there is another kind of 'split' which is the most curious of them all. It is what we might call a 'theological' split. It is 'curious' because it is not immediately clear how people, basing themselves on the same Sacred Scriptures, being animated by the same religious spirit, sharing the same religious concerns, trying to solve the same religious problems, can yet differ in their interpretation of their common Sacred Scriptures.

It may happen that the main body of believers will consider a given interpretation to be inconsistent with, and even contrary to, the accepted common belief. In such a case, such an interpretation will be considered as a 'heresy'. At other times, an interpretation, no matter how different it may be from another interpretation, will be given due respect and accepted as one among other possible interpretations. In such a case, one can speak of a 'theological pluralism' existing in the same religion. Noteworthy is the fact that in Hinduism, Sankhya, Vaisesika and Purva Mimamsa, though so different from the Vedanta in their interpretation of Sruti, were never considered to be 'nastikas'.

§22. We observe too in each of these religions, a kind of *dynamic growth*. None of them can be said to be found in the self-same state as when they emerged ages ago. A certain essential and fundamental 'sameness' is preserved, the Sacred Scriptures continue to be the norm of orthodoxy and the source of inspiration, but a certain kind of 'difference' – a difference in continuity – gradually develops over the years.

Many factors can account for this growth and development, the most important of which is obviously the growth and development in human consciousness in general and in religious consciousness in particular. Social and political factors both on a national and, particularly today, on an international level, have their repercussions on man's religious consciousness.

Another factor worth mentioning in particular has certainly been a certain kind of 'cross-fertilization' between religions. The influence of Judaism on Christianity (Christianity can be very well considered to be an off-shoot of Judaism), of Judaism and Christianity on Islam, of Hinduism and Islam on Sikhism, of Hinduism on Jainism and Buddhism, of Buddhism on Confucianism, Taoism and Shintoism, etc., is obvious. Less obvious perhaps is the influence of Zoroastrianism on Post-Babylonic Judaism and consequently on Christianity, of Christianity on Mahayana Buddhism and on modern Hinduism, etc.

§23. This dynamic growth does not mean a continuer linear progress, as it were. All these religions have had their ups and downs, times of decline and times of revival. Reform movements and 'renaissance' periods are frequent happenings.

Most interesting phenomenon in most of these religions is the presence throughout the years of their history of people who confess to have experienced in a kind of direct and personal way the 'truth' taught by them. These we shall call 'mystics'. Often they initiate the religious reforms and are the inspiration of mystic movements. (E.g. the Merkabah and Kabbala mystical movements in Judaism, Sufism in Islam, the Spanish and Rhineland mystics in Christianity, the Ramakrishna movement in Hinduism, etc.).

§24. If there is one phenomenon which is specifically a modern one, it is the ever-growing need, on the part of many people belonging to different religions, *for mutual understanding and collaboration*. Never before could one witness the relative ease with which representatives of these religions can meet to share their religious beliefs and experiences.

The World Parliament of Religions was inaugurated in Chicago towards the end of the last century. Since then, inter-religious meetings are held periodically in different countries of the world. Studies in Comparative Religion are always on the increase. This is certainly a sign of the times – accountable, to a great extent, by some of the factors listed at the beginning of our study...

Chapter 2

THE WORLD RELIGIONS IN THEIR HISTORICO-EXISTENTIAL EXPRESSION

§25.We now proceed to present the world'S main religions in their historico-existential expression. Our presentation, given its brevity, can only serve as an introduction to each religion and as an invitation for a closer and detailed study of each one of them.

We shall follow as far as possible, in the presentation of each religion, the order of the 'common phenomena' which we have already described. Such an order serves us as a kind of 'model' by which to try and find our way through the complexity which any lived religion is.

1. JUDAISM

§26. Judaism traces its origin to Abraham whom God called and chose to be the father of his chosen people. God thus enters into a covenant (*berith*) with his people: on its part, the people are to be faithful to Him and worship and serve Him alone; on His part, God is to bless, multiply and protect it. This covenant was confirmed and given a more concrete form through Moses to whom God gave the Torah (Law) on Mount Sinai after the people's deliverance from their years of bondage in Egypt. Though the original meaning of the circumcision is not clear, it seems to be the sign of this covenant.

§27. No matter how gradually the ancient Hebrews passed from a probable henotheistic to a monotheistic concept of God, Yahweh, at least from the time of the Babylonian captivity, is the One, Righteous, Holy and Almighty God, creator of heaven and earth. Idolatry is a betrayal. The righteous man is he who is faithful to God's Will as manifested to His people. But God is always ready to forgive; his punishments, which often take the form of persecution and other sufferings inflicted on them by other peoples, are a call to repentance. From time to time

God sent the people prophets to warn it of its infidelities. God is also the Lord of History, and will send the Messiah to fulfill His providential plan and restore the House of Israel. The belief in the immortality of the soul and its reward or punishment in an after-life seems to have taken a long time to develop.

§28. The Sacred Scriptures (simply called the 'Torah') comprises the Pentateuch, the Nebiim (prophets) and Kethubim (other writings such as Song of Songs, Ecclesiastes, Book of Job).[8]

Since the Torah is the Divine Will on the people, the Judaic morality is totally commanded by it which is explained and commented upon in much detail covering, in minute detail all aspects of life by the Talmud ("instruction").[9] The *Midrash* ("investigation") is a collection "of commentaries of the Torah both of its legal aspect (halacha) and of its spiritual aspect (haggadah). The *Targum* is a kind of unofficial explanation and paraphrases of the Torah in Aramaic.

§29. From the patriarchal times, the offering of sacrifice was the main religious cult of the people. Different kinds of sacrifices were offered, the main one being the holocaust in adoration of God. From the time of King Solomon, and up to the destruction of Jerusalem by the Romans (70 A.D.), the Temple was the center of worship. Since then the synagogue replaced the Temple and the rabbi the priest. Rabbinical Judaism, however, dates as far back as the time of the Babylonian exile.

Up to today the Jews celebrate their religious life in many rites and rituals. Among the rites, one can mention: circumcision, bar mitzvah ("son of the commandment") by which the thirteen-year old boy is fully admitted in the religious community, kiddushin ("sanctification") or marriage rite, kaddish or prayers for the dead. Rituals are performed both at home (e.g. the kiddush, the ceremony of sanctification on the eve of the Sabbath) and at the synagogue on the Sabbath and on Festival Days (the more important of which are: Rosh Hashanah or New Year, Yom Kippur or Day of Atonement, and Pesachim or the Passover, Sukkoth or Feast of Tabernacles, Hannukahor or Dedication to commemorate the Maccabees victory, Purim or the feast of Lots to commemorate deliverance from Persians, Shabuoth which recalls the giving of the Torah to Moses, etc.). Notice how most of these feasts recall the wonderful dealings of God with His people.

§30. Already in ancient times, there existed various sects in the heart of Judaism – the best known being the Pharisees, more 'orthodox' in their belief and practice,

---

8 The canon was established at the synod of Jamnia in 100 A.D. For criteria were used to determine which books were canonical: conformity to the Pentateuch, its being written not later than Esdras, in Hebrew and in Palestine. Thus such books as Ecclesiasticus, First Maccabees, Tobias, parts of Daniel, Esther, Judith, Wisdom, Second Maccabees were rejected as apocryphal.

9 Composed of Mishna ("study by repetition", 3rd cent. A.D.) and Gemara ("complement" 4th-6th Century).

and the Sadducees, more 'liberal' in the interpretation of the Torah and who rejected some tenets of common belief like the existence of angels and spirits, the resurrection of the dead and survival after death. The Karaites (8th cent.) were rigidly 'fundamentalists'.

In the middle Ages, with the discovery of Aristotle by the Arabs, great attempts were made to give a rational foundation to the faith like the existence of God, the nature of revelation, the relation between knowledge and faith, the eternity or createdness of the world, the attributes of God, etc. The philosophical work of Moses bar Maimon,[10] though held in the highest esteem, created tensions and later nearly split Jewry into two. By contrast, Jehuda Halevi (1080-1141) represents the extreme opposite: Judaism is not based on reason but on the experience of Israel, on the wonderful works of God and not on speculative reason; Israel is a mystical community, the heart of mankind, whose election and suffering are inextricably interwoven, suffering being the very mark of its election.

§31. Judaism has had, besides the ancient prophets, its mystics. Philo of Alexandria (30 B.C.-50 A.D.) taught that God is known only by intuition rather than by reasoning, although His nature unknown. Bahya Ibn Pakuda (11th cent.) is the major representative of a mystical movement. Author of Duties of the Heart, he recommends complete abandon in the hands of God, detachment from worldly desires and actions, and a consuming love of God. (Noticeable is the secondary importance he gives to the history of Israel as such).

But the two best known mystical movements in Judaism are the Merkabah ("the throne") mysticism expressing the absolute majesty and transcendence of God and the Kabbalah ("oral tradition") mysticism expressing the self-manifestation of God through the 'sefiroth' (potencies). The Kabbalah main text is the Zohar attributed to mosses de Leon (14th cent.), It is particularly interesting that, uncharacteristically of Judaism, it speaks of 'female' aspects (particularly the 'shekinah') of God who, however, in Himself, as 'en sof' ("infinite"), is so unknowable that not even existence can be predicated and therefore is 'ayin' (as "nothing"). The kabbala is a mystical expression of the inner life of God, of His immanence in the world, of the phenomenon of sin and of the final'union' (and not merely 'communion') with God. It survives today in a mitigated from in Hasidism ("piety") mainly due to the writings of Israel Baal shem Tob (18th cent.).

§32. Today, Judaism is branched off in three movements: Orthodoxy pioneered by authors like Samson Hirsch, Reform under the influence of liberal theologians

---

10 Known as Manimonides, lived in 12th centuary. Born in Spain but selled in Egypt. Had a considerable influence on Thomas Aquinas. Best known is his list of thirteen articles resuming the Jewish faith: God as creator, his unity, incorporeality, eternity, obligation to pray to Him alone, truth of prophecy, Moses as father of all prophets, Torah as given to Moses and its irreplacability, God's omniscience, judgment, coming of Messiah, resurrection the dead. Author of *Guide of the Perplexed*.

like Moses Mendelsohn (18th cent.), who not only demythologizes such key Jewish beliefs as prophesy, revelation, election and Messianism, but insisted on the updating of many of its religious practices and customs, and conservatism which tries to strike a balance between the two.

Zionism, the movement for a 'return to the Holy Land, and the building up of Israel as a nation, spearheaded by Theodore Herzl, which resulted in the creation of the modern state of Israel strengthened after the European pogroms.

2. ZOROASTRIANISM

§33. Though Zoroastrianism (or Mazdaism) counts today only 200,000 adherents, (mostly in India, known as Parsees, but about 30,000 in Teberan and Sharifabad, known as Gabars), and hence it is by no means a world-wide religion, we are including it in our study because of its peculiar characteristics, the probable influence it has had on Post-Babylonic Judaism (and hence on Christianity) and its presence in India.

Zoroastrianism takes its claim from Zoroaster (the Greek form of Zarthust) who probably lived in the 6th cent. B.C. in what is now called Afghanistan. He was a reformer of the ancient Iranian religion which bears a great resemblance to the Vedic religion. At first he met opposition and persecution; after some time in exile, he converted King Vishtaspa. His teachings spread to neighboring countries including Persia and became the official religion of the great Persian Empire till their defeat by Alexander the Great in 330 B.C. Eight books of the Old Testament make reference to them. Cyrus is called Yahweh's 'Messiah' (Isaias 45:1), his 'shepherd' (ibid. 44:28) with independence and the foundation of the Sassanian dynasty, Zoroastrianism becomes the state religion – till the conquest of the dynasty by Moslem armies in 651 A.D. Persia (now Iran) is a Muslim (Shiite) country. Zoroaster is said to have been slain at the age of seventy-seven by invaders.

§34. Zoroaster is believed to have received the commission from Ahura Mazda (or Ohrmazd, "the Wise Lord") to proclaim Him as the One, good, holy Lord, Creator and sustainer of the world and thus to spread the true and universal religion. Ahura Mazda's attributes (clearly personified) are Asha (righteousness), vohu mana (good mind), khshathra (goodness), armaiti (wisdom), haurvatat (wholeness), ameretat (immortality). These are 'amesha spentas' ("holy immortals").

At the very beginning of existence, the Holy Spirit declares enmity to the Evil Spirit (Anro Mainyus or Ahriman), and thus a cosmic conflict is waged between the Truth (asha) and the Lie (Druj), between Good and Evil, between Light and Darkness. The heavenly spirits (prominent among whom is Mithra) had to array themselves behind one or the other. Similarly, man has to choose, in full freedom and responsibility, for the triumph of Truth. He has to cooperate, if he is righteous, (ashvan,), for the triumph of Truth. He does so by "good thoughts, good words and good deeds". Honesty, purity,(both moral and ceremonial), charity towards the poor, hospitality, devotion to duty figure prominently in Zoroastrian ethics.

After death, the good will be reworded in heaven (behesht or "most excellent" place), the bad punished in hell. Those whose good deeds equal bad deeds go to a "place of equilibrium". A future saviour (Saoshyant or "bringer of good fortune") is expected. A General Resurrection will renew the entire world, the damned will be saved, the final triumph of the Good over Evil will be complete.

§35. The Zoroastrian Scriptures are the Avesta ("wisdom") only a fraction of which is today extant. It includes the Yasnans or prayers to be recited by the priests when offering sacrifice, the Gathas, seventeen in number, are hymns attributed to Zoroster himself, the Vendidas, or Law against Demons, expound rules to be observed in the various circumstances of life in case faults have been committed (in the first two chapters the story of creation is narrated as well as the story of Yima the Iranain Noah), the Yashts or hymns of praise, addressed to heavenly spirits, the Visprat or invocation to all the lords, and what is known as the 'Little Avesta' consisting in texts, prayers, etc.

The cannon was fixed as late as the 4th century A.D. or, as some believe, as late as the 11th century. Some scholars believe that the Avesta as we have it today differs completely from the old one.

What we could look as 'tradition' in Zoroastrianism is the so-called *Pahlavi Books* (9th century) which includes: Bundahishn (cosmogony) Menck-i- khairat (answers to questions), Denkart ("book of religion" containing legendary biography of Zoroaster).

§36. The heart of the Zoroastrian cult is the worship of Ahura Mazda through hymns of praise and the offerings of gifts (bread, milk, haoma). Blood sacrifice as well as intoxicating haoma had been forbidden by Zoroaster. The chief religious symbol is the fire (or the sun). Various ceremonial purifications, including the initiation ceremony is prescribed. Priesthood is hereditary. There are various ranks of priesthood: the ervad (lowest rank), the mobed (priest of the Fire-temple the most sacred of which is called Atesh Behram) and the dastur or high priest.

The principal feasts are the New Year, the spring and autumn equinoxes dedicated to Mithra, the Gahambars at the change of the seasons, Farvardagan devoted to the spirits of the dead, the Khordad-i Salon, the birthday of Zoroaster. Each month used to have a festival in honor to one or other of the yazads (minor deities – which was a later development! – like Tir, bringer of rain; Spendarmad or earth; Bahman, protector of cattle; Ardivisur, giver of welfare and fertility; Sarosh, guardian of life, etc).

Of course, Zoroastrians are well-known for their Towers of Silence (Dakhma). Burning the corpse pollutes the fire and burying it pollutes the earth.

§37. A monotheistic and dualistic concept of what we might call the 'Ultimate' alternated for a long time in the history of Zoroastrianism. Though today there can hardly be any doubt about the monotheism of Zoroaster himself, the origin of Ahriman remained a serious dilemma. The dilemma is this: Ahura Mazda cannot be the origin of Evil, but if He is not, He cannot be said to be the origin of everything. Zoroaster speaks of the Holy Spirit and of the Evil Spirit as "twins", and in some places, he speaks of the former as the "son" of Ahura Mazda. So can one deduce that the Evil Spirit too is his "son" – since, after all, the Evil Spirit is evil by "choice" and not by nature? Still, it is the dualistic view which finally prevailed by the time the Pahlavi Books were written. Some of Zoroaster followers, to solve the dilemma, posited *Zurvan-i Akanarak* ("Infinite Time") as the Ultimate and progenitor of both Ahura Mazda and Abriman. It was only during the last century that the Parsees in India began to question the dualistic position and to return to the original monotheism.

It is easy to see how the dualistic position could have given rise to Manicheism (from Manes, its propagator in the 3rd century A.D.). It started as a Zoroastrian sect. The monotheist sect drove Manes into exile in India. On his return, he was favored for a time by the Persian Emperor, but after having lost his favor, he was flayed alive and put to death. His disciples spread his teachings to all parts of Asia, North Africa and Europe. Before his conversion Saint Augustine was a Manichean. Manes had absorbed enough of Christianity too to make his teachings attractive beyond the Zoroastrian world. As developed by his disciples, man has two souls: a soul animating the body and is the creation of Evil and a soul which is part of the World-Soul or Christ. All material things are evil and the cause of evil. Jesus, Buddha, Zoroaster and Manes have been sent to help man in the struggle against Evil and to liberate him.

§38. Zoroastrians came to India in the wake of the Moslem invasion. They landed at Sanjan in 716 bringing with them the sacred fire. They kept regular contact with their co-religionists in Persia (what had remained them, called the Iranis). In the 18th Century, the *Qadmi sect* was for which reverted to the Iranian calendar. The rest, opposing them, called themselves the *Shahanshabis* ("royalists" maintaining that their calendar was that of the ancient Persian Kings).[11] But more important still, we observe a movement of 'reform' which tries to go back to what it considers to be the simple original religion – as contrasted to the movement initiated by *Bahramshah Naoroji Schroff* (end of 19th century) and called *Ilm-i Khshnoom* which while adhering strictly to ritual and tradition interprets the scriptures in a 'mystical' way.

11 The Quadmis are found only in Mumbai and Surat; the old Parsee stronghold of Gujarat remain strongly attached to their own tradition.

Parsees themselves, or at least a number of them, are aware of the dwindling number of their co-religionists, of the difficulties with their hereditary priesthood, and of their uncertain future.

3. CHRISTIANITY

§39. From a historical point of view, one can rightly say that Christianity began as an off-shoot of Judaism, or even as a Jewish 'sect'. After the crucifixion by the Romans of Jesus of Nazareth, his disciples claimed that he was the 'messiah' ("the Christ") promised to mankind from the beginning of the world by Yahweh and expected so ardently by the people of Israel. It was at Antioch that the disciples of Jesus began to be called Christians (1st century A.D.).

Jesus Christ is the central tenet of the belief of Christianity. By His life, death and resurrection from the dead, Jesus Christ is the savior or Redeemer of mankind from sin. Yahweh had revealed Himself in him, Indeed, Jesus Christ is the 'Logos' become flesh(*"ho logos sarx egeneto"*), he is now 'the Lord' (*ho kurios*).

It is then by faith in Jesus Christ that man is justified and saved- justification and salvation themselves being a gratuitous gift (grace) conferred by God through Jesus Christ. The Church is the community of believers in Jesus Christ, a community of faith and worship expressed in Baptism and the celebration of the Eucharist. The Church is commissioned to spread the Gospel (euangelion or 'good news') to all men till the Lord comes again at the end of time to judge the living and the dead.

In the light of its belief in Jesus Christ and his unique relationship to Yahweh, the primitive Christian community already began to express its belief in God as: Father (or simply 'God', ho Theos), Son of God (or simply 'the Son', the Lord) and Holy Spirit (or 'the spirit of the Father' or again 'the spirit of the Son'). Thus, the Incarnation and the Trinity became to be the principal characteristically 'mysteries' of Christianity. However, since very early times, the Christian Community included in its profession of faith (creed) other tenets of belief inherited from Judaism (and most likely too from Zoroastrianism) – always interpreted in its new light – regarding the resurrection of all the dead, final judgment, hell and heaven.

§40. As for the Scriptures, Christianity retained the Scriptures of its parent religion as a part of its own – and this is something unique in the history of religion (It retains also those books which were rejected as uncanonical by the Jewish Synod of Jamnia – see supra §28 note). The reason for this was that Christianity saw in the 'election' of the people of Israel a providential plan for the coxing Jesus Christ. But, of course, Christianity has its own specifically Christian Scriptures which consist in the writings of the disciples of Jesus Christ (Mark, Mathew, Luke and John-whose writings form the Four Gospels- Peter and James, and Paul who had never known Jesus personally but who soon became, with Peter the greatest apostle of Christianity outside of Palestine and Christianity's greatest theologian).

Hence, the distinction between the 'Old Testament' (the Jewish Scriptures) and the 'New Testament' (the specifically Christian ones).

For 'Tradition' (in the sense that we have been understanding the term), Christianity considers the writings of the early writers (from the end of the 1st century down to the 8th century) as especially authoritative. Hence the title 'Fathers of the Church'. As outstanding among them, one could mention, Clement of Rome, Polycarp of Smyrna, Ignatius of Antioch, Irenaeus of Asia Minor, Clement of Alexandria, Justin of Naples, and particularly Athanasius, Jerome, Augustine, Gregory of Nyssa, Basil, John Chrysostom, etc.).[12]

§41. Christianity has known a chequered history. Already from the 4th century, theological disputes began to splinter it into 'sects' and threaten its unity. Already during the time of the apostles, the question arose as to whether Christians should continue to observe the Torah. The question was settled at the Council (the very first) of Jerusalem.

The great questions, however, regarding Trinitarian matters (the 'consubstantiality' of the Logos with the Father, the divinity of the Holy Spirit) and later Christological matters (the one 'person' of Jesus Christ, his two 'natures' divine and human, his two 'wills') and other matters regarding discipline and cult (e.g. the veneration of images) were settled by the first eight Ecumenical Councils (from that of Nicea I held in 325 A.D. to that of Constantinople IV held in 870 A.D.). The teachings and decisions of these eight Councils are held today by all major Christian Churches. The so-called Nicene-Constantinople creed is professed by all of them. But this already resulted in Christian sects- some of which are still extant today- which rejected the decisions of one or other of the Councils.

But the first great schism occurred in the 11th century when the Eastern Churches broke away definitely from Rome. The cause was not a sudden one. It had been preceded by smaller and temporary tensions. The addition in the Creed of the 'Filioque', done in the West, had already been strongly objected to by the East. But that, today, seems to be of little importance compared to what is today the main – and perhaps only – cause of division between what has come down to be known as 'Roman Catholicism' and 'Orthodoxy': the former conceives of the Church as one Church with the Bishop of Rome as supreme Pastor and Teacher who enjoys full jurisdiction and the charisma of 'infallibility' – he being the Vicar of Jesus Christ and the successor of Peter – whereas the latter conceives of the Church more as a federation of autocephalous Churches (There are today fourteen such autocephalous Orthodox Churches with the Patriarch of Constantinople as the "first amongst equals").

12 In Christianity, "Tradition" acquires a theological meaning: the 'unwriten' faith handed down orally from generation to generation.

§42. The second greatest split occurred in the Western Church itself with the Reformation in the 16th century preached by Martin Luther, John Calvin and Ulrich Zwingli. The spark which started Luther seems to have been what he considered to be abuses in the Church in matter of doctrine and practice (e.g. the question of 'indulgences'). The Reformation itself was the beginning of the Church's splintering off further and further. Independently of the Reformation, the Church in England severed its communion with Rome in the time of Henry VIII and definitively in the time of Elizabeth I. During the course of the centuries such theological questions as the relation between the Scriptures and the Church, between 'faith' and 'works', between 'grace' and 'freedom' or the number of the sacraments, the way to explain the Eucharistic presence, etc. – not to mention such canonical questions as the celibacy of the clergy, or other questions regarding marriage and divorce, etc. – were causes of dissent and division. Today, however, the main cause of division seems to be more or less the same one which divides Orthodoxy from Roman Catholicism.

Under the name of 'Protestantism' one generally includes such Churches as the Lutheran, Calvinist (or Reformed), Anglican (or Episcopalian), Presbyterian, Baptist, Methodist and some others. These all retain the fundamental Christian Faith as we presented it at the beginning of this section on Christianity.

Other groups, however, because of their rejection of what the majority of Christians consider to belong to the Christian faith, can hardly be called 'Christian'. Among such groups, one could mention: the Quakers, the Mormons, the Adventists, Jehovah's Witness, Unitarians, the Salvation Army, etc.

§43. All religions had their times of persecutions. Put it was Christianity perhaps second only to Judaism, which was the most persecuted of all. The first three centuries of its history saw intermittent periods of persecution under the Roman Emperors (especially Nero, Decian and Diocletian). It was the 'age of martyrs'. Martyrdom, or the prospect of martyrdom, gave rise to a typical Christian spirituality: relinquishing all things, detaching oneself from all worldly concerns, giving up even one's life for and in union with Christ. The result of this is expressed in the hermetical life of the 'Desert Fathers' (mostly in Egypt). The fourth century saw Basil of Caesarea" and the fifth century Benedict of Nursia, the former in the East and the latter in the West, organizing the monastic life. Monastic life has greatly developed ever since and adapted itself to the different needs of the times (cf. the Cisterian Order, the Mendicant Friars, the Contemplative Orders, Apostolic Orders and Congregations, the Secular Institutes, etc.).

§44. All this flowered in great current of mystical life. Nearly every age and every county in the west as well as in the East. In the west, mystics express their experiences of the ineffability of God, their union with God though Christ in the spirit (pseudo-Dionysius, Augustine, Gregory of Nyssa, John of the Cross, Teresa of Avila, Ruysbreck, Eckhart, Catherin of Genoa, Catherine of Siena, and a host of others); in the East , they express their experience of 'theosis' or deification by grace (Gregory Palamas, Maximus the Confessor, Issac the Syrian, Simeon called the new 'theologian'John of the Ladder, and many others). The center of monastic life in the East is still the peninsula in Macedonia, Mount Athos, which in the 18th century published the *Philokalia*, a collection of the ascetical and mystical teachings of Eastern Orthodoxy from the 4th century to the 15th century. *Hesychasm* or 'the prayer of Jesus' method of prayer has had a great influence in the East.

§45. Nearly all religions gave rise to philosophical speculation and in most of them too Philosophical speculation remained subject to and in function of religious belief. Anselm of Canterbury (d.1109) is created with being the initiator of what later became to be known as Scholasticism, the philosophical movement in the Christianity of the Middle Ages. Scholasticism, however, is not the monolithic system it is sometimes thought to be. It attained its highest peak in Thomas of Aquinas, but the Augustinian trend, the Scotisttrend and later the Suarezian trend remained strong. Thomas Aquinas sought to show how many religious truths (e.g. the existence of God) are discoverable by discursive reason, even those religious truths which can be known, only through 'revelation' do not conflict with the principles of discursive reason. Thus he sought to distinguish, without separating, philosophical speculation and theological thought. It was only in the 16th century that, in the heart of Christianity, philosophical systems began to emerge either independently of, or even contrary to, the Christian faith – or, at least, to what was generally considered to be the Christian faith as philosophically explained:

§45. a. One striking phenomenon in Christianity today is the ecumenical movement. An ever-growing awareness of the essential unity of the "Christian Church is bringing Christians together. Efforts are made to overcome theological disagreements and to recapture that unity, in doctrine and practice, which marked the Christian Church at the time of the apostles. Already in the last century, federations of local Churches began to take place. The ecumenical movement resulted, in 1948, in the World Council of churches.[13]

On the part of the Catholic Church, the Ecumenical Council Vatican II certainly opened a new phase in the history of Christianity-not only by its ecumenical attitude but also by its opening religions of the world elongated -

4. ISLAM

§46. Muhammad was born In Mecca in the 6th century A.D. Orphaned at an early age, brought up by his paternal grandfather. Worked in the caravan trade for a widow Khadija, later married her and had four daughters. Spent time in solitary prayer. At the age of forty, he emerged as the prophet of a new revelation,

13 In 1947, the Church of South India came into being by the fusion of Anglicans, Presbyterians, congregations and Methodists.

a reformer of what he considered to be the polytheism of his time, the evil practices and the social injustices which surrounded him. That was in 612 A.D. For ten years, he suffered opposition from the religious leaders and the wealthy. In 622 A.D. he was invited to Medina to act as peace-maker among its warring inhabitants. He departs together with some of his converts among whom his wife and uncle. This *hijrah* ("departure") will mark year one of the Muslim era. At Medina he gradually assumes political and military control. In 630 A.D. (8 A.H.) he attacks Mecca, his native city, with an army of ten thousand men, breaks down the idols of the Kaaba, rebuilds the temple and into its foundation sets the same black stone which Arabs had kissed for centuries. Mecca remains the religious centre of Islam, but Muhammad returns to Medina his political capital. Arabian chieftains vow submission to him. He continues to send expeditions and to issue norms of conduct. In 632 A.D. (10 A.H.) he makes the pilgrimage to Mecca, along with forty-thousand people. The following year he dies in Medina of fever.

§47. Muhammad proclaimed the existence of One, and only of One God, whose name Allah had been known among the Arabs from ancient times but which had been buried, as it were, under the rabble of other deities. Allah is the absolute Lord, the Almighty Creator of all, Judge of all men, the Compassionate and the Merciful.

From the very beginning, Allah sent his prophets, starting from Adam (safi ullah, "the chosen of God"), Noah (nabi ullah, "the prophet of God") Abraham (khalil ullah, "the friend of God"), Ishmael (dhabi ullah, "the sacrifice of God"), Moses (kalim ullah, "the converser with God") down to Jesus (kalimat ullah, "the word of God"). He himself is the last and the seal of the prophets; he is rasul ullab, "the apostle of God". All these prophets, preached Islam or Submission to God. The Quran is the complete revelation made to Muhammad through the mediation of the Archangel Gabriel. The word literally means "recitation", but the book is believed to be not a new creation but the revelation of its archetype in Heaven, parts of which having been already revealed to the preceding prophets.

§48. It is then the duty of man to be submissive (muslim) to God and to worship only Him. Faith witness (shahada) – in one's heart, by oral profession and by the performance of the prescribed works- is the expression of this submission. The basic prescribed works, often referred to as "the pillars of Islam" are: frequent repetition of the kalima; daily prayer (salat), especially at daybreak, noon and at sunset; alms-giving (zakat); the fast (saum) during the month of Ramadan; and, if possible, a pilgrimage (hajj) to Mecca at least once in one's life-time.

§49. At the end of time, there will the resurrection of the dead, final judgment and eternal reward for the believers in Heaven and eternal damnation for the unbelievers.

§50. The definitive form of the Quran was settled thirty years after Muhammad's death – under Othman, the third Caliph. It is universally accepted by all Muslims as authentic. It is divided into one hundred fourteen surahs, arranged in order of length.

Along with the Quran – and of equal divine authority – is the Hadith (literally "tradition") or Sunna (literally, "the beaten track") which consists of saying and actions of Muhammad to serve as a complement to the Quran. By the 9th century A.D. (3rd. A.H.) six collections were critically edited by al-Bukhari, Muslim and four other men.

Orthodox Muslims also recognize igmah (community agreement) and gijas (the principle of analogy or comparison between a new situation with a similar one in the past) as authentic source of doctrine and practice.

§51. Although the idea or feeling of an Islamic 'community' (umma) is strong in Islam, faith (iman) and its practice (din) based on the Quran being the bond of unity, Islam is not an institutional and priestly community. For years, the religio-political authority was wielded by the Caliph. Learned scholars (ulama) now interpret the law.

§52. The greatest split in Islam occurred thirty years after Muhammad's death. The issue – a religio-political one – regarded the succession of Muhammad as head of the Muslim community. The majority maintained that the successor should be elected by popular acclaim. (The immediate successor of Muhammad was Abu Bakr, the father of Muhammad's favorite wife Aisha and one of his first three male converts. He had already had to quell rebellions but saved Islamic unity, Abu Bakr's successor was Umar, the leader of the great expansion of Islam, who after the two-year Caliphate of Abu Bakr, ruled for ten years before he was assassinated. The third Caliph was Utman (or Othman) who did not belong to the Hashimite tribe of Muhammad. After his assassination, Ali, Muhammad's cousin and son-in-law became Caliph. With his death and the abdication of his elder son Hasan, the rival tribe, the Umayyads, gave the Caliphate to Mu'awiya and later to his son. Husain, the second son of Ali was urged by supporters to seek the Caliphate the result of which was the massacre at Karbala. Islam remains divided till the present day into the "Sunnites" and the "Shiites", the former being the 'traditionalists', the latter being 'of the sect of Ali'.

§53. The Kharijites not only recognized the right of the community to elect its leader but also believed that the community can depose him if he is guilty of sin. They take their name from their fact of 'secession' from Ali's sect. This led to other important theological controversies. Who is the true Muslim? Who is to judge whether one is sinful? What is sin? Are human actions predestined by God or are they free? The Murjites as postponed judgment, since the dividing-line between Muslim and non-Muslim was known to God alone. But if the Kharjite-Murjite controversy was political in origin, the Jabarite-Qadarite controversy was more theological. For the Jabarites, 'jabr' or the over-ruling power belonged to God and hence human actions were predestined; for the latter, man possessed 'qadr' or power over his actions. The position favouring human freedom was taken up by the Mutazilites, with whom began the 'kalam', i.e., rational investigation into this or that tenet of belief. They represent the Rational movement in Islam, under the influence of Greek Philosophy when it was translated into Arabic and commented upon (cf. Avicenna, 11th cent., and Averroes, 12th cent.). They called themselves the people of "Unity and Justice" – of Unity because they argued that to hold the Quran as eternal and uncreated constituted 'shirk' (blasphemy associating an equal with God), and of Justice because they maintained that God must act in justice with man. Among other things, they attacked all anthropomorphism (tashbih) attributed to God and asserted that human reason is the ultimate criterion of truth. But the most important split remained that of the Sunnites and the Shiites (the latter gradually developed the doctrine of the "hidden Imam" or Mahdi, they celebrate the Muharram to commemorate the massacre at Karbala, have their own commentaries on the Quran known as Akhbar, replace 'igmah' and , 'gijas' by the authority of the Imam, some of them add to the 'shahada' the phrase "and Ali is the representative of Allah" while others tend to look on him and the succeeding Imams as incarnations of the Godhead. The Shiites gradually branched off into various sub-sects, the more important of which is the Imamiya (or "the Twelvers") and Isma'iliya which include the Bohras, the Khojas (followers of Aga Khan), etc.

§54. Islam has had its great mystics. Well-known is the mystical movement called Sufism (from 'sof', wool). Already from the 8th Century A.D. (2nd cent. A.H.) names like Hasan and Rabi'a, both of Basra become famous for their intense and pure love of God. Significant is the experience of 'fana' or 'annihilation in God' in Dhu'n Nun and Bistami (9th cent.) and others of the 'oneness of Being' (wahdat al-wujud) in Ibn'Arabi (13th cent.). Many sufists were exiled or, like al-Hallaj put to death for their seemingly pantheistic views. AI-Ghazzali (d. 1111 A.D.) is famous for his efforts to reconcile Sufism with Orthodoxy. In India, Sufism survives in the four 'fraternities' (khandan): chisti, suhrawardi, qadiri, naqshbandi, and other minor ones, the tombs of the founders of which are centers of pilgrimage (ziyarat).

5. HINDUISM

§55. Hinduism traces its origin to Vedic times. Vedic literature comprising the Samhitas (recited praises, chanted hymns, sacrificial formulae, magic charms), the brahmanas (descriptive and prescriptive commentaries on the ritual sacrifice), the Aranyakas (texts explaining the sacrifice in an internal and symbolic sense) and the Upanishads (teachings about the one, all-pervading, ineffable Brahman and the atman's identification with it- a realization in which moksha consists) are believed to be Sruti and the basis for further development. Acceptance or rejection of the Vedic Sruti marks what is 'Astika' or 'Nastika'. One generally dates the Vedas from 3000 B.C. to 600 A.D.

In view of the long history of development of Hinduism down to modern times, its various philosophies (darshanas), its religious sects, it is indeed difficult to speak of Hinduism in general without committing the error of over-generalization and undue simplification. Hence what follows is meant merely to be a kind of 'way of approach' to Hinduism as a whole.

Apart from Samkhya (which posits Purusha and Prakrti as ultimate co-principles), Purva Mimamsa (which posits the Veda as eternal and authorless and rejects Brahman), Hinduism can be said to be the experience of Brahman and of atman's oneness with Brahman. However, this 'oneness' is variously conceptualized as is the phenomenal world's relation to Brahman. Moksha consists, as said, in the realization of this atman-Brahman oneness, or in other words, in liberation from avidya and punar-janma caused by karman. Final deliverance is assured (only denied in the dvaitic conception of Brahman-atman, see below). Brahman is nirguna – is saccidananda – but as Ishwara he is saguna. From time to time he appears in the avatara (the more important are Krishna and Rama) "for the protection of the good, the destruction of evil-doers and the re-establishment of dharma." There are different margas to moksha: karma-marga, bhakti-marga, hatha-marga, raja-marga and jnana-marga. Theoretically at least, the ideal life passes through the four ashramas,

Authoritative "traditional" literature (smrti) comprise: sutras (especially, srauta, gryha and dharmasutras); itihas, i.e., the Mahabharata which includes the Bhagavadgita and the Ramayana; the darsanas (samkhya-yoga, nyaya-vaisesika, purva and uttara mimamsa. These date from 600 B.C. to 300 A.D. Then there are the Puranas, the Agamas, etc., covering the period between 300 A.D. till end of the first millennium A.D. Tradition considers the Vedantasutra of Badarayana and especially the Bhagavadgita nearly as sruti.

Religiously speaking, the three main 'sects' in Hinduism are the Vaisnavites, the Saivites and the Saktas. Each has its own Scriptures alongside the Vedas (the pancharatra samhita, the agamas and the tantra); reveres its saints and treasures their mystical teachings (Alvars and Marathi saints, the Adiyars or Saivite saints); has its own system or systems of philosophy (the Vedanta, Saiva Siddhanta, and the Tantric Kaula, Samaya and Mishra) favors its own cult, religious practices, etc.

More interestingly still – from our point of view – is to observe what we have in our General Introduction called 'theological splits'. We have already referred to the earlier darshanas. But even in Vedanta, the Brahman-atman relationship is variously conceived and explained (cf. Shanksra's advaita, Ramanuja's visistadvaita, Madhva's dvaita, Vallabha's suddhadvaita, Nimbarka's dvaidadvaita).

§56. An interesting phenomenon which we observe too in Hinduism down to today is the apparent lag between 'popular' Hinduism and the highly 'speculative' Hinduism of the University or academic world. Hinduism retains many elements of what we shall later call 'primeval' religion dating back to puranic times and even further back – to such an extent that some observers speak of an 'outer' and of an 'inner' Hinduism (the former indicating the 'idol' worship, henotheistic attitude, magical beliefs, taboos, apparent superstitions, etc.; the latter referring to the more interiorized, spiritual and contemplative aspects of Hinduisms).

§57. During the Muslim period (1200-1757 A.D.), we notice the appearance of many saintly men and the emergence of vernacular religious literature. In the North, Ramananda propagates the devotion to Rama and Tulsidas translates the Ramayana in Hindi. In Bengal, Caitanya spreads devotion to Krishna-Radha. In Maharashtra, Tukaram, Ramadasa sing their love to Vishnu (under the name of Vitobha) as does Mira Bai to Krishna in Rajputana, etc.

§58. This time too, saw the emergence of Sikhism founded by Guru Nanak (1469-1539). Like Kabir before him, Nanak, a family-man and an ascetic, felt the underlying unity between Islamic intransigent monotheism and the apparent polytheism of Hinduism, emphasized the worship and service of God over and against external ritualism and pilgrimages and preached brotherhood among Muslims and Hindus. He was succeeded by ten Gurus. The Sacred Scriptures of the Sikh religion is the *Adi Granth*, compiled by the fifth Guru Arjun (16th cent.) – to be distinguished from the *Dasam Granth* ("tenth scripture" compiled after the last Guru) – and consist in the sayings and writings of the Gurus, of Moslem (notably Kabir) and Hindu ascetics and other men who accompanied the Gurus on their journeys.

The main symbol of worship in Sikkhism is the Adi Granth itself. On important feast-days, a ceremony of non-stop reading is performed by relays of worshippers (known as the Akhand Path).

§59. Originally very pacificist, the Sikhs found themselves obliged to form themselves into a military group to defend themselves against attackers. Today both as a religious tradition and in their customs, they are clearly distinguishable from the rest. (They wear the five K's: 'kes' or long hair on head and chin, 'kungha' or comb, 'kuchha' or short drawers, 'kara' or steel bracelet and the 'kirpan' or steel dagger. They abstain from smoking and alcoholic beverages, etc.). But, of course, more important are the typically Sikh religious rites: children are given names which begin with the first letter of the page at which the Granth happens to be opened; youths are initiated in the religion by drinking sweetened water out of a common bowl (sign of casteless brotherhood), couples are married to the singing of hymns from the same book while they walk around it four times; at the point of death, hymns are read aloud in the dying person's ears and chanted as the flames consume the corpse.

§60. The end of the last century and the beginning of the twentieth witnessed a Hindu religious revival. Ramakrishna and his spiritual and social-movement, led by Vivekananda, is an outstanding example; One cannot fail to mention Sri Ramana Maharishi. One cannot help noticing in such swamis, a breath of vision

– which to some may appear to be a syncretistic attitude – a symbiosis of bhakti and jnana, of popular piety and deep contemplation. One can also mention Ram Mohan Roy, founder of Brahma-samaj which reacted against what it considered idolatry and polytheism and began the movement against such social customs as 'sati', enforced widowhood, polygamy, caste-system, etc. Now it is internally divided and enfeebled. Similarly, Dr. Atmaram Pandunang founded the Prarthana Samaj to foment religious life and work for social reform.

Hinduism began to be better known to the West through the activities and writings of Tagore, Aurobindo, Radhakrishnan, etc.

§60. a. Hinduism has been not only be 'matrix' of Jainism and Buddhism, as we are going to see, but also a constant source of influence on these religions even when these religions, now independent religious traditions, spread as far away as Tibet, China and Japan.

Hinduism as such was never – unlike Buddhism and Islam – a 'missionary' religion. It has been only relatively recently that Hindu swamis thought of travelling to Europe and America to spread their religion. But in India itself, we cannot fail noticing the influence of Hinduism on the Indian Christian Church itself…

6. JAINISM

§61. Jainism, like Buddhism, can perhaps be better understood in the context of Hinduism to which, in most respects, it is a reaction. It is a reaction against the authority of the Vedas, the Vedic deities and the upanishadic Brahman, as well as against the sacrificial and brahminical ritualism and the caste-system. But Jainism retains the Hindu fundamental beliefs in karman, samsara and moksha – even though it interprets and explains them in its own way.

§62. Vardhamana Mahavira (5th century B.C.) not only was a contemporary of Buddha, but like him, is reported to have been a prince (or son of a wealthy tribal leader), left home to become an ascetic, obtained enlightenment after years of fasting and meditation, soon gathered disciples and died in his seventies. In Buddhist texts, he is referred to as Nataputta (against whose disciples Buddhists raise a lively controversy).

§63. Jainism interprets *karman* as the hold of the body and matter on the individual 'jiva'. 'Jivas' are uncreated and eternal. So also is 'ajiva' (matter, motion, rest and space). Because of evil actions, subtle material particles 'bind' the jiva, burden it and weigh it down. This accumulated matter remains in the jiva throughout its cycle of births and deaths (samsara). What distinguishes the higher from the lower forms of life is the amount of matter. The way to liberate the jiva from its bondage is austerities (tapas) – both spiritual (meditation, reverence to spiritual masters, faith, confession of one's sins to the guru or sadhu) and corporeal (fasting- even unto death – bodily mortifications, rigid control of the senses).

Mahavira (or jina, the 'great hero' or 'victor') is the last of twenty-four tirthankaras ("ford-builders"). Their lives and teachings serve as a guiding influence on the believers. Liberation, achieved solely through one's own efforts, is the attainment of nirvana, a perfect and freed state consisting in infinite perception, omniscience and omnipotence, and eternal bliss: it is a state of "godhead".

§64. To attain liberation, the jiva has to pass through fourteen steps of purification (gunasthanas), after the fifth of which, man becomes a sadhu, after the thirteenth, a tirthankara, and finally a siddha. The sadhu makes five great vows (mahavrata); ahimsa – the virtue which with daya (compassion) is perhaps the greatest virtue insisted upon in Jainism – truthfulness, honesty, chastity and poverty. Safeguards, as well as restraints (guptis) are prescribed: restraints of the mind, of speech and of bodily movements. Ten principal duties (dharmas) are enjoined on the sadhu, and to a lesser extent, on the layman too: control of anger, forgiveness, humility, simplicity in word and deed, detachment, etc. Thus knowledge, faith and good conduct are considered to be the "three jewels" of Jainism.

§65. It is perhaps in the matter of cult that Jainism underwent certain developments which seem to some to be contrary to the original teachings of Mahavira. Temples, worship of ancient Vedic deities, prayer to Mahavira and the other tirthankaras, festivals, found their way into Jainism. The educated Jain, however, would find that prayer useful psychologically.

§66. Jainism remained a well-organized community with its four orders (tirthas) and presents a more homogenous front that does Buddhism. The principal split occurred around 80 A.D. The Swetambaras ("white clad") differed from the Digambaras ("sky-clad") in that the latter maintained that the monk should renounce to all property and even go naked, whereas the former, though believing that is theoretically true, looked on nudity as no longer possibility because of the "degeneration of the world". Other points of difference regard the Digambaras' insistence that images of the tirthankaras should be represented with downcast eyes and naked, their belief that Mahavira was celibate, that once liberation is attained (jivanmukti), one should go entirely without food or drink, that women cannot attain liberation before they are born as man and should not be accepted as nuns. Another important point of difference regards the Scriptures.

As a rule, Jains are nirgrant has ("people without a book"). The Digambaras maintain that the original books containing the teachings of Mahavira were destroyed. They recognize however as authoritative for their sect the works of certain patriarchs (second to ninth century A.D.). The Swetambaras adhere to a biblical canon, called the Agamas (or Siddhanta), established about a hundred years after the death of Mahavira by the Council held at Patali-Putra (today Patna) and given final Shape in the fifth century A.D.

§67. During the course of time, very full commentaries and Independent treatises were written. The *Tattvavarthadhigamasutra* is considered extremely authoritative by both sects. Meaning literally the "aphorisms to attain knowledge of the truths", it is a systematic treatise about the seven fundamental truths of Jainism: jiva, ajiva, asrava ("afflux" of matter into the jiva), bandha, samvara ("halting" of the afflux of matter) nirjara ("elimination" of accumulated matter), moksha. It was commented upon by Umasvati (3rd cent. A.D.) and is recognised by both sects. Siddhasena Divakara (7th cent.), Haribhadra (8th cent.), Hemachandra (12th cent.) and Mallisena (13th cent.) are worthy of special mention.

Characteristically Jain is the philosophical conception of being as indeterninate (anekantavada) because of which it is possible to pass many judgements on any one object, all of which are true but only partial true – and therefore relative (syadvada). Since the senses and reason cannot overcome the limits of materiality, only the transmission of absolute knowledge guarantees the simultaneous comprehension of "all points of view" (naya). This cannot help reminding one of the Buddhist madhyamika and the religious import of both to overcome discursive thought in pursuit of religious meta-discursive insight...

7. BUDDHISM

§68. We have already remarked that Buddhism, like Jainism, can be better understood in the context of Hinduism. Buddhism, like Jainism, is, fundamentally, the same kind of reaction to Hinduism as Jainism is. Both Buddhism and Jainism react to the same aspects of Hinduism, and both retain some fundamental Hindu beliefs (like karman, samsara, moksha). But here Buddhism differs as much from Jainism as it does from Hinduism, Besides, Buddhism, as we shall soon see, underwent certain developments unknown to Jainism.

§69. We have also referred to a certain parallelism in the life of Mahavira and Buddha. Mahavira (the 'great hero") and Buddha (the "enlightened") are titles given them by posterity. Interesting also from a religious phenomenological point of view is the fact that the lives of both were later described in Jain and Buddhist scriptures respectively as replete with extraordinary, 'supernatural' events. The real name of Buddha was Siddhartha Gautama (called also Sakya Muni from his clan). He was, as we said a contemporary of Mahavira.

§70. The originary teaching of Buddha can be best summarized in the arya-satya ("noble truths'): all phenomenal existence is dukkha (sorrow): suffering is caused - and caused by 'craving'; there is a cessation of suffering – which is brought about by the suppression of craving; there is a way which leads to this cessation of suffering. This way is the Noble Eight-fold path: right view, right resolve, right speech, right action, right living, right effort, right thought, right concentration (samadhi). It can be resumed as: right conduct (shila), right concentration, and wisdom (prajna). Buddha calls it *madhyama pratipat* or 'middle path' in that, doctrinally it stirs midway between eternalism and nihilism, and practically, between self-indulgence and undue self-mortification. Buddha also identifies it with Dharma (the "Law").

Buddhism explains samsara by its doctrine of *pratityasamutpada* ("the causal wheel of dependent origination). The primordial cause of suffering is avidya (ignorance) which causes karmic forces which, in their turn, cause initial consciousness. This causes the psycho-physical organism which, in its turn, causes the six sense-organs. These cause sense-object-contact which causes sense-experience which causes thirst for sense-enjoyment (trsna). This thirst causes clinging to such an enjoyment, which causes the will-to-be-born which, in its turn, causes birth (or re-birth) which, finally, causes old age and death.

§71. Earlier Buddhism further explained the theories of *ksanabhangavada* (momentariness) or of the impermanent nature and uncaused perpetual flux of all things. All things are the agglomeration of the five skandhas, or aggregates, namely: matter (i.e. momentary atoms of earth, water, fire and air), feeling, perception, disposition and consciousness. Hence it denied the upanishadic 'atman'. Freedom from samsara is nirvana or the "blowing out" of this agglomeration. If it is spoken in terms of bliss, this is to be understood in a negative sense (that is as non-suffering). Gautama Buddha was only a man whose mission it was to teach the dharma leading to bodhi ("enlightenment", or awakening, realization). The ideal for man is the *arhat,* the one who is thus enlightened.

§72. The Scriptures of earlier Buddhism is the Tipitaka ("the three baskets") written in Pali. It is divided into three parts: the Vinaya (discipline of the samgha or the Order of monks), the Sutta (teachings of the Buddha, stories about his life, etc.) and the Abhidamma (doctrinal speculation). The present canon was probably compiled by the Third Buddhist Council at Pataliputra, in the 3rd century B.C.

The non-canonical scriptures (what we have called 'tradition') is vast. It includes such works as Milinda-Panho, Dipavamsa, Mahavamsa, Visuddhi-magga and commentaries on the Tipitaka (all written in Pali).

§73. The first split occurred a century after Buddha's death. The original issue was, a question of interpretation of the vinaya. It resulted into the split between the*sthaviravadins* and the *mahasanghikas*. The former counted elven schools of philosophy, the latter nine. Of all these, the most important are the *Sarvastivada* and the *Sautantrika* schools.

§74. By the beginning of the Christian era, a movement began to let its presence strongly felt – a movement which finally divided Buddhism into two clearly distinguished religious traditions: *Theravada and Mahayana*. Calling themselves "the big Vehicle" (as contrasted to the Hinayana or "small vehicle"), these Buddhists, tracing their doctrine to the Buddha whom, they claimed, the hinayanists had misunderstood, developed their doctrine in *bhutatahata* ("suchness") as the ultimate principle of existence. It is sunyata ("Vacuity") as it is ineffable and transcends all particular forms and concepts, but is called by different names according to the different phases of its manifestations. Hence it is dharma as norm of existence; it is bodhi as enlightenment; it is nirvana as a state of bliss attained after egoism has been overcome; it is *paramartha* or the highest Truth;it is *bhutakoti* or the essence of being; it is *tathata*, reality itself or *tathatagarbha* or the womb of life and existence, etc.

There also developed the doctrine of the Buddha's *trikaya* (three bodies). Gautama is the *nirmanakaya* or "assumed body" or phenomenal aspect of the Buddha; Buddha's "blissful body" is the *sambhogakaya*, his manifestation to Himself and to the elect; his "cosmic body" is the *dharmakaya*, the *Tathagata* or Absolute Itself.

The ascetic ideal becomes the *boddhisattva* who enlightened though he be, defers his final entry into nirvana to help others achieve enlightenment, thus sharing in the Buddha's *mahakaruna* ("great compassion") and maitri ("love"). It is thus easy to understand how hundreds of buddhas and buddhisattvas soon peopled the Mahayana 'heaven' (the four principal ones being: *Sakyamuni, Amitabha, Maitreya, Avalokitesvara*).

§75. The Mahayana Scriptures are Mahayanasutras (which include: *Sadharma-pundarika* or "The Lotus of the Wonderful Law", *Prajna-Paramita* or the perfect Wisdom", etc.)

Non-canonical but authoritative literature is immense. The two principal philosophical schools are *Shunyavada* (Aahvagosha, Nagarjuna, etc.) famous for its doctrine of reality as 'sunya' and for its madyamika dialectics, and Vijnavada (Asaga, Vasubandhu, etc.), known also as Yogachara, which speaks of reality as 'consciousnesses'.

§76. A "third Vehicle" is also spoken of – namely Mantryana (the "Vehicle of the mantra"), known also by many other names, such as *vajarayana* (the "Vehicle of the Diamond"). It is Tantric Buddhism and where, it is reasonable to suppose, the perduring influence of Hinduism on Buddhism is most apparent. It made its appearance in the 7th century A.D. It lays stress on rites, on the recitation of mantras. It developed its own esoteric practices, etc. It has its own Scriptures. Its amalgamation with Tibetan religion gave rise to its Lamaism (8th century). A characteristic of Lamaism is the belief that the Dalai Lama (the great Teacher) is the Nirmanakaya of Budha Avalokita, and that it is possible to determine – by highly intricate calculations – his successor who would have been conceived forty nine days after the predecessor's death. Similarly, the Panchen Lama is the Nirmanakaya of Buddha Amitabha. Philosophically, however, Mantrayana is Mahayanist, particularly vijnavadin.

§77. Theravada Buddhism spread to the South Eastern Countries (Ceylon, Thailand, Burma), whereas Mahayana Buddhism spread to the North Eastern ones (first to China and then to Korea and Japan). In India, Buddhism reached its Zenith under Ashoka (3rd century B.C.) but by the 10-11th century, it all but disappeared.

Besides the classical philosophical schools (e.g. the San-Lun which is Madhyamika and Fa-hsiang which is Vijanavada) we find in China and later in Japan, comprehensive philosophical schools based on one or other of the sutras (the most important of which is Tien-tai or Tendai in Japanese). More noteworthy, however, are Tsing-tu (Japanese Jodo) or the 'Pure land' set which is the Chinese and Buddhist bhakti. Devotion to *O-mito-fu* (Japanese Amida)- the Indian Amitabha - plays a central and basic role. It is pietist, stresses faith, requires reliance on the Scriptures. In China it was founded by Tan-Luan in the 5th Century A.D. but did not find its way to Japan before the 12th century when it was introduced into the country by Honen. An interesting development was due to Honen's disciple, Shinran, who acting on a divine inspiration, left the monkhood to spread Jodo among the lay people. Thus, Jodoshinshu ("The True Pure Land" sect) made its beginning.

§78. By way of contrast to Jodo, Chan (Japanese Zen) – from Sanskrit 'dhyan' – is meditative, stresses insight, and requires reliance on the guidance of the master (roshi). The Indian Bodhidharma is credited with having introduced Chan into China, in the 6th century A.D. – Chan branched off into two sects. In Japan, they are called Rinzai, began by Eisai in the 12th century (it is the Zen made known to the West by D.T. Suzuki) and Soto, began by Dogen in the following' century (which in fact is the more popular and more numerous).

Both Rinzai and Soto lead the adept to satori (enlightenment) but they differ in many respects. Rinzai practices the use of koans ("riddles") to empty the mind of thoughts and discursive thinking; Soto scorns their use and favours instead one's sitting in the faith that one is Buddha and observing objectively such thoughts as may pass through the mind. Rinzai does not rely on any Scriptures whatsoever; Soto does the same except for the teachings of Dogen, its first patriarch. Soto, unlike Rinzai, uses prayers for worldly blessings and looks on its first patriarch as a Boddhi-sattva.

§79. Tantric Buddhism also found its way to China and Japan. In China, it was introduced by three Indian missionaries in the 8th century and in Japan by Kobo Daichi, the following century. In China, it is called Chen-Yen, whereas in Japan it is called Shingon ("True Word"). Shingon is famous for its attempt to amalgamate Buddhism with Shintoism as we shall see later. Buddha Vairocana is the Absolute but is manifested in Buddhas, Boddhisattvas, devatas, animate and inanimate things. Purificatory rites include: confession of sins, taking refuge in the 'Triple Jewel', preaching the Dharma, application of merit for the benefit of others. The use of mantras is central.

These different schools and sects have always been, on the whole, tolerant of one another. In Japan, one notable exception to the rule is Nichiren (named after its founder in the 13th cent.). For him, salvation consisted, and consisted only, in faith in the Lotus Sutra, to be expressed in the formula 'Namu Myoho Rengekyo'. He was particularly violent against Jodo and Zen. The Soka Gakkai in Japan of today pushes its intolerance to extremes.

§79. a. Buddhism in China and Japan has had a long history and many vicissitudes. Sometimes it was favoured, sometimes it was banned – depending on the favour or disfavour of the Emperor. But how it could accommodate itself to the local religions, permeate them and, to a large extent, absorb them, will be better understood when we shall have given a close lock to these ancient Chinese and Japanese religions, particularly Confucianism and Taoism in China, and Shintoism in Japan.

Since the Communist take-over in China, Buddhism in that country, like all other religions is, presumably, suppressed. But, it seems, its thousands of temples and monasteries have been preserved as cultural monuments. In fact, Buddhism has been a great source of inspiration in all the artistic fields (architecture, painting, sculpture, etc.), and it is still too early to say to what extent the Chinese Buddhist spirit has been extinguished. Though Buddhism never became the official State religion in either China or Japan, it's nearly two-thousand-year history in these countries must have surely left its indelible mark on the spirit of the people. In Japan, Buddhism is very much alive. As we shall see later, Buddhism remains the chief source of inspiration for the so-called 'new religions' in Japan of today.

8. CONFUCIANISM

§80. Confucius (Latinized form of Kung-futzu) lived in the 6th century B.C. Born in the state of Lu (now Shantung province of China), he is said to have been dedicated himself from a very early age to study of ancient Chinese religion end ceremonies. Soon he acquired a reputation for learning and disciples flocked around him. First as secretary of justice and then as Prime Minister of the state of Chou, he labored to put his religious, moral, social and political ideals into practice. Failing in this, he quit and for the next fourteen years he travelled with disciples to different states. At the age of sixty-eight, he returned to his native state and spent the remaining years of his life teaching and editing the classics. He is said to have died at the age of seventy-two and to have been buried in Lu (the present city of Chufu).

§81. Confucius' saying that he was "no originator but a transmitter, a believer in and admirer of antiquity" is often quoted. It is clear that he felt his mission in life to recall his contemporaries to the 'golden past' of their history where perfect harmony (cheng) between man and man, subjects and Emperor reigned supreme. 'Cheng' is also the Tao, the way of the natural law governing the universe. It is Tien Ming or "the Will of Heaven". It is true 'Heaven' is more often spoken of in impersonal terms, but it is also identified with Shang-Ti (the Supreme Ruler, called also Tien-Ti or Heavenly Ancestor).

According to Confucius, the 'four cardinal virtues' (wu chang) which must permeate all human inter-relationships are: jen (goodness, benevolence, humaneness, requiring insight in and sympathy for the other's nature and needs); yi (justice, righteousness, formulated in the 'golden principle': "never do to others what you do not like them do to you"); li (a sense of propriety – which has a wide range of meanings, like good manners, correct observance of rites and ceremonies, modesty, a sense of decency); chih (wisdom, the ability to distinguish between right and wrong). To these some Confucianists add a fifth: hsin (good faith, truthfulness, loyalty) but others include it in yi.

The basic human inter-relationships are five (wu lun): that between father and son – and hence filial piety (hsiao) is the model relation on which all other relationships are to be patterned; between husband and wife; between an older and a younger brother; between friend and friend and between ruler and subject. With these as basic, all other human inter-relationships can be founded.

§82. The Scriptures of Confucianism are known as "The Five Classics and Four Books" (Wu Ching and Si Shu). The Wu Ching are the ancient Chinese Classics which Confucius edited. They are: Shih Ching or Book of Odes, a collection of song and sacred hymns; Li Chi or Book of Rites, a record of government system and rituals of the early Chou dynasty; Shu Ching or Book of History, containing chiefly kings' proclamations; "Chun Chiu" or "Annals of Spring and Autumn", a chronicle of events based on the history of the state of Lu (and which is the only work attributed to Confucius) and I Ching or Book of Changes, expounding a philosophy of mutations in human events, originally a system of divination based on changing arrangements of the lines of an octogram but which developed into a full philosophy for human conduct in varying circumstances. (A sixth classic, Yueh Ching or Book of Music, has been entirely lost). – The Si Shu or Four Books are: Ta Hsueh or "The Great Learning", Chung Yung or "The Golden Mean", originally two chapters from the Book of Rites but later developed into two independent books expounding the teachings of Confucius; Lun Yu or "Analects of Confucius" consisting of the master's saying collected by disciples and which is the most popular of all; and finally Meng-chi or "The Book of Meng", Meng or Mencius being the most effective spokesman of Confucianism and whom Chinese regard as the "second sage".

§83. It was only 300 years after Confucius' death, that Confucianism became the official creed of China - which in the meantime had been united and become an Empire. The Classics became the principal study of scholars and statesmen. By the sixth century A.D. a sacrifice, second only to that offered to Shang-Ti, was offered to Confucius. By the beginning of the eleventh century, Confucius was officially declared "the Sagest of Sages" and by the beginning of the twentieth, he was given equal rank with the highest 'ancestors'.

§84. It is often pointed out that Confucianism is a 'this-worldly' religion, that Confucius was skeptical, or at least uninterested in the 'spirits' revered by the ancients and by his own contemporaries, that he was concerned not with any 'after-life', but with the ethical, social and political reform of his times. The 'silence' of Confucianism on 'other-worldly' matters could be compared to the silence (or alleged silence) of the Buddha about 'meta-physical' questions. (An example of this, the answer of Confucius to a question regarding the state of the dead, is often quoted; "Till you know about the living, how are you to know about the dead."*Analects*, 11, 11).

Apart from the fact that such and similar answers can be differently interpreted and the fact too that the Analects often refer to Tien, one must never forget that Confucius edited the Classics and encouraged people to study and put them in practice. Besides, and above all, this is already to pre-judge the question what 'religion' is – something which we have to reflect upon in the philosophical part of our study.

And it is a fact that Confucianists continued to revere the ancient 'deities' especially the Sky, the Earth, the Sun and the Moon. Sacrifice to Shang-Ti was offered by the Emperor (called by the title of "the Son of Heaven"), and by him alone, on specific times during the year. Ancestor cult, so typically Chinese (recall the famous question regarding the 'Chinese rites') remained one of the mainstays of Confucianism. Numerous temples continued to be built, animal and food offerings made. (Temple functions wore performed by regular Government officials. Feng-shui or fear of offending the 'spirits', continued to be a potent factor in the consciousness of the people.

§85. The chief counter religious movements in China have been Taoism (of which we shall soon speak) and Buddhism (introduced into China, as we have seen, by the first century A.D.) till the three, not before periods of struggle, came to be recognized as "the Three Jewels of China", each religion influencing greatly the others.

But there were other rivalries causing splits within the mainstream of Confucianism. Motzu (or Moti) reacted against what he thought to be an exaggerated ceremonialism inherent in Confucianism and emphasized instead universal love. One of the two most controverted issues in Confucianism regarded survival after death. Wang-Chung (1st cent. A.D.) subscribed to a whole-hearted fatalism. The other question regarded whether human nature was essentially good or essentially evil. Confucius and Mencius had taught that it was essentially good. Hsuntzu (4th cent. B.C.) taught that it was essentially evil. Yang Hsiung (1st cent. A.D.) and Han Yu (8th cent. A.D.) attempted compromise positions.

§86. *Neo-Confucianism* is the name given to a movement initiated by Cheng Yi (11th cent. A.D.) and especially by Chu Hsi (12th cent.) which gave a philosophical interpretation to Confucianism teachings. The basic position is that Tao is the Ultimate Reality and Yang-Yin, the active- passive dual principle forms – the material reality. Man's nature (li) is a part of the Ultimate Reality, but his substance (chi) is material. The aim of moral improvement is to recapture one's nature. Chu Hsi drew heavily on the Classics which he amply commented – but it is clear that he was greatly influenced by Taoist and Buddhist teachings. His commentaries on the Classics were compulsory reading in government schools till the beginning of present century. Neo-confucianist schools differed particularly with regard to the meaning of Ko-Wuh ("investigation of things"), some interpreting it more in terms of reason, scientific exploration, others more in terms of insight, contemplative meditation.

§87. What we said about Buddhism in China after the Communist take-over, applies equally, If not more to Confucianism. Recently, an anti-confusianist propaganda flared up. This is easy to understand: certain aspects of Confucianism (e.g. appeal to tradition, idealizing an imperial structure of society, etc.) do not accord with a revolutionary, communist spirit.

9. TAOISM

§88. Taoism is a name used to cover several religious movements running parallel to, and often against, Confucianism. It was not earlier than the second century B.C. that some of these movements converged to give rise to what we today can call by that name. Still, Taoism can be traced to Lao-tzu, Lieh-tzu (contemporaries of Confucius) and Chuang-tzu (4th century B.C., the Mencius of Taoism). The famous book Tao-Teh-Ching ("The Book of Tao and Teh") is often ascribed to Lao-tzu.

§89. Taoism can perhaps be best understood in its confrontation with Confucianism. Both seek to live the Tao, but whereas Confucianism looks to the historical past as the Ideal, stresses moral, social and political harmony and is chiefly, even if not exclusively, concerned with 'this-worldly' welfare, Taoism looks for its Ideal in a pre-historical past when man was immersed in the 'totality of being', stresses spiritual, individual and contemplative harmony and is greatly concerned with immortality.

§90. Taoism then seeks harmony with the Tao. To achieve it, it is not so much action which is required, but, on the contrary, wu-wei ("non-action"), a kind of letting oneself be – in accordance with one's nature, in spontaneity, simplicity of life, and in the vital rhythm of the natural order of things. Man's main task in life is therefore to know the Tao. The Tao is indeed ineffable and invisible, but it is, at the same time, the origin of everything that has a name and a form. As such it cannot be 'being', it can only be described as 'emptiness'. But it is also that 'oneness' which explains multiplicity. From It sprang heaven and earth and therefore It is "the progenitor of all things in the world". Through Its Teh (often translated as 'power'), It is all-pervading. In Itself, it is weak and humble, but through Its Teh, it is strong and active. In Itself, it is restful and at peace, but through Its Teh, it is creative and governs all things.

To know the Tao, and to live in harmony with It, the 'good man' must forsake all activism, retire within himself, act naturally and give himself to thinking and meditation. He must let things follow their course, shun artificialities in learning, social relationship and general conduct. Only by reflecting the Tao in oneself, can one find peace and contentment, only thus can the State be rid of war and even of the very need of a governmental system.

§91. Though the Tao is beyond 'being' and 'cognition', it is apprehended in its first emanation, namely the "One". This "One" is the first and greatest 'deity' in Taoism. Throughout the years, it was called by different names, for example, Yu-Huang (the "Pure August"), or, more commonly, Tien-Shih (the "Celestial Master"). From this "One", other emanations or 'deities' followed. All these were given due worship and gradually a priestly system developed.

§92. The Tao-Teh Ching, mentioned already, and the Chuang-Tzu Chintz; (*The Book of Chuang-Tzu*) can be rightly considered to be basic texts of Taoism. It was only as late as the 15th century A.D. that the Tao-Tsang was compiled. It is patterned on the Buddhist Tipitaka and contains about 1,500 works. It is divided into: a first section which deal with the 'jade purity' of the saints; a second section dealing with the 'highest purity' of those who are really united with the Tao; and a third section dealing with the 'greatest purity' of the Immortals.

§93. Taoism, like Confucianism, underwent many vicissitudes in Chinese history, till it became, as we mentioned earlier, one of the "Three Jewels" of China. Lao-tzu, like Confucius, ended up by being given the highest religious honors.

It can easily be understood how Taoism proved to be a rival, for long years to Confucianism on the one hand, and how it could absorb so many Buddhist elements on the other. It survived more as a spirit permeating many different sects rather than a well-knit religious tradition.

Some sects sought immortality, conceived as a prolongation of life in a subtler body on blessed islands presided over by deities, by means of drugs, herbs and breathing exercises; others by merits obtained through the performance of good deeds. (Lu Tung Pin, 8th century A.D. is an outstanding figure for his cataloguing merits and demerits).

Sects whose monks practiced a Buddhist-like asceticism (e.g. the Chuan-chen sector or "Perfecting the True" sect) flourished side by side with esoteric sects well-known for their magic, sorcery, and orgiastic practices (e.g. the Tien-shih Tao or "Taoism of Celestial Master").

Bhakti Taoism found expression in the worship of Yu-huang ("Pure August") the equivalent of O-mito-fu of Tsing-tu Buddhism.

§94. At the beginning of this century, there developed two sects worthy of note. The I-Kuan Tao ("Pervading Unity Tao") believed in the "One" as the root of all things and which penetrates and permeates all existence. Cosmic periods of prosperity and calamity follow one another. Men are saved by Wu-sheng Lao-mu or the "Old Mother transcending Life". During World War II,it was very active in North China. The Tao-teh Shah (The Society of Tao and Teh) called also Tao Yuan or "The Hall of the Tao", believed in Tai-i or "The Greatest One". Its central building consisted of five halls for worship, scripture reading, meditation, preaching and performing acts of charity. It preached a kind of community between heaven and man in matters of the spirit and a human world brotherhood. In the Temple, are placed symbols not only of Confucianism and Buddhism but also of Islam and Christianity.

95. If we are to believe some reports, Taoism has been granted official recognition under the Communist regime. The China Taoist Association was officially founded in 1957. Temples are being rebuilt (The esoteric sects – which, in any case, were mostly underground – have been suppressed). The aims of the Association are to promote the Taoist tradition, help the Government in the Socialist reconstruction of the country, take part in the country's movement for world peace, etc.

In any case, the Taoist love and beauty of Nature without and within man, the effort to bring harmony between the two, the cultivation of the best ethical qualities in man, the peaceful life of the Temple and the quiet struggle for self-purification and union with the Tao, are Surely in consonance—with the Chinese spirit.

10. SHINTOISM

§96. The word 'Shinto' is the Chinese rendering of the Japanese Kami-no- michi ("the Way of the Kami"), used especially in the 6th-7th century A.D. to distinguish the local Japanese religion from 'Batsudo'("the Way of the Buddha").

The Kami are 'powers' spoken of in personal or impersonal terms, dreaded or revered according to whether they are good and benevolent or bad and malignant. Their number is said to be myriads. At first, there was an initial chaos, then the sky and the earth became differentiated. From a white cloud between them, there first emerged Kunitokotachi no Mikoto (the "One Who Established the Eternal Land") or 'mid-Sky Master' who produced 'High Producer' and 'Divine Producer', the three together called "the Three Creator Kami". In subsequent lineage two 'Kami' stand out for their special importance: Izanagi (the "Male Who Invites") and Izanagi (the "Female Who Invites"). After his sister's death, Izanagi followed her to the Land of Darkness to look for her, but was repelled by the dirt and pollution he found there. On washing his left eye, he produced

Amaterasu Omikami, the Sun Goddess; on washing his right eye, he produced Tsukiyomi no Mikoto, the Moon God and on washing his nose, he produced Susanoo no Mikoto, the God of the Withering Wind of Summer.

§97. Gradually, Shinto cult concentrated in the worship of Amaterasu to whom the Mikados, the Emperors of Japan, traced their lineage till the Second World War. She is venerated at the famous temple at Ise, a center of national pilgrimage. Every twenty years, the temple is demolished and another one, patterned exactly on it, is built on an adjacent ground. The cult is conducted by a royal princess assisted by seventy-three mandarins (cult functionaries). Amaterasu is described in terms of peace, love, purity, righteousness and generosity.

§97. Cult is also performed at home round an altar and in innumerable temples (ginja). Prayers, gifts and praises are offered to the 'kami'. Special feasts and festivals are held generally connected with agricultural events (e.g. rice-sowing, harvest, etc.).

Though no elaborate system of ethics was drawn up till the 12th cent. A.D. (the Butshido, literally "knightly behavior"), lists of "heavenly offences" (amatsutsumi whose prototypes were Susanoo's crimes against Amaterasu) and "earthly offences" (kumitsutsumi) were known. No distinction is made between intentional and unintentional offences. All need to be purified which can be done by imi (abstention from strong drink, from food not purified by a holy flame, from hearing of music, from sexual relations, etc.), by harai (offering of gifts by a mandarin on behalf of the offender), by the recitation of norito (mantras), and especially by misogi (rites, particularly, the use of water and salt). Offences are conceived as dust which pollute man. The celebration of Oharai (semi-annual "Great Purification") occupies an important place in Shintoism even today.

§98. The basic texts of Shintoism are the Kojiki ("Record of Ancient Matters) and the Nihon Shoki ("Chronicles of Japan"). They were compiled, however, as late as the 8th century A.D.

Other traditional texts acquired during the years considerable importance. To mention a few: Manyo-Shiu ("Collection of Ten Thousand Leaves" 8th cent.), Jogen-Shiki ("Rules of ceremonies", 9th cent.), Warongo ("Oracles", 16th cent.), Bushido already referred to, etc.

§99. It is easy to understand how under Buddhist influence (from middle of 6th century A.D.), the kami began to be gradually identified with the numerous Buddhas and Bodhisattvas. We have already seen how Buddhism succeeded so well to spread in Japan. The Buddhist sect which most influenced Shintoism was Shingon. This sect soon developed the idea of honji suijaku: 'honji', the basic, real religion is Buddhism; Shinto is 'suijaku' the partial 'local manifestation'. Or at least Buddhism and Shintoism were only two aspects of the same reality and of the same belief – which led to the conception of ryobu Shinto ("dual Shinto").

§100. From the 15th century we witness an attempt to purify Shintoism from foreign elements and to revive it in its original purity. This renaissance of shintoism (fukko Shinto) found expression in the Yuiitsu Shinto ("The One and Only Shinto") movement. Here the idea of 'honji suijaku' is reversed: 'honji' in shintoism, 'suijaku' is Buddhism, Confucianism, Taoism, and the rest. This movement of reform was carried on thanks to the writings of scholars such as Kamo Mabuchi and Motoori Noringa (18th cent.) and Hirata Atsutane (19th cent.)

§101. Shintoism proliferated into innumerable sects. No less than 140 of them existed at the beginning of this century. One could distinguish between 'mountain sects', 'purification sects' end 'faith-healing sects'. Of the latter, the one which is most flourishing even today is Tenri-kyo ("The Religion of Divine Wisdom") founded by Nakayama Miki in the 19th century, through a revelation she received. Her writings consitute, with the ancient Chronicles, the basic Scriptures. Her teachings go back to 'proto-Shinto' (term used to refer to pre-Buddhist Shintoism) but are clearly influenced by Buddhist sources, especially by Jodo and Shingon.

§102. To give a cohesive and natural character to Shintoism, an attempt was made to distinguish between State (or Shrine) Shinto from Sect Shinto. Irrespective to what private sect one belonged, one had to show allegiance in one way or another to the official religion of the State (Catholics were allowed by the Church authorities to show such an allegiance for it was regarded as a mere civil expression of patriotism).

Japan's defeat in the Second World War marks a landmark in Shintoism. By an Imperial Rescript, promulgated in 1946, the Emperor Hirohito disclaimed lineage from Amaterasu and hence the title to religious veneration. The belief of many Japanese that the mission of their country – "the land of the kami", the first to come into existence – was to dominate over the rest of the world, was thus shattered. State Shinto was abolished.

§103. All this has had a double affect. On the one hand, a religious vacuum, as it were, was created; but on the other hand, a host of so-called 'new religions' (shinko shukyo) arose to fill this vacuum. As examples of these, we could mention F.L. Kyodan ("The Brotherhood of Perfect Liberty") which with its aesthetic orientation, describes life as art and God as the artist of artists; Itto-en ("The Garden of Light") which practices 'active prayer' in social service; Odori no Shukyo ("The Dance Religion") which practices dance as a means of attaining enlightenment and the 'non-self' (muga) and particularly Rissho Kosei Kai ("The Community of Truth and Fellowship") which, in the words of its founder Nikkyo Niwano, is organized "in order to realize a happy world by making efforts to perfect men's personality through the pious intercourse of many people and the harmony of the believers on the basis of the true meaning of Buddhism."

These 'new religions' are not mutually exclusive. Not only are they extremely tolerant one of the other - with the exception of Soka Gakkai ("The World-Creating Society") which is militantly aggressive – but they accept the fact that one could adhere to one or more of them. Indeed the Japanese do not find it at all strange that they be Shinto, Buddhist and Confuciant at the same time. Though most of these 'new religions' are fundamentally Buddhist, they are clearly influenced by Hinduism, Christianity – and not least of all by their ancestral religion, the religion of "the land of the rising Sun".

Chapter 3

NOTES ON CONTEMPORARY "PRIMIEVAL" RELIGIONS

§104. No Phenomenology of Religion can be said to be complete and satisfactory. Religious 'phenomena' are too wide to be all studied. This would be much more the case if such a Phenomenology of Religion, no matter what method it adopts, leaves out other religions than those main ones which we have touched upon – and these religions are indeed very numerous!

But precisely because of their number, it is indeed extremely difficult to speak of them in general. If it is already very difficult to generalize on any one religion, it is obviously much more so to generalize on many of them. But this is not the only difficulty.

The first difficulty is to find a term suitable to designate them. The term 'primitive' is often used to designate those religions professed by people whose culture is thought to be still in its initial stages. However, apart from the fact that the term 'primitive' has acquired today a pejorative connotation (namely 'savage'), a better knowledge of these people and their religions has shown that in many cases, their culture and their religion is far from being 'primitive' at all! Often their social customs, kinship systems, etc., are indicative of a highly sophisticated culture. Again a better understanding of the nature and function of religious belief (as we shall see in the second part of our study) is helping one understand better the nature and function of the religious belief of these people. – Again, other terms, such as 'animistic' 'tribal' do not seem to be appropriate either – at least to cover all of them.

For these and other reasons, we prefer to use the term 'primeval' – with the full awareness, however, that this term has its disadvantages. By 'primeval' we want to indicate the fact that these religions (and cultures) are presumed to have been less influenced by certain characteristically modern cultural developments (for better or for worse!).

§105. In fact, these people we are referring to – in India, Africa, Australia and New Guinea, South America, etc. – generally live in small, homogenous social units, more or less cut off from the rest (because of jungle, desert, ocean, mountainous regions, long distances, etc.). Generally they live by one kind of labor (food-gathering, hunting and/or fishing, herd-keeping). Their habitat is simple: bamboo, mud or clay huts enough to give them shelter from the sun and the rain (and wild beasts). One could go on listing elements which would permit one to say that these peoples are presumed to have been less influenced (or un-influenced at all) by such modern cultural developments such as the modern metropolis, means of transport and communication, education in the natural sciences and abstract thought, trade and commerce and social services, etc.

On the other hand, these peoples often exhibit a refined culture and civilization of their own. (Hence the misleading terms of 'savage' or 'uncivilized' when applied indiscriminately to them!). We have already referred to the existence of social customs and kinship systems which often reflect a highly developed culture. Here we refer too to the existence of artistic skills (e.g. sculpture on wood, clay, stone and bronze), paintings, and general know-how in techniques in hunting, fishing etc., and above all to the systems of keeping law and order amongst themselves – all of which cannot be highly admitted and appreciated.

§106. There are other difficulties in studying these religions. One big difficulty is the absence of Scriptures and other written (e.g. historical) documents. This has led some to classify these religions as 'non- literate' (or 'non-Scriptural') religions. The term has the disadvantage of being only 'negative' (like 'non-Christian', 'non-Hindu', 'non-Muslim'). But it certainly brings out the fact that a common phenomenon in all these religions is the absence of Scriptures – which, given our 'historico-existential' method which we have adopted for our phenomenological study of religions, is for us particularly significant. – Another big difficulty is, in many cases, the indirect sources of information. Ignorance of the language and of direct access to the heart and mind of the people, much of our information of these religions is based on 'interpreters', on external observation. Added to that, that often these people recent 'outsiders' poking their nose into what they consider to be too sacred to be made known and divulged to these. Often some religious 'secrets' are withheld even from members of their own group till their 'initiation'; others are made known only to a very select few (e.g. the elders). – A final difficulty which can be mentioned is the fact that it is often very difficult, if not impossible, to say to what extent these people have not been influenced, at some time or other in the past or present, by external cultural and religious factors and therefore to what extent they are 'primeval' (in the sense we are understanding the term).

Notice that by 'primeval' we do not want to imply that a study of these religions can lead to any certain conclusions as to what the religion of 'pre-historic' man must have been – as some ethnologists, in former days, were led to think. These people, and therefore their culture in general and their religion in particular, have had their centuries- long history...

§107. Given these preliminary remarks, what can one reasonably say about these 'primeval religions' – from a historico-existential point of view? Can we observe any common phenomena?

One very striking phenomenon is the fact that all these people possess a religious lore the origin of which they attribute to their 'ancestors'. This lore is handed down from generation to generation. Sometimes, these ancestors are conceived to have been half-human and half-animal (as among some Australian aborigines). Sometimes, this religious lore is believed to have been taught to their ancestors by 'spirits'.

In every case, this religious lore is to be kept intact, memorized faithfully and passed on from generation to generation in its integrity. It must be jealously guarded from the non-members of the group and often from members themselves who have not yet been 'initiated'.

This religious lore is full of stories of how the world began, of how man first made his appearance on earth, of their ancestors, of what happens after death, of 'spirits' and their commerce with men, of ancient heroes and their deeds in past ages, etc.

Certainly noteworthy is the fact that very often this lore speaks of a Spirit who is above all other spirits. He is often identified with the Sky or the Sun. Often he is spoken of in terms of a man who is married, has sons. Frequently he is bisexual. He is both good and fearful. Often he is thought to be a rewarder of good men (giving them success in hunting, health and prosperity) and a punisher of evil ones (sickness and death, floods and draught, failure in hunting and other misfortunes are attributed to him). Often, as in Africa, he is conceived of as a mysterious power pervading all things, capable of doing anything, knowing and seeing everything. But he is withdrawn from general commerce with men (due to some fault or other of theirs). It is only on special occasions that he is propitiated (e.g. epidemies), otherwise recourse is had more often to the spirits. In Africa, he does not figure in art (except in Ghana, Kenya and Rhodesia). He is called by different names: Mulungu, Leza, Nyambe. The idea of such a supreme spirit is found from one end of the American continent to the other.

§108. Offerings of animals, first fruits, prayers are made to the spirits – both to the good ones and to the evil ones – to propitiate them, to placate them. Cult-dances, with dancers using masks representing spirits, are often performed. Such dances re-enact the stories of their religious lore and thus renew the vital forces causing rain, fertility of the soil and of their women, success in hunting and triumph in warfare, love, speedy dispatch of the dead to the abode of the ancestor. They are commemorative drama performances.

Often specific places are allotted for purposes of cult and some kind of 'altar', niche, mound of earth, is built. Certain objects, particularly awe-inspiring (like a big mountain, big oak, round boulder, etc.) are often said to be inhabited by the spirits and hence given particular creation. Similarly, carved images and other artifacts are used in cult.

Often a cult functionary is specially appointed – if the office is not hereditary – to perform cultural acts. This is to be distinguished from what ethnologists came to know by the name of 'shaman', that is an interpreter of the will of the spirits known to him in trances, dreams or through strange omens. Often the chief of the group is the cult functionary.

A very common phenomenon is the rite of 'initiation' when the boy, now come of age, and having gone through preliminary stages, is fully considered an adult member of the group and introduced to the secret religious lore. This often happens at the age of puberty and sexual initiation is often linked with it. – Similarly, other important dates for the individual or the group are marked with religious rites and feasting (e.g. a birth, marriage, death; new harvest, triumph in warfare, success in hunting, etc.)

The ancestors themselves are often propitiated. Sometimes they are believed to be still in contact with the group.

§109. Noteworthy is the fact that all these peoples know that there are certain actions which should not be done and others which should be done. This has been taught them by their ancestors who learned it from the spirits (if not, from the supreme spirit himself. Similarly with certain customs to break which, even if unintentionally, is punishable by the group.

As we have said already, certain offences are punished by the spirits or by the Supreme Spirit himself. Certain calamities are signs of his wrath for misbehavior. Often, however, these calamities are attributed to evil spirits – or even, as in some places in Africa, to a great evil spirit, a brother or son of the Supreme Spirit.

Certain rites are prescribed to expiate the fault and wash away contamination which results from it.

§110. Another common, but by no means universal, phenomenon is the idea of what ethnologists call the 'totem', that is an animal or plant which is recognized to have some special relation to the group as an ancestor, protector and a rallying factor. The group bears its name. It is usually forbidden to eat the totem – except, on special occasions, when a communal sacrificial meal is eaten to invigorate in the group vital powers.

The chief or head of the group is often considered to be a personification of the totem. As said before, the social system of these peoples is often highly complicated.

Social customs, like their moral behavior, – indeed the two go together – are a part of their religious lore.

§111. We mentioned above cult dances. Often such dances are thought to be productive of the intended effect provided they are performed exactly as they should and even irrespective of the will of the spirits. The effect intended can be either beneficial (e.g. rain, fertility) or malignant (e.g. death of the enemy). Very widespread among such people is this idea that a rite, a practice, by virtue of its exact performance and irrespective of anything else produces its result. The user of such a practice came to be called by ethnologists a sorcerer (or if female witch). Hence, the use of charms (or amulets) against spells (or incantations) used by the sorcerer against somebody to ward off the evil intended by him or to ward off evil in general. The use of such practices came to be known as 'magic' (white magic, if the intended result is beneficial; black magic, if the intended result is evil). If the practice imitates the result intended (e.g. pouring of water to produce rain) it is known as 'homeopathic' magic; if some action is done to an object which bears some relation to the person on whom the result is intended (e.g. burning a piece of cloth once worn by the person to cast on him some evil) it is called, 'contagious' magic.

PART FOUR

RELIGIOUS LANGUAGE

"That religion is strong which in its ritual and its modes of thought evokes an apprehension of the commanding vision. The worship of God is not a rule of safely – it is an adventure of the spirit, a flight after the unattainable. The death of religion comes with the repression of the high hope of adventure." (A. N. Whitehead, *Science and the Modern World*, 1933 ed., p. 239)

INTRODUCING THE SUBJECT

§1. Two questions have to be clearly distinguished. Take this statement: "God exists": One question is to ask whether this statement is 'true', that is, whether it corresponds to a state of affairs; another question is to ask what this statement 'means', that is what is meant by the terms 'God' and 'exists'. The first question is a question about 'truth', the second question is about 'meaning'.

§2. It is clear that though these two questions are logically distinct, they are very closely inter-related. In fact, if I find that the terms 'God' and 'exists' (as applied to 'God') are unintelligible, I simply cannot even raise the question whether the statement "God exists" is true or false. The critical question (about 'truth') is to be settled, indeed raised, only if the logical question (about 'meaning') is answered in the affirmative. In simpler terms, one can only try to prove whether a statement is true or false if one knows what one is talking about!

§3. Philosophers have always been interested in the study of language, or more precisely, of the phenomenon of human speech as such. Often, philosophical problems were raised and answered through a linguistic approach. (For example, Socrates tried to raise and answer moral problems by examining what was precisely meant by the terms 'good'. In Medieval Europe, philosophers grappled with the meaning of 'universal' terms, etc.).

This is particularly true of religious language, that is, of language used with reference to God (or the 'Transcendent', 'Ultimate Reality'). All the great philosophers of antiquity – Sankaracharya, Nagarjuna, Maimonides, al-Ghazzali, Thomas Aquinas – faced the question how it was possible, or impossible, to employ terms, ordinarily used to describe objects, events, persons – all of which fall under man's empirical experience – with reference to an Absolute, and hence non-visible, non-tangible, Reality.

§4. This question can become for one more serious if one pays heed to what many mystics – belonging to many religious traditions - say about the 'ineffability' of God (or the Absolute, the Ultimate Reality). Since concepts and words borrowed from empirical experience are in no way adequate to speak of God, and, even more, they can be very misleading, ordinary knowledge of God is simply 'ignorance'.

Hence, for one to attain as true knowledge of Him, it is necessary for one to 'go beyond' anything which the human mind (by its reasoning and imaginative faculties) can conceive or imagine. Mystical 'apophatism' renders, therefore, our question more acute: is human language, when used to express God (a meta-empirical Reality) at all meaningful?

§5. The Scholastic answer to this question is in the affirmative. We shall examine this answer during the course of our study. At this introductory stage of our enquiry, we content ourselves with pointing out that in view of the modern problematic, this answer would need perhaps to be re-thought.

§6. In fact, the modern problematic is somewhat different from that of antiquity. We said that the logical and the critical questions are closely inter-related. In antiquity the critical question had not yet passed through the crucible of modern Empiricism and of Transcendental Idealism (for example, of the Kantian type) – to speak, only of these two philosophical movements.

§7. With the rise of Neo-positivism, in the early fifties of this century, in Germany, and the increased interest in the study of the nature and function of language- to which, for reasons which we shall see, Philosophy was reduced- religious (as well as metaphysical and moral) language was wore and more looked upon as meaningless.

§8. Needless to point out the importance, therefore, of our study. The alleged meaninglessness of religious language presents a serious challenge to the religious believer. If religious language is meaningless, the religious believer not only cannot justify his religious belief (i.e. proves it to be true and not false) but cannot even raise the very question of its justification. He is hence condemned to total silence (which is of a different kind from the 'mystical silence'!). Even if he were to appeal to the authoritativeness of some kind of 'divine Revelation' (Sruti, etc.) or some kind of 'mystical intuition' (anubhava, etc.), the religious believer will have to acknowledge the unbridgeable gap between ordinary language and religious language.

§9. But we shall not undertake our study for mere 'apologetic' purposes. A philosophical reflection on the nature and function of language, i.e., a Philosophy of Language, in general and of religious language in particular, is being recognized more and more today to be an indispensable tool for a better understanding of religious belief itself. Even though 'Faith' (the sense of the Numinous) is supra-conceptual and supra-notional, it is thematizad in 'belief' (and therefore in concepts and words, that is in language). It is normally through and by means of religious language, that is, thematized belief, that one is led to deeper (or higher!) levels of religious consciousness.

Such a Philosophy of Religious Language can facilitate that mutual understanding between adherents of different religious traditions whose tenets of belief seem, often enough, to be so mutually exclusive. It can help a better appreciation of, but at the same time a more insightful appraisal of one's sacred Scriptures.

§10. As is clear, we shall not attempt to cover the whole field of Philosophy of Language. Our direct interest is its relevance to Religious Language. We shall have therefore to leave many things unsaid with regard to Philosophy of Language understood in a more comprehensive sense.

Again, as it was pointed out already, many of the difficulties which arise with respect to religious language, arise too – for much the name reasons – with respect to metaphysical and moral language. Here, we shall be concerned, at least directly, with difficulties arising with respect to religious language.[14]

It is to be noted too that since modern philosophy of Language and the philosophical movements which preceded it – arose in the West, whenever 'religious language' was spoken of both by those who were against it and by those who were for it, it was understood to refer to theistic, particularly Christian, religious language. But it is clear that it can refer to any language about a Transcendent (Absolute, Ultimate Reality, etc.) intended by all the World religious traditions. And it is in this latter sense that at take religious language to mean.

14 We treat of moral language from a linguistic point of view (i.e. of Meta-Ethics), in our *Ethics* (cyclostyled notes), § 9-17 et passim.

Chapter 1

ANALYTICAL LINGUISTIC PHILOSOPHY

§11. In its earlier stages, modern Philosophy of Language started as an analysis of language as such - hence the name.

Actually, one might say that such an analytical linguistic philosophy was a confluence of three streams:

1. Empiricism (dating from Robbes, Locke, Hume in England and Mach in Germany) which reduced knowledge to sensations and facts to sense data. Knowledge is confined to what is empirically given.

2. Symbolic Logic (Whitehead, Russell) which applies the mathematical method to formal logic. Words stand for logical symbols and the logical structure of propositions, considered as self-contained units (hence 'logical atomism'), is translated into strict rules (e.g. of implication, exclusion, equivalence, etc).

3. Linguistic Philosophy proper (Moore, Wittgenstein) which studies the nature, scope and limits of language. Different kinds of propositions are distinguished. Rules are established to differentiate between 'meaningful' and 'non-meaningful' statements.

§12. Analytical linguistic philosophy passed through two main phases known as 'logical positivism' and 'logical empiricism'. There are certain fundamental assumptions which run through both phases, but there are also no less fundamental divergences.

A. General assumptions:

1. The primary subject-matter of Philosophy is linguistic significance. That is, its task is to clarify the purpose of language and the ways by which language can attain it.

2. Hence, Philosophy qua Philosophy (that is Philosophy understood in the sense described) is empirically uninformative. Unlike the natural sciences, it does not tell us anything about any 'state of affairs'.

3. The proper 'locus' of significance, or meaning, is the proposition. It is in the proposition that one is to look for 'manning'.

4. The function of philosophy (thus understood) is to engage in a logical analysis of language.

B. Divergences

These divergences – which will become clearer later – concern the precise nature and purpose of language, the meaning of 'meaning' and the proper method of logical analysis.

1. LOGICAL POSITIVISM

§14. Known also as 'neo-positivism' (originating in the so-called 'Vienna Circle' with Schlick, Carnap, Neurath and others best represented in England by Whitehead, Russell, Wittgenstein and Ayer) is led by its 'scientific conception' of reality to see in the language of physics the paradigm of all meaningful language (hence 'physicalism'), In its radical form, logical positivism is not much favored today. But the following principles are held even today by quite a few authors.

1. There are two kinds of cognitive (i.e. informative) prepositions or statements: the *analytical and the synthetical.* An analytical proposition is a proposition whose meaning is already clear by an analysis of the terms used. In fact, it is 'tautology'. Its function is either to establish verbal conventions or to relate ideas among themselves. It prescinds completely from 'facts' and is therefore uninformative about actual 'State of affairs'. Analytical propositions are those used in mathematics and logic. Only analytical propositions are necessarily true. A synthetical proposition, on the other hand, is a proposition whose meaning is not immediately clear from an analysis of the terms used. Its function is to affirm or deny 'facts' – facts, that is, of actual reality. Only they are informative about actual 'state of affairs'. Synthetical propositions are those used in the natural sciences. They can never be necessarily, but only hypothetically true-that is, their truth or falsity always remains open to confirmation or denial by experience and observation.

§15. 2. The 'Meaning' of a proposition is the method of its verification. By 'meaning' it is here meant the 'logical equivalence' (and not the psychological act of 'intending'). This principle shows us how to translate a given proposition into other logically equivalent propositions (called 'protocol statements'). If no such method is possible, that is, if the proposition cannot be verified, such a proposition has no 'meaning', it is 'meaningless' (or 'non-sensical'). This principle came to be known the 'verification principle', and the analysis based on it as 'verificational Analyses'.

3. A non-analytical (i.e. synthetic) proposition which, by definition, purports to state something about factual reality, must be *empirically* verifiable. If it cannot be thus proved true or false by empirical means, such a proposition is 'meaningless', it simply makes no sense. (Notice, therefore, that 'meaningless' does not mean 'false'; it means 'cannot be proved either true or false). At best, such a proposition has only an 'emotive' meaning for it expresses some kind of emotion of the speaker (or writer). But such an 'emotive' meaning is not informative about factual 'state of affairs'. An 'emotive' meaning is to be distinguished from 'cognitive' meaning.

4. In virtue of such an analysis, moral, metaphysical and religious propositions are meaningless. At most they have only 'emotive' meaning.

§16. 5. The 'verification principle' gradually underwent two modifications. In its original and radical form, to 'verify' meant to 'verify conclusively'. It was soon realized, however, that understood in such a 'strong' sense, a verificational analysis was simply impossible. That meant that all general statements, including all laws of the natural sciences would be meaningless. Only analytical propositions can be verified conclusively. Hence, to 'verify' was given a 'week' sense, that is, to 'verify probably'. One is then to ask what facts count for or against such a proposition being probably true (or false). – The other modification was simply a shifting of emphasis from the enquiry into facts which would count for the proposition being true to an enquiry into facts which would count *against* its being true. In other words, if a proposition cannot be proved false – by empirical experience – such a proposition is meaningless. Hence this principle came to be known as the 'principle of falsifiability.[15]

§17. We have just pointed out that for Logical Positivism, moral, metaphysical and religious propositions (and therefore moral, metaphysical and religious language) is 'meaningless'. As we said earlier, Logical positivism is not much favored today. Hardly any author will be happy to be called a Logical positivist, today. But the above enunciated principles are shared, to a smaller or greater extent by the following authors (among others).

Thus for Ayer, since religious language is empirically unverifiable, it is 'meaningless'. At most it has an 'emotive' (but not 'cognitive') meaning. But if theism is meaningless, so also is atheism. In both cases one claims to speak of God (to prove the existence of God in the first case, to disprove it in the other case): in both cases, one speaks a *meaningless* language. Flew tries to show that such facts as evil and the freedom of man render the very idea of God logically contradictory. Since religious language is unfalsifiable, it is meaningless. Of course, the believer

15 Other suggestions to modify the principle further have been made. For example: "an ostensible statement of fact is significant if, and only if, it can in principle, be verified by human experience."

can always qualify his statements- till the statements "die the death of a thousand qualifications". For Williams, believing in an 'incomprehensible' (therefore meaningless) God is no different from non-believing. According to McPherson, in spite of religious experience, religion belongs to the sphere of the 'unsayable'. Newell-Smith argues that it is illogical to explain alleged miracles by 'supernatural' agencies. A. Maclntyre discusses religious experience (such as visions and voices) and concludes that such an experience does not yield, of itself, any evidence for or information about anything other than the experience itself. Similarly be develops at some length what he thinks to be the logical inconsistencies in any talk about God, including that used in the arguments for God's existence. For C.B. Martin, religious language based on an allegedly 'direct experience of God' is very much like psychological (e.g. esthetic) language. Mackie and Findlay go even further. For the former, religious language is not only 'meaningless' but even self-contradictory. This he shows from the very existence of evil. For the latter, the very idea of God as a 'necessary being' is a logical absurdity.[16]

2. LOGICAL EMPIRICISM

§18. We have already pointed out the general areas of disagreement between Logical Positivism and Logical Empiricism (see supra, §13). This will be brought out better in the following contrast:

1. Whereas in Logical Positivism language is considered as a kind of impersonal and quasi-objective entity in itself, in Logical Empiricism, language is understood to be a social, inter-subjective complex. The significance or import of human-language cannot be fully appreciated by a mere formal study of language considered in the abstract. One could distinguish between 'language' (formally and abstractly considered) and 'speech' (existentially and concretely considered).

Consequently, whereas in Logical Positivism the purpose of language (or at least of 'meaningful language') is mainly, if not exclusively, to 'inform' and therefore the paradigm of language (considered as a means of communicating information) is scientific language, in Logical Empiricism the purpose of language is manifold according to the various 'significant-situations' of the speaker and hearer (Wittgenstein, abandoning his earlier position, speaks, in his later writings, of different 'language- games').

§19. 3. Again, whereas in Logical Positivism, 'meaning' is understood as 'the method of verification', in logical Empiricism, 'meaning' is understood is terms of use or function. Hence the principle: *the meaning of the language is found in its use or function*. A 'meaningful' proposition is therefore not a proposition which can be (empirically) verified, but a proposition which has a specific function to play. Verification analysis is thus replaced by *functional analysis*. The functions of language are many.

16 For reference, see Bibliography.

4. In logical Empiricism, the two chief techniques used in revealing the 'meaning' (and therefore the 'function') of a proposition: the 'paradigm-case technique' (comparing an unclear word or phrase in the proposition with a clear use of the same word or phrase as used in another proposition) and the 'significant comparison technique' (comparing the use of a proposition with the use of another activity purporting to do the same function).

§20. To apply all this to religious language. It is certainly interesting to see how various authors assign various 'functions' to religious language (which, therefore, they would consider 'meaningful'). Many, however, consistently with their Empiricism, refuse to accept a meta-empirical referent. Some whom we referred to in the context of Logical Positivism do also make use of functional analysis to establish their position. Needless to point out that some others while setting great store by functional analysis are no empiricists at all.

Thus, according to Braithwaite, the function of religious language is to express the speaker's intention of 'acting in a certain way'; the function of Christian religious language, in particular, is to express the Christian's intention of acting in an 'agapeistic way of life'. Hepburn refines this theory. According to him, the function of religious is to express man's ultimate moral choice which legislates for all the aspects of his life. Van Buren, deciding that religious language cannot refer to any meta-empirical Reality, attempts a 'secular meaning' of the Gospel and of its message. In much the same way, Miles attempts to show that the function of religious language is to transmit 'message-giving parables'. Wisdom argues that the function of religious language is to express reality in a certain kind of 'structure' or pattern. Similarly, according to Hare, the function of religious language is to give one a certain kind of 'blik' or view of the world.

§20. Other authors insist more on the function of religious language to express one's inward feelings or convictions. Thus for Smart, religious language is a kind of instrument to heighten one's religious emotions. For Coates, religious language expresses, more particularly, one's sense of 'feeling assured with the world'. Similarly, according to Leon, religious language expresses finite man's 'acceptance of the world in awe'. Speaking of death, MacKinnon shows how religious language's function here is to state that man, in spite of death, does really matter. More generally still, Allen sees in the function of religious language an expression of man's 'postures' or attitudes towards existence. For Zuurdeeg, religious language is a 'convictional language', that is it expresses one's inward convictions which it is not possible or even desirable to prove as veridical.[17]

§22. We are now in a position to proceed to what we think a more comprehensive Philosophy of Language in general and of Religious Language in particular could be. We shall content ourselves with *general indications.*

17 For reference, see Bibliography.

Our reflections will be grouped under *two main headings*; an evaluation of Analytical Linguistic Philosophy in general and of its relevance to Religious Language in particular, and our personal stand on Religious Consciousness and Religious Language.

Chapter 2

TOWARDS A PHILOSOPHY OF RELIGIOUS LANGUAGE

§23. We began our study by pointing out the logically distinct but closely interrelated questions regarding 'truth' (the critical question) and 'meaning' (the logical question). Our brief exposition of Analytical Linguistic Philosophy, albeit a brief one, must have surely brought this out clearly. One can wonder whether it is at all possible to answer the logical question without having solved first the critical question, but, on the other hand, whether it is at all possible, or even 'meaningful' to try and solve the critical question without having decided on the meaning of the terms one is going to use in its discussion (and therefore without having solved the logical question).

§24. That is the reason why we think the logical question is much more serious than it might seem at first sight. That is the reason too why we think too that several attempts which have been made to answer the logical question by appealing, for example, to the authoritativeness of Divine Revelation and of the Inspired Word as recorded in Sacred Scriptures – which authority one must accept in 'Faith' – or to the self-authenticating religious, particularly 'mystical' experience, in which man encounters God directly and understands the Divine Reality by a kind of religious insight, etc., are not completely satisfactory. Such terms as 'Divine Revelation', 'Inspired Word', 'Sacred' (as applied to the Scriptures), 'Faith', 'religious' or 'mystical experience', 'encountering God', 'Divine Reality' are all religious terms. And it will not certainly do to use such terms in an argument where the question at issue is precisely the 'meaning' of such terms!

§25. What is more, such attempts take it for granted, consciously or unconsciously, that on the one hand, 'Revelation' (Sruti, Quran, etc.) is a revelation, or divine disclosure, of the words themselves and not only of the 'reality' which these words signify – and thus no distinction is made between the 'reality' revealed, or experienced, and its conceptualization and notionalization, so to say, by the recipient of the divine revelation or the experiencer (the prophet, the rishi, seer, etc.) – and that, on the other hand, and conversely, 'Faith' is in the words themselves and not only in the 'reality' which the words signify.[18]

§26. We could address such a criticism of ours to the attempts made by such authors as Crombie, Mitchell, Farmer, Farrer to vindicate the logical meaningfulness and purposefulness of religious language. Our evaluation of Analytical Linguistic Philosophy takes another direction.

1. EVALUATION OF ANALYTICAL LINGUISTIC PHIOSOPHY

§27. The 'challenge' which Analytical Linguistic Philosophy makes to Religion should therefore be taken with all radical seriousness. It should be constantly borne in mind that not all analytical philosophers – deny that religious experience could be valid (i.e. 'true') for the experiencer; but the question remains whether the language he uses to express his religious experience to others is or can be 'meaningful' to these others who have not made the same experience. To put it differently, the question is whether religious experience is at all 'communicable' or at least, whether religious language can serve as a means of communicating to others – for, after all, whatever language is, it is also that – religious truth. If not, religious language should be simply regarded as having only 'emotive' meaning; if yes, how could religious language possibly do it.

§28. The great lessons we willingly therefore learn from Logical Positivism, or at least some of them, are the following:

(a) Religious language, like language in general, is subject to logical analysis, to rules of logic and reason. If it proves recalcitrant to such an analysis and such rules, religious language does not mean what it says. It has therefore not only to say what it means but also to give account for its recalcitrancy.

(b) Religious language as such is *not descriptive of empirical reality*. Believers claim for religious language a 'cognitive' meaning about a 'supernatural Reality'. Hence no matter how many other 'meanings' or 'functions' functional analysts discover in religious language (conative, emotive, convictional, etc.), unless religious language fulfils the claim of believers, it is no religious language at all. To do so, one has not only to justify one's use of 'Reality' qualified as 'supernatural' but also to account for the alleged claim that language can be 'cognitive' (or informative about 'state of affairs') without being descriptive of empirical reality.

18 The theory of 'literal Revelation' does not hold much favour today with an increasing number of Christian Theologians. Sporadic voices are heard today in Hinduism and Islam against a belief in a corresponding 'literal' Sruti and Quran respectively. As for "Faith", the opinion of St. Thomas is often quoted: "The act of the believer does not stop at what is enunciated but at the reality."

(c) Religious assertions (or propositions, statements) are *notempirically verifiable.* Useless to claim they are in principle verifiable or falsifiable –eschatologically! For 'eschatologically' is already a 'religious term' – which needs precisely to be logically justified! And it is not enough to claim that religious assertions have to be accepted in 'Faith', for first one has to understand what is one has to so accept, in 'Faith' (i.e. what the assertion logically stands for). Similarly, as religious assertions are not empirically verifiable, so too they are *empirically falsifiable.*

§29. However, according to us, Logical Positivism is vitiated by its radical Empiricism – an Empiricism which is the 'presupposition', uncritically taken for granted, of its Philosophy of Language. Hence:

(a) Consistently enough with its Empiricism, Logical Positivism limits the notion of 'fact' to empirical fact, and that of 'factual' to actual or possible sense-experience. If Empiricism can be shown to be philosophically unwarranted presupposition, this limitation will also be shown to be unwarranted and Arbitrary. – Similarly, Logical Positivism narrows down the meaning of 'explanation' or 'verification' to scientific (empirical) explanation. The same criticism applies.

(b) It has been successfully argued by critics of the 'verification principle' – with whom we concur - that on the strength of the same principle, it is itself 'meaningless'! In fact, it purports to be a "non- analytical statement (otherwise it would be a 'tautology') and yet it is impervious to 'verification' by empirical experience. In other words, it cannot be proved true or false by empirical tests – and hence it is 'meaningless'!

§30. (c) Paradoxically enough, Logical Positivism can be shown to be unfaithful to its own empirical techniques – and hence radically inconsistent with itself. For it takes without empirical proof (and hence as "dogmatically and a-prioristically") that:

1. The primary, indeed the exclusive function of language is to inform. It arbitrarily excludes other possible functions (which Functional Analysis subsequently brought out).
2. There are only two possible kinds of cognitively 'meaningful' propositions – and that 'non-meaningful' propositions are merely 'emotive'.
3. The paradigm of language is scientific language (a position which some Logical Positivists, like Wittgenstein later abandoned).

§31. At this stage of cur discussion, we content ourselves with this overall and general evaluation of Logical Positivism. A more comprehensive criticism will have to wait for the more positive exposition of our position on the Philosophy of Religious Language. But it will be helpful already from now to pass a general remark on the position taken by some Logical Positivists whom we referred to above. Mackie and Flew fail to make a critical examination of the terms 'good and evil' as used in religious language. Findlay confuses 'logical' necessity with 'metaphysical' necessity. Williams uncritically takes 'Incomprehensibility' as the logical equivalent of 'insignificance'. Similarly, the 'paradox' is often taken as the logical equivalent of 'logical contradiction' and its function, even in ordinary speech, is overlooked. McPherson at least tends to confuse 'inexpressible' (or 'unsayable') with 'not-knowing' and fails to bring out, or to bring out sufficiently, the essential discrepancy, or lag, between 'knowing' and 'saying'. On the whole, it can be said that such authors (e.g. A. MacIntyre) fail to critically examine, with respect to the 'proofs' of the existence of God, other possible kinds of 'proof' than the 'logical proof' which they criticize.

§32. Perhaps most importantly of all, such authors (e.g. Martin) confuse religious experience with 'psychological experience'. At least they fail to examine critically the possibility of different layers or depths of human consciousness...

These general remarks will be justified and clarified curing the remaining part of our study.

§33. We learn equally great lessons from Logical Empiricism. As we have seen, Logical Empiricism helped in the overcoming of the narrowness of Logical Positivism and opened wider vistas; it has accomplished this by its insistence on the nature of language as a social, inter-subjective reality, by its bringing out the many purposes of language and by its defining 'meaning' in terms of 'function'. Hence we agree:

a) Religious language, like human language in general, is understandable only as a social, inter-subjective reality. Such an understanding requires that it be taken in the whole human context – the believing community, in our case – in which it is used.
b) Religious language has, or can have, a multi-functional character. Functional analysis has brought this very forcibly. Only that we do not limit the function of religious language, as some authors do, to this or that function. This will become clearer later. Religious language, in fact, expresses *of* man much more than other aspects of human language (e.g. logical or scientific), whatever else besides it also expresses (that is, according to us, of 'God'). And the fact that religious language does express things of man – in other words that it does have always and necessarily, an 'existential' meaning, must be constantly borne in mind.
c) Religious language has consequently an 'emotive', 'conative', 'existential', 'convictional' (and other) meanings...

§34. But after all has been said and done, Logical Empiricism - as the name implies- remains shackled and fettered with the same kind of *Empiricism* which we criticized before. And hence much of what we said earlier applies equally here. But more particularly;

a) Logical Empiricism fails to distinguish, between psychological experience and religious experience, or rather it reduces the latter to the former.
b) It ultimately renders religious language subjectivistic and arbitrary (Would the believer be interested in his knowing what my 'blik' or my 'way of structuring reality' or my 'conviction' is unless I can communicate to him the ground, the support, the justification, for it?).
c) As to the principle of 'falsifiability', Logical Empiricism fails to distinguish between different kinds of religious language itself. Functional analysis has done well in distinguishing between different kinds of languages but it has taken religious language to be of one kind. We readily admit that one kind of religious language is falsifiable – as we shall see later. But paradoxically enough whereas for Logical Empiricism only what is 'falsifiable' is 'meaningful', for us what is empirically falsifiable is not what is directly and primarily expressed in religious language!

2. RELIGIOUS CONSCIOUSNESS AND RELIGIOUS LANGUAGE

§35. One thing is being realized more and more is that a much more comprehensive study of language is needed than the one Analytical Linguistic Philosophy, at least in its earlier stages, presented.

If language is a social, inter-personal reality, various factors have to be studied. There is first the speaker who wants to 'say' something; there is the spoken (or written) language he uses as a means of his saying it; there is the hearer to whom the speaker wants to 'say' it. It is true, one can study language as a kind of independent reality. In fact, throughout the course of time, language acquired this kind of autonomous reality: words came to have definite meanings (and thus dictionaries to be written; misuse of words leads to unintelligibility and often to humor and laughter), relation between words came to be formalized in certain structures (and thus formal logic, and more recently symbolic logic emerged), etc. But this aspect of language is only one aspect of language considered as a social, inter-personal reality, or as an inter-subjective communication. It is the syntactic aspect.

A more important aspect of language is the use made by it by the speaker. Language, considered as an inter-subjective communication, can never be abstracted from the speaker – from what he wants to 'say' (to communicate, to convey), from the way he wants to 'say' it, from his purpose in 'saying' it, etc. This aspect is the pragmatic or the interpretive aspect of language.[19]

But still a more important aspect of language is the way language, or more precisely, the speaker through the medium of language, 'says', or communicates

19 Ferre, op. cit., pp. 148ff.

to the hearer. How does language express what the speaker wants to 'say' in a way that this is communicated to the hearer? This is the semantic aspect of language.

These three aspects or dimensions of language must be taken together. Over emphasizing one aspect to the exclusion of the others leads to a failure to understand language as human speech.

§36. If language is an expression of what the speaker wants to communicate to the hearer, we must begin our study of language – particularly of religious language – from the speaker.

Let it be said at once that we shall not be concerned here with showing the existence of or describing man's religious consciousness.[20] Our main interest here is not a confutation of empiricism but the 'meaningfullness' of religious language. Vow, whatever religious language is, it is an expression of religious consciousness.

This can be readily understood if we stop to reflect that in point of fact, language in general is an expression of some aspect or other (or some layer or other) of human consciousness in general. It would be interesting to know how primitive men began to form meaningful sounds (words) through the medium of which he communicated to other men. But it would not be unreasonable to suppose that before he formed the sound 'bear' he was conscious of the existence, nature, etc., of this animal which he distinguished from other things (other animals, trees, other men, mountains, etc). The sound 'bear' was an expression, indeed a *sign* of his consciousness of the animal signified. He experienced (by sight, touch, bearing, etc.) the animal (cf. the 'species impressa') became conscious of such an animal as characteristically itself and distinct from other things (cf. 'species expressa') and signified it by a word.

Of course, today man 'inherits' words. The baby experiences by sight, touch, etc., something and mummy tells it "a teddy-bear"... But here like in the case of primitive man, two things are at work: sense-experience and the awakening of consciousness. Notice, however, that whereas for visible, tangible things, sense-experience seems to be co-extensive with consciousness, consciousness is not circumscribed by sense-experience.

This is borne out by language itself. In fact, such words as 'if', 'when' 'and' 'how' 'why', 'although' etc., do not describe any object of sense-experience. Again, words like 'beauty', 'truth', 'unity' do not refer to any object of sense-experience.[21] No matter how we explain the 'mechanism', so to speak, of the awakening of

20 S Azzopardi, *Philosophy of Religion*, JDV, pp. 3-6.

21 Beauty, like light, is, paradoxically enough, invisible. Similarly, truth, unity, etc. What is seen is the object. These terms, therefore, express man's 'reaction' (poetically, aesthetically, etc.) to the object. One way to distinguish between a 'concept' and an 'idea' would be to reserve the term 'concept' to what an object is, and the term 'idea' to a verbalisation of an 'apperception' of consciousness. For other parts of language other than nouns (e.g. verbs, conjunctions, prepositions, adverbs, etc.) we could reserve 'term' or 'notion.'

consciousness, the possibility of knowledge etc. (e.g. by positing, with Kant, the a-priori categories of pure reason), and even if we were to concede, as we do, that sense-experience is the 'occasion' (but not the 'cause') of the awakening of human consciousness, thus taking a mid-way course between radical Idealism and radical Empiricism, our position is that language is the expression of human consciousness and not of sense-experience alone.

§37. Hence *the poly-valency of human language*. A sentence, or even a single word, can be the carrier of different meanings – in accordance with the different levels of human consciousness which it expresses. For example, the word 'good', expressive of sense-experience means one thing (i.e. pleasant), expressive of esthetic experience (or esthetic consciousness) means another (i.e. 'beautiful'), expressive of moral experience (or moral consciousness), means still another (i.e. 'should be done'), etc.[22]

This means too that a word is or can be charged with an over-plus of meaning which can only be indicated by the tone of voice (e.g. 'come!' as an imperative, expressing my wanting you to come), the general attitude and gestures, the surrounding circumstances, etc. If language, considered as a social, inter-personal reality, is speech, speech is a human act, or rather a series of acts (uttering words, referring to something, causing an effect on the hearer, performing something).[23]

But, paradoxically enough, this means to the *limitations* of language "Man has constantly to invent new words to express what he means – words which neither his mother-tongue nor foreign ones may be able to provide him with. If he is unable to invent a new word, he will find himself obliged to use an already available word, but by so doing, the word for him acquires a now 'connotation'. Even by the passage of time, or as used in a particular cultural or linguistic context, a word often acquires 'connotations' over and above its general meaning (or 'denotation'). Again, if a word stands as a sign, as we have said, for the thing known (or 'designated'), the more the latter is understood, the greater power of signifying the "sign" acquires. A sign is always approximative, tending more and more to the reality signified, but never co-extensive with or exhaustive of it.

§38. We said that language is expressive of consciousness. We made reference to different aspects or layers of consciousness. We do not have in mind here psychological levels of consciousness in the sense of Freud or Jung, but what we elsewhere[24] call appetitive, noetic, esthetic, erotic, agapeistic, moral, religious levels of consciousness. Without going into the finites of our description of religious consciousness which we give there, it would be enough for our present purposes, to describe it in the way which we shall present in a moment.

22 Salvino Azzopardi, *Ethics*, pp. 8-9.

23 Thus Searle distinguishes: utterance-act, propositional-act, perlocutionary-act and illocutionary-act. See Bibliography.

24 Salvino Azzopardi, *Philosophy of Religion*, pp. 6-7.

This is to say that we consider as of the highest importance in our enquiry, the semantic aspect of religious language. Such questions would have to be raised and answered: what is the relation between religious thought and religious language? What is the 'referent'in religious language? How does religious language 'refer' to it? What is the meaning of 'religious meaning'? What is the 'religious context' which gives a proposition a religious meaning? What is the special feature, if any, of religious language which makes it differ from scientific, poetic, moral language? Is there one or many religious languages?

§39. If language, considered in its totality, that is as human speech, is an expression of human consciousness with the purpose of 'communicating' something to another, we must now recall what we say elsewhere about *religious consciousness.*

It would suit our purposes here to describe religious consciousness as the consciousness of God (the Absolute, Ultimate Reality). We distinguish this religious consciousness (which we would also call 'Faith') from 'belief', that is from a conceptualization and verbalization of 'Faith'. We recall that religious consciousness, like human consciousness in general in its different levels, can be more or less awakened, more or less explicit.

We have just said that religious consciousness is the consciousness of 'God'. The first question a linguistic analysis would be: "What do you mean by God?" If we wanted to put this question in more philosophical terms, we would ask: "What is the formal object of religious consciousness?" The difficulty in answering this question consists in the fact 'God', strictly speaking, is no 'object' at all! (He is the 'Subject' par excellence). As self-consciousness is the ground and support of other aspects or layers of human consciousness- and the 'self' is, by definition, net an 'object' (ob-jectum) but the 'subject' of consciousness, so too, according to us, religious consciousness is the ground and support of self-consciousness... To say the same thing from another angle: 'God' as 'Ultimate "Reality', is not an 'object' amidst another objects, not even a 'subject' amongst other 'subjects', not a 'reality' along with other 'realities'. He is the ground, support, origin, source, or as we prefer to say, the ultimate metaphysical intelligibility of objects and subjects, of reality and being itself.

Notice now that if language is an expression of consciousness, and religious language of religious consciousness, religious consciousness precedes religious language (logically not chronologically). In other words, man has become conscious of 'God' before he could 'speak' about Him. In the words of St. Thomas, man can arrive at knowing *that* God exists before he arrives at knowing who God is (and therefore at being able to 'say' things about Him, to 'speak' of Him).[25] We could express this by saying that man can become more and more conscious that the empirical world, and himself included, with its change, causation contingency, graded perfection and finality, cannot be its own ultimate intelligibility - an

25 Cf. *Contra Gentes*, III, 38.

ultimate intelligibility which has to be 'posited' therefore in, by and through 'something' (or 'somebody') else. Or again, man can intuit that empirical reality is net exhaustive of, commensurate with the totality of reality and that therefore there must be an 'overplus' to empirical reality giving it intelligibility and meaning.

§40. These considerations make the semantic question of religious language more acute. If consciousness is awakened through the medium of sense experience, and if 'God' is not an 'object' perceptible by the senses, how can language, which is an expression of sense-awakened consciousness, say anything 'meaningful' at all about God?

Notice, first of all, that tr.is applies too, to a lesser extent, to language about the 'self' (which is not an 'object' and not directly sense-perceptible). And this is the reason why mystics say that the 'Self' is ineffable – which they distinguish from the 'psychological' or 'empirical' self which is precisely experienced as 'object'. It cannot be described, therefore; it can only be intuited.[26]

But before we try to answer the question we raised, it is necessary to distinguish between different kinds of religious language. There is first of all, religious language of direct intuition. This is, according to us, the primary religious language. It is the language used by one who makes personally and intuitively the experience of God (of the Absolute, Ultimate Reality). The other kinds of religious language are derivative of this. We can signal out religious language of a doctrinal and pedagogical purpose, used either by the one who makes personally and intuitively the experience of God or by those who derive their religious language from him to instruct others, and religious language of systematized and academic nature, used to present religious doctrine in a coherent, explainable, defendable way.

Needless to point out that these different kinds of religious language often overlap. But a phenomenological study of the history of religions can easily justify our distinction between these different kinds of religious language.[27]

§41. Similarly, a phenomenological study of religion can easily justify our further claim that religious traditions, with their beliefs, cult and morality, originate from different direct and personal experiences of God (Absolute, Ultimate Reality). Belief, cult and morality are the existential expression of this sense or experience of God (experienced in different ways and therefore, given also the existential situation of the experiencer, expressed in different ways).

But this is to say that the ultimate referent of religious language is God or rather God as experienced that is God and man's 'relation' to Him (man's experience of Him). Everything else in religious language is, according to us, expressive of, based upon, and conducive to this ultimate referent. It is this ultimate referent – if

26 Mystics distinguish therefore between the psychological self (soul, aham, etc.) from the real (transcendental) self (the spirit, substance of the soul, guha, atman, etc.).

27 S Azzopardi, *Philosophy of Religion*, Chapter III.

we prefer, twofold ultimate referent – which distinguishes religious language as such from moral, esthetic, scientific language, etc.

Our claim not only agrees with the teachings of many mystics of most religious traditions that God (the Absolute, Ultimate Reality) is in Himself (as non-experienced) ineffable because unknowable – except perhaps in the highest peaks of mystical consciousness – but also brings out better into relief what we think to be valuable in the position of many functional analysts as well as their fundamental shortcoming. We recall that according to these religious language is essentially existential, it is a language about man, of his experience, of his emotions, of his intention to act in a certain way, of his conviction, of his way of seeing things, etc. (see supra §20-21). Their fundamental shortcoming is their failure – because of their empiristic prejudice – to go beyond that and see the ground and support of this existential expression itself.

§42. Now we have to face the 'basic question raised above' (in § 40). The question is: How does religious language, particularly in its primary form, refer to God (the Absolute, Ultimate Reality)?

Having said what we had to say what we 'mean' , by 'God', it should have become clear, that religious language cannot signify God in the same way that language – which we said to be composed of concepts and words which are fundamentally 'signs' – signifies 'objects'. Religious language cannot therefore describe God in the same way that it can describe objects, subjects (in a psychological or empirical sense) or events of empirical experience. Religious language cannot deduce or induce God by strictly logical (merely discursive) arguments based on merely logical premises or sense-perceptible facts.

But religious language shares with language in general the power to evoke deeper (or higher) levels of consciousness, for example, of the 'self' – in our case, of 'God'. Hence our question about the ways of 'referring' to God is actually a two-fold question, or, if one likes, two logically distinct but closely inter-related questions. One question is to ask how religious language evokes the consciousness of God ("that God exists") and the other question is to ask how religious language can speak meaningfully about 'God. Once consciousness of Him is evoked or aroused ("who God is" or "how to predicate attributes to God"). This brings us back to the questions as raised, among others by St. Thomas, and even further still, to the questions about 'truth' and 'meaning' which we raised at the very beginning of this study.

We need not go into the first question. We treat of it at some length elsewhere.[28] Suffice it here to stress the fact that, at least according to us, arguments or proofs for the existence of God are not merely logical, discursive proofs. Their function is evocative of a deeper (indeed the deepest) level of human consciousness – the

28 See opp. cit. 72-75 *Ethics*, pp. 72-75 and *Philosophy of Religion*, pp. 14a-14b.

religious consciousness. They harness the intuitive (or apperceptive) power of the intellect through the medium of the discursive reason. But as yet this intuition or apperception is pre-conceptual. And precisely because it is pre-conceptual, the question (the second) question arises: How can language refer to God or how is it possible to speak meaningfully about God?

§43. In the religious literature of the world and in the teachings of mystics and religious philosophers from ancient times, we can discern at least three ways of referring to God. St. Thomas calls them: the way by remotion (or negation), the way of analogy and the way of eminence.

1. Way of negation. This is closely linked to apophatism. According to St. Thomas, it is the 'principal way' (C.G. 1, 14). It consists precisely in denying what God is not. It has a strong tradition in Christianity, through the influence of Plotinus and pseudo-Dionysius.[29] In Judaism, Maimonides stresses the apophatic nature of religious language to such a degree that St. Thomas found himself obliged to react. But best known for this apophatic way are the Upanishads and – especially the Buddhist Madhyamika.[30]

Logically conceptually, of course, this way really does not 'say' anything about God (the Absolute, Ultimate Reality) – it refuses precisely to do so. But his apophatic 'silence' is the diametrical opposite of the agnostic or sceptic non-committal. It is the 'learned -ignorance' of Nicolas of Cusa. In fact, it is born out of a deep consciousness of the 'ineffability' of God as Ultimate Reality, as Absolute and therefore of the radical inadequacy of human language to 'define' (which is to 'limit') Him in concepts and words.

Still, this apophatic way has the power of evoking – especially if both contraries are denied (e. g. 'being' and 'non-being', 'spirit' and 'matter', etc.) – what this very denial or negation designates. Notice that many predicates we attribute to 'God' are, in spite of appearances, negative (e.g. 'spirit' i.e. non-matter; 'eternal', i.e. 'without being and end'; 'infinite', i.e. without limitation, etc).

§44. 2. Way of analogy. This is the Kataphatic way. Pseudo- Dionysius calls it 'the way of causality'. In fact it is based on the intuition that if 'God' is the

29 Pesudo-Dionysius, see especially his Mystical Theology. For Example: "(God is) neither one, nor oneness, nor godhead, nor goodness; nor is He spirit according to our understanding, nor filiation, nor paternity; nor anything else known to us or to any other beings, of the things that are or the things that are not…" (chapter V. For the apophatism of St. Thomas, see our Philosophy of Religion), p.16.

30 An example from Upanishads: "Caturtham, the sages think, is neither inwardly nor outwardly cognitive, nor cognitive both wise, not a mass of cognition, neither cognition nor non-cognition. It is the unseen, non-felt, ungraspable, uninferable, unimaginable, indescribable essence of the knowledge of the one atman, the negation of all phenomena, peace, bliss, non-duality, to be realized." (Mandukyopanishad, 6). Nirvana is neither being nor non-being, neither 'both being and non-being', nor 'neither being nor non-being', according to Madhyamika.

ultimate intelligibility (metaphysical cause) of empirical reality, empirical reality must somehow or other reflect, point to the ultimate reality. To the extent that it does reflect and point to it, one can make use of concepts and words denoting objects of empirical reality of designate or to evoke Ultimate Reality. But to the extent that it does only reflects and point to it, one cannot make use of such concepts and words and attribute them to Ultimate Reality in a univocal way. For St Thomas, analogy stands midway between pure univocity and pure eqivocity (S.Th. I,13, 5 in c.).

That the theory of analogy as a way of 'referring' to God is not without its difficulties is clear. Already in early Scholasticism, a tension arose as to the more correct way of understanding it. One way (analogy by attribution: what is predicated of God is applicable to Him in a true (formal) sense but not in the same way as to creatures, since, precisely, God is the ultimate cause whereas the creatures are creatures: hence only God can be called 'good' formally, the creature only derivately) tends towards univocity. The other (analogy of proportionality: what is predicated of God is applicable to Him in a true sense and applicable to the creature also in a true (formal) sense but in both cases, this applicability is proportionate to the natures of each) tends to equivocity. Various attempts have been done to distinguish and sub-distinguish.[31]

A recent criticism has been made of the analogy of proportionality that the proportion admits of two unknowns (the 'nature of God' and whatever is predicated of Him *as* proportionate to His nature).[32] Our answer to this criticism is that the objection will hold water if it is used to 'prove' God's existence, but not otherwise. As we said before the 'existence' of God – in a confused, Vague, supra-conceptual and intuitive manner-is already presupposed as having been posited before one tries to 'speak about' Him (to say 'who' God precisely is, to attribute predicates to Him). Again, the analogy of attribution is said to amount to a tautology: whatever can produce an effect can produce an effect. Our answer is this analogy, even if it does not tell me 'more' than what I knew before – vaguely, confusedly, etc. – helps me to explicitate more and more in my conscious awareness what is it that I intuit pre-conceptually and intuitively.

We accept, however, that one function of analogy is to be "one means of providing criteria for the disciplined use of ordinary language in theological contexts." But this is not the whole significance of analogy.

§45. Religious language makes ample use of similes and metaphors. These fall under the general category of analogy – especially if analogy is justified more for its evocative power of signifying than for its descriptive (or 'attributive') function. Scholasticism, however, distinguishes analogy in the strict sense from metaphor in that the former predicates attributes to God 'intrinsically', whereas the latter only

31 This whole question will be treated both in Metaphysics and in Philosophical Theology.

32 F. Ferre, *Languages, Logic and God, Language, Logic and God*, pp. 72-77.

'extrinsically'. (But here Scholastics differ: for some, for analogy to be 'intrinsic' it has to be that of attribution, for others, on the contrary, for analogy to be intrinsic, it has to be that 'of proportionality'. Needless to say that only 'simple perfections' (those which do not imply any imperfection and are therefore better than their contraries can be attributed to God, according to the Scholastics, by analogy and intrinsically.

A simile, by its nature, can easily be understood to be non-literally true. If it is developed into a story, it is a 'parable'. Not much difficulty in that. The difficulty is with the metaphor, for most religious language is couched in metaphorical language which can easily be understood in a literal sense. And when the metaphor is developed into a story, it is an 'allegory'.

It is only when the metaphor or the allegory is believed in literally that we call it a 'myth'.When it is recognized for what it is – as a story appealing more to the imagination and feelings rather than to logic and reason – in other words, when it is mythologized, and its function of expressing or signifying religious truth perceived, it is understood to be precisely a metaphor or an allegory. Here it is a question of what we elsewhere call a deepening of religious consciousness, a transit, as it were, from the 'mythic' to the 'mytho-logical' level.[33]

§46. 3. Way of eminence. Pseudo-Dionysius, and after him St. Thomas calls this way the way of 'transcendence' also. St. Thomas does not develop his thought on this subject as much as he does on the subject of analogy. Letting ourselves to be inspired by Pseudo-Dionysius and by St. Thomas commentary,[34] we give our own way of understanding it.

As analogy stands 'midway' between – and therefore transcends! – univocity and equivocity, so too the way of eminence stands midway – and therefore transcends – both affirmation and negation, the kataphatic and the apophatic ways. Or again, as analogy affirms the reality signified and denies the way of signification (e.g. when God is said to be "personal being" analogy affirms 'personhood' and 'being' in God but denies that what is meant by these terms is affirmed of God in the same way as it is affirmed of a human person), the way of eminence affirms and denies at the same time what is affirmed of God. (Hence such expressions of God as a "supra-personal being", "infinite Being", "super-essential being", "the Absolute" or "Ultimate Being").

To speak of "affirmation and negation at the same time, indeed of affirmation by negation and negation by affirmation, would sound to be logical nonsense or conceptual meaninglessness. And it would certainly be if one were to take what is intended or 'designated' as descriptive of any object (person or event) of empirical experience. But here again, the function of religious language, is not descriptive

33 S. Azzopardi, *Philosophy of Religion*, pp. 5-6.

34 Pseudo-Dionysius, *De Divinis Nominibus*, commented by St. Thomas in his *In Dionysium.*

but evocative. In fact, even in ordinary human speech, we make use of paradox to express something for which asimple affirmation or a simple negation would be hopelessly inadequate. Paradox is a very common way in all the Religious literature of the world of expressing religious truth. We further justify its function by our 'dialectical' approach to religious Faith.[35] If a term or a proposition cannot refer to 'God' if not partially, 'tendentially' and therefore imperfectly, it needs to be at the same time denied and its dialectical opposite posited. This 'positing', however, is in itself already an affirmation which needs, in its turn, to be denied... Needless to point out that this 'coincidence of opposites' (in the terms of Nicolas of Cusa)[36] is not effected on the level of discursive thought which necessarily proceeds by affirmation and negation, by analysis and synthesis, by deduction and induction -but on the level of 'intuitive thought', or 'intellect' or 'understanding', which St. Thomas calls "the united powers of intuition and reason."

§47. Analytical Linguistic Philosophy continues to arouse interest in the subject of religious language and thus to make the work already began by historians and philosophers of religion more relevant to the understanding of one's own religious tradition. Already a long time ago, Rudolf Otto brought out in better relief the non-rational (i.e. intuitive, supra-discursive) element in religious 'Faith'. Paul Tillich insisted on the continuum of religious consciousness and human consciousness in general, and especially on the symbolic nature of religious language. Mircea Eliade helped re-discover the religious evocative power of the religious myth, of the religious signs and symbols. Rudolf Bultamnn helped us become more and more aware, even if one refused to accept all his conclusions, of the necessity of 'demythologizing' religious language in terms of contemporary 'world- views'.

But a host of lesser-known authors have also, more recently, made valuable contributions to a fuller understanding of religious language, its specific meaning, its peculiar function and its manifold logic. Thus Ian Ramsey, brings out in more contemporary terms, the nature of religious language as 'disclosure' (evocative) language, as a language 'purveyor of insight', interpreting analogy as a asymptotic way of referring and the way of eminence as a 'model with qualifiers'.[37] F. Ferre makes quite a comprehensive critical evaluation of modern linguistic analysis in general and of various authors in particular and shows how a one-sided emphasis on one or other of the logic of religious language has led to a failure to understand not only religious language but language as whole, as human discourse.[38]

Functional analysis Itself, as we have seen, has made, in its way, a considerable contribution to an understanding of religious language, but many authors marred

35 Op. cit. pp. 11-13.

36 Nicolas of Cusa, *Of Learned Ignorance* and the *Vision of God.*

37 I. Ramsey, *Religious Language,* especially, chapters I and II.

38 F. Ferre, op.cit.

their efforts, according to us, not only by their one-sidedness but also, and especially, by their radical and fundamental empiric pre-suppositions.

There is still a long way ahead of us in this field of study. But all these modern insights, bringing out better the dynamic power and at the same time the crippling limitations of human language,especially when man expresses his experience at the deepest (or highest) level of his consciousness. And this leads us to pass a final concluding remark.

Chapter 3

CONCLUDING REMARKS: THE NECESSITY OF A HERMENEUTICS OF SCRIPTURES

§48. All the World Religions have their Sacred Scriptures – 'sacred' precisely because they are either believed to have been 'inspired' by God or at least believed to record faithfully and in an authoritative and unchangeable way the experience and teaching of the initiator of the religious tradition concerned (Hence the Idea of "revelation', 'sruti', 'Quran', etc.). In non-Scriptural religious traditions, oral tradition serves the same purpose, it is believed.

A so-called fundamentalist, 'literal revelation' belief has, however, been a cause of much misunderstanding between adherents of different World Religions especially when certain really or apparently mutually- exclusive beliefs are found in different Scriptures. But today, at least in Christianity and, as we have had already the occasion to point out, in other religious traditions, it is recognized more and more that the Scriptures too are couched in human language. And to understand their religious import, a better understanding of human language in general and of religious language in particular is a necessity. Hence, necessary too is a hermeneutics (the science of interpreting) the Scriptures themselves. The underlying principle is that no matter how 'inspired' the Scriptures are, they are written by man, conditioned as he is by his 'existential situation' (language, culture, personal temperament and character, social milieu, his own and his contemporaries' needs, the exigencies of his time and place, etc.), and in human language. Our study has helped us to become more and more aware of what all this involves.

§49. Such a hermeneutics implies a lot of things, e.g. a *textual criticism* which tries to establish the original text; a *documentary criticism* which tries to establish the author and when, where, why and to whom he wrote; *source criticism* which tries to establish whether the author relied on or even reproduced earlier texts; *form criticism* which tries to explain the origin of the text by working out its 'History' prior to the permanent form it took: *literary criticism* which tries to establish the different kinds of literary forms found in the text, (e.g. doctrinal maxims, controversies, narrative, etc.) and the style, linguistic characteristics distinctive genius of the author, etc.

§50. But perhaps more important still, such a hermeneutics will have, if possible, some kind of rule by which what is strictly of religious import be distinguished from non-religious elements found in the scriptures (e.g. historical, geographical, scientific, social, political). And through what is of religious import, to discover, or re-capture the ordinary religious experience which gave rise to the scriptures. Hence an understanding of religious language – and of what we have been trying to drive at during the whole course of this study – is obviously of the highest importance. Religious language (with its concepts and words, categories of thought and patterns of speech, its negative, analogical, eminent ways of referring, its allegorical and symbolical manners of describing, its own kind of 'meaning' function and logic, etc.), can only evoke, in the depths of the heart, God, the Absolute and Ultimate Reality and our relation to Him in an ineffable Union.

BIBLIOGRAPHY

Allen,E.L. "The Great Argument," *The Expository Times*, Vol. 58, 1947.

_______ "The Arguments for God's Existence," *The Congregational Quarterly*, Vol. 30, 1952.

Allison, H.E. "Faith and Falsifiability," *The Review of Metaphysics* 22 (1962): 499-522.

Alston, W. P. *Philosophy of Language*. New York: Prentice-Hall, 1965.

_______ "Language: Philosophy of" *Encyclopedia of Philosophy*, Vol. 4.

Austin, J.L. "Other Minds," in *Logic and Language* (ed. A. Flew), 2nd Series.

_______ "Performative-Constative," in *The Philosophy of Language* (ed. J.R. Searle), 1971.

Bochencki, J. *Logic of Religion*, 1965.

Braithwaite, R.P. *An Empiricist's View of the Nature of Religious Belief.* Cambridge: CUP, 1955.

Campbell, J.T. *The Language of Religion*. New York: The Bruce Pub Co. 1971.

Charlesworth, M. "Linguistic Analysis and God," *International Philosophical Quarterly*, Vol. 1/1, 1961.

Christian W. *Meaning and Truth in Religion*, 1964.

Clarke, W.M. "Linguistic Analysis and Natural Theology," in *Proceedings of the American Catholic Philosophy Association*, Vol. 34, 1960.

Clifford, P.R. "The Factual Reference of Theological Assertion," *Religious Studies* 3 (1967): 339-346.

Coates, J.B. "God and the Positivists," *The Hibbert Journal*, Vol. 50, 1952.

Copleston, F. "The Meaning of the Terms Predicated of God," in *Contemporary Philosophy*. (ed. Copleston, F.) London: Burns and Oates, 1956.

Corbishley, T. "Do the Mystics Know?", *The Hibbert Journal*, Vol. 50, 1951.

Cox, D. "The Significance of Christianity," *Mind*, Vol. 64, 1955.

Crombie, I. "Theology and Falsification," in *New Essays* (ed. A. Flew), London: SCM Press, 1955.

_______ "The Possibility of Theological Statements," in *Faith and Logic* (ed. B. Mitchell g.v.).

Crystal, D. *Linguistics, Language and Religion*. London: Burns an Oates, 1965.

Evans, J.L. "On Meaning and Verification," *Mind,* Vol. 62, 1953.

Ewing, A.C. "Religious Assertions in the Light of Contemporary Philosophy," *Philosophy*, Vol. 32, No. 122, 1957.

Fawcett, T. *The Symbolic Language of Religion*. London: SCM Press, 1970.

Ferre, F. "Is Language About God Fraudulent", *The Scottish Journal of Theology*, Vol. 12/4, 1959.

_______ *Language, Logic and God*. New York: Harper and Bros., 1961.

Findlay, J.N. "Can God's Existence Be Disproved?" in *New Essays* (see u. Flew).

Flew A. and MacIntyre (eds). *New Essays in Philosophical Theology*. London: SCM Press, 1955.

Flew, A. "Theology and Falsification," *Ibid.*

_______ "Philosophy and Language," *The Philosophical Quarterly*, Vol. 5.

_______ *God and Philosophy*. London. 1966.

Flew, A. (ed) *Logic and Language*. Oxford: B. Blackwell, 1955.

Ganguly, S. *Logical Positivism*. Calcutta: Allied Pub, 1967.

Glasgow, W.D. "Knowledge of God", *Philosophy,* Vol. 32/12, 1957.

Hare, R.M. "Religion and Morals" in *Faith and Logic* (ed B. Mitchell q.v.).

_______ "Theology and Falsification" in *New Essays* .... (see under Flew).

Hawkins, D.J.B. "What do the Proofs of the Existence of God Purport to Do?" *The Clergy Review*, Vol. 37, 1952.

Hepburn, R.W. "Demythologising and the Problem of Validity," in *New Essays* .... (see under Flew).

_______ *Christianity and Paradox*. London: Watts, 1958.

Hick, J. "Man's Awareness of God" in *Religious Belief and Philosophical Thought* (ed. W. A. Alston), New York: Harcourt, Brace and World, 1963.

Hick, J. (ed). *Classical and Contemporary Readings in the Philosophy of Religion*. New York: Prentice-Hall, 1964.

Hill, W. A. "Religious Experience as a Court of Appeal", *The Hibbert Journal*, Vol. 53, 1955.

Hodges, H.A. "What is to Become of Philosophical Theology?" in *Contemporary British Philosophy* (ed H. D. Lewis), London: George Allen & Unwin, 1956.

Jones, O.R. "The Challenge of a Contemporary Philosophy to Religion," *The Hibbert Journal*, Vol. 53, 1955.

Kellenberger, J. "The Falsification Challenge," *Religious Studies* 5 (1969): 69-76; 243-249.

Klocker, H. R. *God and the Empiricists*. Milwaukee, 1968.

Leon, Ph. "The Meaning of Religious Propositions," *The Hibbert Journal*, Vol. 53, 1955.

Lewis, C. "On the Logic of Belief Claims in Religion," *The International Journal of Philosophy and Religion* 5 (1974): 162-175.

Lewis, H. D. (ed) *Clarity is Not Enough: Essays in Criticism of Linguistic Philosophy*. London: George Allen and Unwin, 1963.

Lewis, H.D. "The Cognitive Factor in Religious Experience," *Proceedings of the Aristotelian Society*, Suppl Vol. 29, 1955.

Mackie, J.M. "Evil and Omnipotence," *Mind*, Vol. 64, 1955.

MacKinnon D.M. "Death" in *New Essays* (See under Flew).

MacIntyre, A. (and A. Flew) eds. *New Essays* (See under Flew).

_______ "Visions" *Ibid.*

_______ *Difficulties in Christian Belief.* London: SCM Press, 1959.

_______ "Is Understanding Religion Compatible with Believing?" in *Faith and the Philosophers* (ed. J. Hick) N.Y: 1964.

MacQuarrie, J. *God-Talk*. London, 1967.

Martin, C. B. "A Religious Way of Knowing" in *New Essays* (See under Flew).

_______ "The Perfect Good," *Ibid.*

_______ *Religious Belief.* Cornell: Cornell Univ Press, 1959.

Martin, J.A. *The New Dialogue Between Philosophy and Theology*. N.Y. 1966.

Mascall, E. *Words and Images*. London: Longman, Green and Co, 1957.

McIntyre, J. "Analogy" *The Scottish Journal of Theology*, Vol. 12, No. 1.

McMullin, E. "The Analytic Approach to Philosophy," *Proceedings of the American Catholic Philosophy Association*, Vol. 35, 1960.

McPherson, T. "The Existence of God," *Mind*, Vol. 59, 1950.

_______ "Religon and the Inexpressible" in *New Essays* (See under Flew).

_______ "The argument from Design," *Philosophy*, Vol. 32, No. 122, 1957.

Meynell, H. *Sense, Non-Sense and Christianity*. London, 1964.

Mitchell, B. "Theology and Falsification" in *New Essays* (See under Flew).

_______ (ed.) *Faith and Logic*. London: George Allen & Unwill, 1957.

Nielsen, K. "The Intelligibility of God-Talk," *Religious Studies*, 6 (1970) 1ff.

Nowell-Smith, P. "Miracles" in *New Essays* (See under Flew).

Ramsey, I.T. *Religious Language*. London: SCM Press, 1957.

_______ *Words About God*. New York: Harper and Row, 1971.

_______ *Christian Discourse: Some Logical Explorations*. Oxford: OUP, 1965.

Reid, A. "Religion, Science and Other Modes of Knowledge," *The Hibbert Journal*, Vol. 54, 1955.

Ryle, G. *Dilemmas*. Cambridge: CUP, 1954.

_______ "Ordinary Language," *The Philosophical Review*, Vol. 62, 1953.

Schmitz, K. L. "Restitution of Meaning in Religious Speech," *International Journal of Philosophy of Religion* 5, (1974): 131-151.

Searle, J.R. *Speech Acts: An Essay in the Philosophy of Language*, 1969.

_______ (ed) *The Philosophy of Language.*

Smart, J.J.C. "The Existence of God" in *New Essays* (See under Flew).

Stace, W.T. "Positivism," *Mind*, Vol. 53, 1944.

Sution, C. W. H. "Philosophy and Religion," *Philosophy,* Vol. 26, 1951.

Tillich, P. "Two Types of Philosophy of Religion," and "Existential analyses and Religious Symbols in Classical and (ed. J. Hick, q.v.).

Upmson, J.O. *Philosophical Analysis*. Oxford: The Clarendon Press, 1956.

Van Bure, P. *The Secular Meaning of the Gospel.* London: SCM Press, 1963.

Vandell, K.P. *Basic Issues in the Philosophy of Religion*. Boson, 1971.

White, M. *The Age of Analysis*. Boston, 1955.

Whitely, C.H. "The Cognitive Factor in Religious Experience," *Proceedings of the Aristotelian Society*, Suppl Vol. 29, 1955.

Williams, P. "Tertullian's Paradox," in *New Essays* (See under Flew).

Wisdom, J. *Philosophy and Psychoanalysis*. Oxford: Blackwell, 1953.

_______ "God" in *Logic and Language* (see under A. Flew).

Wittgenstin, L. *Tractatus Logico-Philosophicus*. London: Routledge and Keegan Paul, 1922.

_______ *Philosophical Investigations*. Oxford: B. Blackwell, 1953.

Zuurdeeg, W.F. *An Analytical Philosophy of Religion*. Nashville: Abingdon Press, 1958.

The Author
Fr Salvino Azzopardi, S.J. (1931-2006)

Indeed Salvino Azzopardi enjoyed bursting into a hearty laugh, and his laughter in company was contagious. He really enjoyed a joke and his optimism diffused a joyous spirit on all round. In any conversation he was gentle and kind and would never ever hurt anyone in the least. He always looked at the bright side of any argument, although he knew well enough how to defend staunchly his point of view. When in the last few months he occasionally writhed with excruciating pain in his chest and stomach, he would softly whisper with a broad smile on his wry face that he was "all right" and that the pain would soon pass.

He relished in being of service to others, and he willingly, nay joyfully, helped others to understand some abstruse or weird problem in philosophy.

Salvino, the fifth child of the Legal Procurator Philip Azzopardi and Giuseppina née Borg, and nephew of the servant of God, Eugenio Borg, his mother's brother, was born on 20th June 1931 at Hamrun, Malta. He had his secondary schooling at the Lyceum and at an early age joined the "Lega", the Hamrun Catholic Action "Milites Christi Regis", where he became a catechist of the young aspirants.

In 1947, at the age of sixteen, Salvino joined the Society of Jesus at Naxxar, Malta, following in the footsteps of his brother Anton who had joined the Society two years ahead of him. He emitted his first vows in 1949 at Naxxar, and then followed the normal course of studies in the Society: two years literature at Naxxar, three years philosophy at Vals in France, a year's prefecting the boys at St Aloysius' College, Malta, and another year at Clongows College, Ireland. Then four years of theology at Heythrop College, Oxon, England, where he was ordained priest on 31 July 1959. Fr Salvino did his Third Year of Novitiate in Florence, Italy, after which, i.e., in 1961, he was sent to the Gregorian University in Rome where in 1963 he took his Doctorate in Philosophy "cum laude".

Back in Malta in 1963, he was appointed House Minister at St Aloysius' College, and a year later, in 1964, he succeeded in fulfilling his ardent desire to go to the Missions. In his first three years in India he filled the post of Secretary of the Bishop of Dumka and of the Regional Superior. He took his final Vows on 2nd February 1965 at Sahibganj in India.

But the Superiors realized that Salvino's real bent lay in teaching philosophy. So in 1967 Fr Salvino was sent to Benares Hindu University to study Hindi, Sanskrit and Indian Philosophy. Yet again, his teaching pursuit was not yet to be, for in 1969 after Benares, Salvino was called to be the Rector of St Xavier's School, Sahibganj, India. But God had other plans for him, for in 1971 Fr Salvino, to his great joy, was appointed professor of Modern and Indian Philosophy and Comparative Religions at De Nobili College, Pune, India, and from 1977 to 1979 and from 1982 to 1986 filled there also the post of Dean of the Faculty. He left De Nobili College in 1990.

During his twenty years at Pune he lectured to hundreds of Jesuit students, diocesan seminarians and members of other religious orders, males and females, Indian and non-Indian. He possessed a particular charism of rendering his students fascinated by his vivid and lucid lectures. The hand-out notes he gave his students went round to other faculties and Universities in India. Fr Salvino was several times invited to read papers on philo-theological subjects at International Congresses, even those non-Catholic, in the United States. He was a good speaker with solid intellectual material and practical ideas to transmit and ever stressing the bright and joyful side of our belief. It sometime happened that after a lecture or a homily the congregation rose up to applaud.

After all those years of intensive intellectual activity in India, Fr Salvino began to feel his health wane. So in 1988 his Superiors advised him to return to Malta to regain his health. The doctors in Malta sent him to London for a heart by-pass surgery, after which he had to spend over a year convalescing in Malta. Fr Salvino aspired to go back to India, but now that the time allowed for his visa and the "No Objection to Return" permit expired, he was stuck in Malta.

This was, however, providential, for in 1990 the Bishop of Gozo asked him to be the Rector of the Diocesan Seminary. Fr Salvino accepted with joy. He loved working for the formation of the future priests. At the Seminary he also lectured on Oriental Religions and gave spiritual talks and counselling to priests and to the people at large. Under the tutelage of the Bishop, Fr Salvino was mainly instrumental in bringing about the affiliation of the Gozo Seminary to the Dominican University "Angelicum" in Rome. This was no easy task for he had to see to it that the conditions laid down by the "Angelicum" regarding professors, library, admissions, assignments, examinations and so on were properly adhered to. Fr Salvino had the onerous task of travelling several times to Rome to settle matters with the "Angelicum" authorities.

After five years of Rectorship in Gozo, Fr Salvino was in 1995 called by the Provincial to be his "Socius". Furthermore, on a request by the University of Malta he was appointed visiting lecturer on Comparative Religions with special emphasis on Oriental Theology. His lectures and tutorials were so vivid that he was once asked by one of his students whether he was really a Catholic priest or a Hindu sanjasi in disguise.

However, though Fr Salvino was happy to serve as socius (secretary) and a visiting lecturer, he thought that those offices did not fill his time and that he was underworked. So when in 1997 he received an invitation to the Professorship of Philosophy at the newly-founded Athenaeum in Sri Lanka, he grabbed this opportunity, even though he was well aware that now at the age of 66, one would normally go into retirement. He rejoiced that he would be entering another new world, the world of Buddhism, totally different from that of Hinduism with which he had been very familiar. His optimism and his apostolic zeal never failed him. He was ready for anything so long as he knew it was the will of God for him manifested through his Superiors. Fr Salvino left for Sri Lanka on 24th August 1997.

Four years lecturing at the Philosophical Faculty at Sri Lanka gave him renewed vigour. With his characteristic smile and hearty laughter, he became an inspiration to all around him. But the visa problem hit him again, and he was forced to return to his native country. In Malta he again accepted to lecture at the University of Malta, but he never abandoned his pastoral ministry.

However, after two years his heart began again to show signs of failure, and this time it gave him serious trouble. He had consequently to give up his lecturing, even though he continued to help students privately with their theses.

From 2001 onwards, Fr Salvino at Loyola House, Naxxar, Malta, carried on with his studies in Sanskrit, Greek and Hebrew. He was also the House historian and put in charge of various small offices. When his health did not permit him to move about freely he stayed in bed and spent time in prayer, listened to classical music and watched DVD films on his computer.

His health grew worse. In 2006 the periodic but frequent severe bouts of stomach and pulmonary attacks made his life miserable. But he never lost his optimism, his cheerful smile and his hearty laugh, nor did he ever refuse to help anyone who asked for his assistance.

On 6th August 2006, the feast of Our Lord the Saviour, his namesake, Fr Salvino, feeling relatively well, accepted an invitation by his niece to lunch at her house. At about 3.00 p.m. he started feeling queer in his chest and hard to breathe. He was rushed back home, and the doctor ordered him straight to hospital. Fr Salvino in bitter pain and hardly able to breathe, received the last rites and just after 9.00 p.m. he rendered his soul to God.

May he rest in the peace of the Lord!

Anton Azzopardi S.J

(Rev Fr Anton Azzopardi SJ is the brother of Salvino Azzopardi)